My Life's Ride

MY LIFE'S RIDE

Rick Valente

Creators Publishing

Hermosa Beach, CA

MY LIFE'S RIDE

Cover art by Coral Black
Cover photo by Jim Lensveld

CREATORS PUBLISHING
737 3rd St
Hermosa Beach, CA 90254
310-337-7003

ISBN (print): 978-1-962693-23-3
ISBN (e-book): 978-1-962693-24-0

First Edition
Printed in the United States of America
1 3 5 7 9 10 8 6 4 2

DEDICATION

To my mom, a beautiful Italian woman who always worked for the church and showed everyone love and respect.

To my dad, an Italian stud who had five brothers, ran an Italian club, and showed me how to be a man and how to show love and respect for others.

To my brother Chas, who was my first inspiration, was always fun to hang out with, and who always had my back when we were growing up.

Mom, Dad, and Chas, may you all rest in peace.

To my cousin Mark, who was like the little brother I never had and would do anything for me and my family, like taking care of my parents during the last years of their lives.

CONTENTS

INTRODUCTION

This is a book about how passion can change your life and inspire you to be fearless to make it a reality. Growing up, my passion was to become a bodybuilder. I envisioned myself winning lots of contests and being on the covers of bodybuilding magazines.

Life doesn't always go according to plan. Sometimes, life throws us a curveball and knocks us on our ass. Over the course of my career, I've learned that how you respond to a crisis can mean the difference between wallowing in failure or figuring out how to turn adversity into an opportunity and find success in a way you never thought possible. My hope is that readers of this book will come away with the tools they need to navigate their lives and understand what is most important in life—to find happiness. The lasting friendships I've made over the years give me the most happiness.

Look, none of us are going to live forever. That's the deal we signed when we were born. If we can touch a life, help a friend in need, then we will have made the world that much better. When we're gone, all that will be left of us are the memories people will have of us.

In writing this book, I've tried to impart what I have learned during the course of my life's journey. You have to have a positive outlook, and you have to look out for making other people happy. No one gets through life on their own. I never did. I don't know where I'd be without the rock-solid friendships I've been blessed to have.

CHAPTER ONE

KNOCKED ON MY ASS

"Everyone has a plan until they get punched in the mouth."
—Mike Tyson

THE MOST POWERFUL PUNCH I EVER TOOK knocked me the fuck out. Right on my ass. But I didn't take this punch in the ring. And I didn't take it from any person, either. Nope. You know where this overhand right came from? Life.

The most challenging week of my life began on Saturday, December 29, 2007. I was forty-nine years old and thought I had life all figured out. I had come from the cold, violent, drug-filled streets of Ansonia, Connecticut, to the sunny, warm, easygoing beaches of Marina del Rey on the Westside of Los Angeles. Just a few blocks from the Pacific Ocean, close enough to feel that cool marine breeze.

Twenty-five years had passed since I first walked into Gold's Gym Venice. During that time, I had accomplished more things than I ever could have dreamed of. At this age, I was basically retired and feeling free and happy. After all those years of hard work, I thought I could relax a little and enjoy the life I had built.

So, on this Saturday night, I was going on a date with a beautiful fitness model named Lori. She was fun to talk with, and I found myself becoming more and more attracted to her. When I pulled up to her house and saw her walking out to my car, I said to myself, "Damn, I'm a lucky guy. Tonight is going to be a good time."

Little did I know how it would turn out.

We made the drive over to Beverly Hills, laughing and flirting the whole way over, and then we pulled up to the valet at Madeo Ristorante. This was my go-to spot. It never disappointed. The ambiance. The pre-dinner drinks. The spaghetti bolognese. Amazing. And, of course, great wine. Italian food and vino. Does it get any better than that?

We did the whole nine yards, including cannolis and cappuccinos. Our energy was riding high as we drove away in my Mercedes. I can't remember if we were going to a club, my place, or wherever. It didn't matter. We never got there.

As we left Beverly Hills, Luther Vandross set the mood. I reached over and held her hand, and that's when my cell phone rang. I ignored it at first, but the ringing wouldn't stop. It was 11 p.m. Who the fuck was calling me this late?

Lori and me

When I finally glanced at my phone, it was a picture of Mom and Dad. If my parents were calling me at two in the morning their time, then something was really wrong.

My brain released a huge flood of adrenaline. My heart rate increased. I know good news can wait until the morning. Bad news can't.

My first thought was that it was about my older brother, Chas. He struggled with heroin and alcohol. He had been in and out of prison and rehab for as long as I could remember. When someone in your family has a drug or alcohol addiction, you are always walking on eggshells, thinking any day could be the day when you get that call with the bad news.

With that thought in my head, I anxiously answered. "Hey, is everything okay?"

My dad responded in a shaky voice. "Your mom fell and broke her hip. She's in the hospital. I just heard back from the doctor and it's bad. Get your ass home right now. I need you."

His words were strong and manly, but his voice was anything but. He seemed scared. He sounded like he had been crying. This was a man who didn't believe men cried. He always used to say to me when I was kid, "Stop your crying or I'll give you something to cry about."

The news made me nauseous. I let go of Lori's hand and said, "I have to get home. I'm sorry."

I explained what happened as I took her back to her place. She wished me well and told me that if there's anything she could do to help, to let her know.

Dad and Mom

"Thank you," I said, and then sped off.

When I got home that night, I booked the first flight out the next morning. I didn't sleep a wink, tossing and turning, thinking about my mom. In the morning, I threw on sweatpants, a hoodie, and dark shades. No bag to check, just the essentials in a small backpack. I jumped in a cab, headed to LAX, and raced onto the plane. Once seated, I felt exhausted, falling in and out of sleep the entire way. That stale-air, shitty-airplane sleep.

Flying from Los Angeles to New York in December throws you for a loop. You leave that sunny "winter" in SoCal, where it's hot in the sunshine and cool in the shade, and head for the real-deal, bone-chilling New England winter. As we flew across the country, the clock jumped three hours ahead and the light turned a gray, ashy color. The lush, green palm trees gave way to leafless, brown, skeleton-looking trees, covered with snow.

I landed at JFK late in the afternoon, headed straight to the Hertz window, and rented a four-door, black Cadillac. I headed north on Interstate 678, just as the sun began to set. Luckily, it was a Sunday, so traffic wasn't crazy. The city opened up, I got on I-95, moved into the fast lane, and let that Caddy run.

My thoughts were swirling as the speedometer needled past 100. I was passing cars like they were standing still, except I couldn't shake this one lady who kept pulling up next to me, waving her arms all crazy. I thought she was a wackadoo, all hopped up on cocaine or something. Every time she'd pull up, I'd pull away, and she eventually gave up.

Later, I went through a toll booth. "Turn your lights on," the dude working the booth said.

Whoops. Talk about being fucking distracted with your own thoughts. That lady was trying to save my life.

I made the hour-and-a-half trip in about an hour. Everything was a blur until I parked in front of my parents' house. It was the same house I lived in for the first nineteen years of my life in Ansonia, Connecticut, a small town next to New Haven, which is one of the most crime- and drug-infested cities in the country. It was no coincidence that so many of New Haven's problems bled into the surrounding neighborhoods.

Our house was located on a corner lot, about a mile off Ansonia's Main Street, in an area called Hilltop, because it was up on the hill above town. We had a yard, a few nice trees, and a fence to keep in our dogs—usually shepherds and Dobermans.

As a kid, our home was a place of peace in the middle of a truly chaotic town. Back then, when I would walk in the door, the aroma of my mom's Italian cooking was the first thing I would smell. She always had spaghetti sauce simmering on the stove. Wafts of garlic, olive oil, onions, and oregano would immediately signal I was in my safe space. I knew that day, though, I wasn't walking into my boyhood home or smelling my mom's cooking.

I took a deep breath, gave myself a pep talk, and got out of the car. It was cold and crisp. The snow on the ground crunched under my feet. I still recall that sound as I walked toward the back door. Italians hardly ever use the front door. Don't ask me why. It's just the way we are.

I walked in and saw Dad sitting on a couch in the parlor. I could tell he hadn't slept or eaten since Mom broke her hip a day earlier. I had never seen him like this. Totally out of it. He stood up slowly, and we hugged each other. And that's when I noticed it tucked in the cushions—the handle of a .38 revolver.

Before I could say a word, he said, "I'm telling you right now, Ricky, if anything happens to your mother, I'm not sticking around."

Dad wasn't one to talk shit, and I realized at that moment the gravity of the situation. It wasn't just my mom in need of help, but also my dad. It was the first time in my life I was going to have to step up and take care of my parents.

After a while, I calmed Dad down, and I told him how much I loved him and Mom and that I was going to do everything in my power to make sure we were going to be okay. After that, he didn't put up much of a fight when I reached into the cushions and took his gun away. Dad was a big gun collector, so to be on the safe side, I went around the house looking for any guns he had stashed that weren't locked up in his gun cabinet.

Dad told me they had taken Mom to St. Raphael Hospital (now Yale New Haven Hospital), where I was born. The plan was for me to check on her, pick up some food, and get back home to feed Dad.

As I walked into Mom's hospital room, my heart raced. I always remembered her as a ball of energy, with a huge, loving smile. And there she was, drooling on herself, high, and nearly knocked out on morphine. This was a lady who never smoked or drank in her entire life. To see her on one of the most powerful drugs in the world was disturbing. She didn't say much. I'm not even sure she knew who I was.

I talked to the doctor and found out her hip was not just broken but shattered. She'd have to have surgery once the initial swelling calmed down, just to see if there could be a way to fix it. At the time, Mom was seventy-eight years old. I knew from studying the body my whole life that this wasn't a good thing. I hoped it would all work out for the best, but I prepared myself for the worst.

I learned later that she had tripped on a rug in our kitchen while cooking dinner for Dad. She hadn't had any major health issues before that. No dizzy spells or tripping incidents. This was just a freak accident. And it would lead to the end of her life.

After visiting with Mom, I headed out to the parking lot, sat in the rental car, and felt the weight of the situation, with all its implications. In my younger days, I would try to out-muscle my problems, but that wouldn't work now. I would need help.

It was getting late, so I hauled ass to Roseland Apizza in nearby Derby and picked up a pizza pie, spaghetti, meatballs, and cheesecake. In our Italian world, this was comfort food.

I got home and found Dad just how I left him. I tried to make him eat, but he didn't have any appetite.

During dinner, I did my best to assure him that everything was going to be okay, even though I wasn't sure of it myself after visiting with Mom and talking with the doctor. He didn't say much in return. It felt weird, just him and me at the dinner table without Mom.

After dinner, I went to the bedroom I grew up in and collapsed onto the bed. I was exhausted physically and emotionally. I fell asleep instantly, and the next thing I remember, my phone was ringing early in the morning on New Year's Eve. I didn't recognize the area code.

Jesus, what now?

I answered with a lump in my throat.

"Hello?"

There was a slight pause on the other end of the phone. It was my brother's daughter's husband.

Chas and me

"Your brother Chas is dead," he said.

His words hit me like a Mike Tyson overhand, right out of nowhere. I was speechless. Instantly numb. I don't remember how that call ended. My mind was fucked up beyond belief, racing a million miles an hour.

And then all my thoughts turned toward Dad. His wife of sixty years was in the hospital, and now his firstborn son, his namesake, Charles III, was dead. All in a span of forty-eight hours.

A day earlier, Dad was so distraught, he was on the couch with a gun. There was no way I could tell him about Chas until Mom's situation was more stable. Whether it was right or wrong, I decided I was going to sit on the news of my brother's death while I handled getting his body back to Connecticut from Arizona and setting up the funeral. Holding the news inside of me was the most emotionally difficult thing I've ever had to fucking do.

My sister Paula, me, and my brother Chas

With bodybuilding, fitness, and nutrition, you can find a book (or a website nowadays) and get the answers and guidance you need. But where's the rulebook for a life crisis? Where's the Charles Atlas guide (one of the first books I had about weightlifting) for dealing with this? There are tons of books about processing and healing after a crisis, but where was the play-by-play when I needed it most?

It felt like it was all on me. My older brother, dead. My mom, hospitalized. My dad, in a state of shock. My sister, avoiding it all. Talk about wanting to lash out and fight the world. This is life, though, right?

Chas

I don't pretend to be the only one having gone through devastating events like this. We all go through it. Life never stops coming at you. It is full of unpredictable adversity, completely out of your control. The one thing you can control, however, is how you respond to it.

I decided to take a long, hot shower, where I bawled my eyes out and screamed at the top of my lungs. I gave myself that time to let it all out. To let it all wash down the drain.

After that shower, I knew I had to be the rock for my parents. If I would focus on them, I would be less likely to focus on my own pain and grief. I would build my own strength by helping build theirs. As I put on my big boy pants, I vowed to handle the situation.

Over the next few days, I snuck around town, figuring out how to get my brother's body back home and coordinate the funeral. It took a couple of days, but once his body finally arrived in Ansonia, I got a phone call from the Italian funeral home director, Robert Ricciuti. He told me to get down to the funeral home right away.

When I got there, he showed me Chas's body. There were black-and-blue bruises all over his body. What the fuck? My brain went crazy with scenarios, but I couldn't do anything about it at that moment. Whatever had happened to Chas couldn't be changed. But taking care of Mom and Dad was something I could at least try and control.

I stood in that cold, sterile metal box and looked down at my dead older brother. It seemed like it was just yesterday that I was looking up to him. He was four years older than me, and I idolized him. There were no words for how I felt as I stood there. I kissed his forehead and said, "I love you bro. I hope you're finally at peace."

As I left the funeral home, I knew I had to break the news to Dad, even though he was still in shock about Mom. In small towns, word travels fast, so it was important that he hear about Chas from me, not someone else.

The next day during lunch, I said, "Dad, I have something to tell you."

I could tell his thoughts went immediately to Mom. Chas wasn't even on his radar, so I told him very simply, "Chas has passed."

My dad heard the words, and it looked like he got punched in the stomach. He was totally sideswiped by the news. He never saw it coming. Boom. Life.

I sat across the table from my tough, military dad. He was reduced to a frail shadow of himself. He stared blankly and said, over and over, in disbelief, "My Chas? My Charlie? How? Why? What happened?"

I wanted to squeeze the pain out of him, but all I could do was gently hug him. My dad broke down and the tears started flowing. I had only seen him cry once. You know his position on crying. Men don't do it. But this day was different. We both cried.

I stayed with Dad until he settled down. Then I gathered my strength to go tell Mom at the hospital. She was more alert than before but still had tubes and wires running in and out of her body. After talking to her about her hip and seeing how she was doing, I kissed her on her forehead and said, "Mom, I have some bad news."

She seemed to know what I was going to say. A mom's intuition, I guess.

"It's Chas. He passed away," I said.

Mom handled the news like John Wayne. Took it right on the chin, kept her composure, looked at me and said, "It finally caught up to him."

Mom held a certain peace about Chas. I think that's because she had lived his death so many times in her imagination.

Back in the day, he'd disappear for days at a time on a binge. I'd watch her sit at the kitchen window crying, worried sick, hoping and praying he'd pull up in the driveway. So, when the day finally came that he didn't make it home, she had already grieved for him too many times to count.

After a while, Mom's concern shifted toward my dad. She wanted to make sure I would look out for him. I assured her I would. With Mom and Dad informed, the next thing I had to do was finalize Chas's funeral plans and say goodbye.

On the day of Chas's funeral, I drove to the funeral home with my cousin, Mark, who helped me immensely during that time and in the years that followed. I am eternally grateful for his love and support. Neither of my parents attended. Mom, in the hospital. Dad, too distraught. They didn't get the chance to say goodbye to their first son.

I was moved to tears by how many people came out to pay their respects and say their goodbyes to Chas—from my cousins and other relatives to close family friends and a few of Chas's old biker bros.

Breeze, who owned a biker shop and built bikes for Chas and me, was there. Joey Cardella and Gary Taylor came to show respect for Chas. Arthur and Jane Goldstein, whom I knew my whole life, also attended the funeral. Another one of Chas's friends, Joey Malardo, showed up, too. It was incredible to see and feel their love. Even my sister showed up. We hugged, kissed, and kept it cordial but didn't talk much.

By far the worst part was the open casket. I don't know why the fuck we did that. It was torture.

I kept replaying Mom's words back in my head, "It finally caught up to him." I couldn't help but think how Chas and I came from the same parents. We grew up in the same house. We roamed the same neighborhood. It could have been me in that coffin. But it wasn't.

I had done my fair share of drugs as a teen, but I ultimately followed my passion for bodybuilding. And it saved my life. I truly believe Chas never found a passion, and that's why he turned to alcohol and drugs.

Oddly enough, when you're working out really hard, it releases endorphins in a manner similar to the way heroin works on drug addicts. We were both chasing that high, but in our own ways.

After the funeral, we had to move Mom from the hospital to a convalescent home while she awaited surgery on her hip. I then had to arrange home care for Dad so I could return to Los Angeles for work.

On that plane ride back to LA, I felt like I was in a heavy fog. Once back in the Golden State, the beautiful sunshine didn't seem to shine so bright anymore.

I was shattered. No one should have to go through this, but there I was, trying to make sense of something that was truly senseless. It was like I was drowning in misery.

I don't know how many days I stayed locked up in my house, but it must have been quite a while because I had received a call from Frankie Cassavetes.

Frankie's a trainer who trains a lot of high-profile athletes and actors. He had asked me to go to Robert Duvall's birthday party with him and Ray Liotta. I hadn't even left the house to go to the gym, so I thought I should get out and try to have some fun.

After catching up with some friends, I sat on the porch, deep in thought about all that had happened with Chas and my mom and dad. Ray came outside and talked to me about Chas and asked how my parents were dealing with Chas's death and Mom's hip. I was so lucky to have friends who understood how your life could change instantly.

When Frankie and Ray dropped me off at home that night, I thanked them both and told them I love them.

Frankie Cassavetes, Ray Liotta, and Robert Duvall at Gold's Gym

Over the next five years, I flew back and forth from Los Angeles to Ansonia more times than I can count.

I helped Mom through four failed surgeries on her hip. One time, she contracted a MRSA staph infection after one of her surgeries and almost died. She was in and out of convalescent homes. She needed a Hoyer lift to get in and out of bed. She had to wear a diaper. *A diaper?*

Mom had always left the house dressed to the nines for whatever that day held. Now it was a hospital gown and a wheelchair. She was the one who took care of everyone, and now she was the one who needed someone to take care of her. It depressed me to see her like this.

Dad was never the same after Mom shattered her hip and Chas died. Mom had always taken care of Dad like nobody's business. He lost weight and his health deteriorated. He had relied on her so much for the necessities of life, and now that support was gone. He had to eventually go on oxygen and use a wheelchair.

When Mom was healthy enough to be home, they'd watch TV together, holding hands in those damn wheelchairs. I was uplifted by how much they still showed their love for each other.

Because of Mom's wheelchair, she had to be carried up the stairs to the back porch and into the house. Eventually, I decided I needed someone to build a ramp back there. Joey Cardella put me in touch with a carpenter he knew, Bobby DiBiase.

Bobby was incredible. It took him two days to build the ramp, and it snowed the whole time. But Bobby never complained. He was there to do a job, and he did it. I'll always be grateful for the work he did. Thank you, Bobby.

Ultimately, I had to hire a team of twenty-four-hour nurses because I couldn't be there full time and my parents needed professional medical care. I also had some relatives drop by and check in on my parents from time to time.

Things started off fine, but then I started noticing stuff missing from the house. Things like Mom's jewelry and Dad's tools. The weirdest things that went missing were buckets of copper piping and vintage swords Dad had in his workshop.

I can't prove it, but I'm pretty sure some of my so-called relatives looted it and sold it for scrap. Shit like that made me sick to my stomach. It was tough to process it all without flying off the handle and beating the shit out of someone.

And if all that wasn't bad enough, the nurses couldn't make it up the hill during snowstorms, and Mom would have to sit around in a soiled diaper. I thought, "Fuck this. Enough is enough."

The inevitable day came when I had to move them out of the house and into an assisted living facility. I flew in from LA, and wouldn't you know it, another snowstorm had hit, which only made things that much worse. In spite of it all, I did all I could to make it happen as smoothly as possible.

Dad had bought the family house in 1957. It was his castle, and he wanted to die in it. Having to move out of his home was devastating. He was so demoralized. I felt awful that I couldn't respect his wishes, but the wheels had come off. Their safety and health were my primary concerns and responsibility.

When the van came to take them away, Dad acted like a cornered badger, full of piss and vinegar. I had to physically remove him from the house to get him to go. It tore me up doing what I knew had to be done.

As we rode away together, I looked back at the house, thinking of my childhood.

CHAPTER TWO

THE FIGHT AT THE ITALIAN FESTIVAL

"To hell with circumstances; I create opportunities."
—Bruce Lee

WHAT IS CHILDHOOD ALL ABOUT? I'm no psychologist, but my guess is it's about experiencing enough shit to discover what your passion is. To figure out your dreams, ambitions, and goals. And sure enough, by the time I was ten years old, I had seen, heard, and experienced enough shit to start to figure things out.

The two biggest influences in my younger years were my family and my neighborhood. A real shocker, right? I mean, what else is there when you're a kid? More specifically, it meant being surrounded by a bunch of alpha males.

It turns out tough guys come in all shapes, sizes, and colors. The truth is, you can't discount any dude based on looks. It's all about heart, that competitive fire in your belly to be the man. It doesn't matter how many people are in a room; in your head, you're the top fucking dog. It's something that's engrained in you, that unstoppable force that makes you want to be the dominant one.

Young stallion

Like a lot of bodybuilders and athletes, I started out as a scrawny, skinny half-pint of a kid with something to prove. To make matters worse, I was pigeon-toed and had to wear those gangly steel braces on my lower legs. The kids were fucking ruthless with the name-calling. Talk about getting a chip on my shoulder.

But hey, a few chips never hurt anyone. Take a listen to Michael Jordan's acceptance speech at the Naismith Memorial Basketball Hall of Fame. He said he didn't have just one chip on his shoulder; he had a whole bag.

Of all the alpha males I've come to know in my lifetime, Dad will always remain the first and most influential one. He was a man's man in every which way. Let me tell you what I mean.

CHARLES W. VALENTE II
May 25, 1928—March 3, 2012

Dad was born in New Haven, Connecticut, to Charles and Mary Valente. He was the oldest of six boys: Norman, Pucci, Nelson, George, and Gary. I can only imagine how those six Valente brothers ran the neighborhood back in the day. Damn, they must have had some fun.

Dad was a tough-love kind of guy, a trait that came from his own pops, my Grandpa Valente, who was as tough as they come. When I was eight, I caught pneumonia and was laid up in bed with chills and a raging fever. One day, Grandpa Valente came over to play cards with Dad and heard I was sick as a dog. I was scared shitless thinking I was going to die when Grandpa Valente popped his head in my room, took a long look at me, and said in his loud, raspy, East Coast Italian voice, "Keep it up and you'll wind up in a box!"

I got better soon after that. I guess that was his way of saying, "I love you."

Dad (center) and his brothers

The Valentes came to America from Sicily around the turn of the century, when Italy's economy was flatlining. There were no jobs there, which led to poverty, violence, and disease. My family did what so many other Italians did—they left a bad situation in hopes of finding a better one. After passing through New York City, they had ended up in New Haven with a bunch of other Italians, Grandpa met Grandma, and they started their big Italian family soon after.

My dad was about five feet, eight inches tall and weighed 170 pounds. He was a good-looking guy, with a quick smile and joke. A military man. His friends called him Chuck or Sonny. He had a solid build despite never working out with weights—everything he did was very physical, from his work (hanging wallpaper and construction) to his passions (hunting and fishing). Dad hung wallpaper so seamlessly that he got jobs all over the East Coast, including New York City. He was a pretty big deal in his trade.

No matter the situation, Dad held his own. He always wanted to be in control, and when necessary, he wasn't afraid to enforce his own code of right and wrong, like the time at my sister's wedding.

Paula married her husband, Norman, when she was eighteen. (I was ten.) At the wedding reception in our church's Italian Hall, everyone was dancing, laughing, and drinking. The mood changed when Uncle Gary, who was a bit of a player, pinched a woman's ass out of the blue. Dad caught wind of it and confronted him.

Dad's family

"What the fuck are you doing? Have some respect," Dad yelled.

Uncle Gary was drunk and wasn't about to back down from anyone, let alone his brother. "What the fuck are you gonna do about it?" he yelled back.

Next thing you know, Dad and Uncle Gary were going at it like they were in a title fight. Soon enough, the cops showed up, and Dad and Uncle Gary wanted to fight them, too! It was fucking crazy. It took a few cops on each arm to drag them off to jail and slap disorderly conduct charges on them. The local newspaper wrote a small article about their scrap. But it wasn't long before Dad and Uncle Gary were back to their old ways, hanging out and playing cards together.

There were tons of crazy stories like that, and Dad had always been in the middle of each one of them. He's been gone for quite a few years, and I wish I could sit down with him and talk about life and everything he meant to me. If I could write him a letter and send it to him up in heaven, it would go something like this:

Dear Dad,

I always looked up to you. Before Elvis, before Bruce Lee, before all the bikers and bodybuilders, you, Dad, were my first idol.

Watching you, day in and day out, taught me everything I needed to know about being a man. You treated Mom with so much respect. You always opened her door, whether it was a car, house, or restaurant. You never raised your voice and always treated her like a lady.

You got up every morning at 5 a.m. and went to work before I even woke up for school. You came home in the evening and never had a single complaint. You were like clockwork. People always ask me where I got my discipline from, and I tell them, "I got it from my dad."

Thank you for your unwavering guidance, and for setting me straight when I fucked up or got out of line. God knows I did that a lot. At the time, I hated getting whipped, but you always made sure to explain why I was being punished, so I learned my lesson. I hope you noticed I never made the same mistake twice.

Thanks for being a hard-ass and making me wake up early

on the weekends to do chores, like mowing the lawn in the summer, raking leaves in the fall, shoveling snow in the winter, and yard work in the spring.

Your Big Three Rules stayed with me forever: 1) Be respectful, 2) Be productive, and 3) If you want something, work for it. It's all I've ever needed to know to achieve my life's goals. That's how I bought my first minibike, remember? When Stevie Piccard from across the street got his minibike, I asked you for one, and you told me that if I wanted it, I had to get a job and work for it. And so, I went out and got a paper route and started cutting the neighbors' lawns. I saved up enough money and bought that bike. And to tell you the truth, had you just bought it for me, I don't think I would have loved it like I did. Earning it felt good. I liked that feeling and still do.

My first minibike

I also loved the way you'd take the time to hang out with me. Like when I was five, you'd sit me down on the couch with you to watch movies. If it wasn't a war movie, it was "Tarzan," or a western with John Wayne. I remember when John Wayne would do something badass, you'd point at the TV and say, "See that? I can do that."

And guess what, Dad? I believed you. In my eyes, you could do anything. Remember when I was in the Boy Scouts and came home with a block of wood, axels, and four little wheels? You took me into your woodshop and helped me build the sweetest little racecar, complete with a custom paint job. It was fast, too! We kicked everyone's asses at the Soap Box Derby. You even made a display case for our winning car and blue ribbon. I still have it.

I loved that you had such strong passions and that you shared them with me. I mean, what kid gets to learn to safely load, aim, and shoot a gun, and learn how to make the bullets? And when you took me fishing, you took the time to make sure I knew how to cast the perfect line.

Thank you for letting me hang out in your man cave with you and your buddies. I loved that basement and all the custom-made pieces, like your gun cabinet and that case you built for your coin collection. You even built that brick bar from scratch! You would all gather around it, and I would hear all your crazy hunting and fishing stories. It was a beautiful thing to see all the camaraderie, the razzing, and the fun.

Dad's man cave

Remember when you took me to St. Sebastian Men's Club? To be a kid in a place like that felt incredible. I'll never forget when Mom called looking for us, and the bartender called out, "Is Sonny here?"

You were sitting right in front of him! You waved off the call, and the bartender said, "Nope, he already left."

When the bartender hung up, we all busted out laughing. You and your brothers popped back another shot and beer, and then we hustled home for dinner. We never told Mom about that. It was our little secret.

I could go on and on about all the things you did for me in those early years, but let me just say this...

I have always been so proud to be your son. When we were out and about in town, people would always yell, "Hey, Sonny! How you doin'?"

When we would go out eating, someone would stop by the table to say hello, and then when you would go to pay the tab, the waiter would say, "It's been taken care of." I saw how you treated people with respect and how people treated you with that same respect. I always felt like I was with a superstar when I was with you in the neighborhood.

St. Sebastian Club

I love you, Dad.

—Your son, Ricky

To have just one more hug, kiss, or conversation—wouldn't that be beautiful? I would give anything to have another day with my parents.

As cliché as it sounds, once they're gone, they're gone. If your parents are still alive, make the time, pick up the phone, and book that trip. Go see your parents before it's too late. Because, trust me, one day it will be. And then what?

My parents loved to tell the story about how they met. I heard it a lot over the years, and it made me laugh every time. We'd be at dinner and someone would ask them, "How did you two meet?"

My dad would get a funny look in his eye, and he'd say, "It was 1946—no, 1947—and I was at the local roller skating rink in New Haven with my friends. We were watching all the pretty girls go round and round. And that's when I saw her and knew I just had to meet her."

"Meet me? More like kill me!" Mom would chime in.

Dad would laugh and continue. "So, when I finally got enough courage, I got out on the rink and skated up next to her, but I couldn't stop and accidentally bumped into her!"

"That's a nice way to put it," Mom would say. "I think you ran me over on purpose!"

They would laugh out loud at themselves. Turns out, Mom fell down and broke her ankle. I'm not shitting you!

Dad and Mom

They were inseparable from that day on and married later that same year. They had my sister, Paula, in 1950, and my brother, Charles III, in 1954. I think I was an "oops." I came along on July 11, 1958. Seven-eleven. That lucky combo. And I've felt that way my whole life. Lucky.

Mom came up with my name, Ricky Dennis. The Ricky part was for one of her favorite singers and actors, Ricky Nelson, and the Dennis part was for her favorite comic, *Dennis the Menace*. She must have had a crystal ball when she named me because I went on to have a career in entertainment and was always getting myself into a little trouble. (Okay, maybe a lot of trouble.)

In 1957, Dad bought the house I would grow up in for $12,000. It was a modest three-bedroom, one-bathroom house. Having only one bathroom was rough. If it wasn't Paula taking hours on her hair and makeup, it was my dad smoking unfiltered Camels while he did his business. Not a pleasant memory!

Me, Chas, and Paula

I barely knew my sister since she was eight years older and always did her own thing. She married right out of high school and was gone before I knew it. My brother was a different story. If Dad was my first idol, Chas was my second. He was one badass dude in his own right.

Before I knew how crazy and respected Chas was outside of the house, I saw him come and go wearing the coolest clothes, like bell-bottom jeans, silk shirts, and platform shoes. He looked like a Hollywood movie star with his leather jackets and stylish, long hair. He was athletic, too. He could pull wheelies on his bike and do backflips into the pool. He never backed down from a dare, either.

Chas and I shared a bedroom until my sister got married. Every kid brother who has shared a room with his older brother knows it's fucking torture. Chas would play practical jokes on me, use me as his whipping post, or wrestle me to the ground to either choke me out or tickle me to death. He'd also do older brother type of shit, like pin me down and drip spit within an inch of my forehead, then suck it back up while laughing his ass off.

I always hated that I wasn't strong enough to toss him off me. It was those beatdowns that gave me plenty of motivation to get bigger and stronger. That's the rite of passage for a kid brother, I guess.

There was harmony in the Valente family during those years. Dad brought home the bacon and served as judge and jury. Mom did everything else—literally, everything. She was the head chef, nurse, chauffeur, laundress, housekeeper, and everything in between.

I was so blessed to witness the everlasting love affair between my mom and dad. They kissed goodbye every morning when Dad left for work and hello every evening when he came home. He treated her like his queen, and she treated him like her king. They had an amazing balance and ease. Like a dance, filling in for the other without ever skipping a beat.

My mom was always an angel. The best woman I've ever known.

GERALDINE SOFIA PUGLISE
February 22, 1929—October 10, 2012

Mom was born in New Haven, Connecticut, to Michael and Mary Puglise. She had two brothers, Tony and Mike, and one sister, Annie. Her parents, like my dad's, were also from Sicily, making me full Sicilian.

Mom was the classiest lady I've ever known. She always matched her shoes, gloves, and hat to her dress whenever she left the house. Her smile brightened any room.

Mom lived for cooking and baking. She loved to make people happy, and feeding them was her way of doing it. Food was her love language. Our love language. We ate family-style, homecooked Italian meals every night. Spaghetti and meatballs, lasagna, baked ziti—you name it, Mom made it, and she made it really well. Mom also fed the church and the neighborhood. If someone was really sick, or if there was a graduation, birthday, funeral, wedding, or newborn, my mom would bring one of her best dishes. She never missed an opportunity to give.

Mom learned her cooking and baking skills from her mom—my grandma, Nonni, who lived a few blocks off Wooster Street in New Haven. Her house was easy to pick out because it leaned to one side. No shit, it was so old, it was crooked. Nonni was one of those grandmas that covered all her furniture in plastic to keep it clean. I left a lot of skin on those couches, peeling my legs off them in the summertime.

Mom's parents and brother Luis

Dad was the luckiest of us all. He got the full force of Mom's loving and affectionate ways. She made it so easy for him. She cooked his breakfast, packed his lunch, and had dinner ready every night. Mom also gave him the choice cut of meat every time. And if they were ever going out, before Dad jumped in the shower, he'd always ask Mom, "Honey, what am I wearing?" And sure enough, by the time he got out of the shower, Mom would have his socks, shoes, pants, shirt, and hat set out for him on the bed. Thinking of that still makes me smile.

We shared so much love through food. There was nothing like Sundays at the Valente house. That special day of the week would start when Dad brought home fresh bagels, cream cheese, and doughnuts from Vonetes on Main Street. I'd sit on a stool at the counter in our Italian-styled kitchen, eating chocolate eclairs while watching Mom chop onions, garlic, and fresh tomatoes for her sauce. She'd throw all the ingredients into a huge pot, add a few spices, turn on the heat, and let it simmer all day long.

Once the sauce started simmering on the stove, it was time to get dressed up for church. Mom would make Chas and me wear suits and ties. And half the time, she'd put us in matching suits. Come on, Mom! We'd load into our big, white Ford station wagon, with Dad singing along to Frank Sinatra, and head to church.

We went to Holy Rosary Parish, located on Father Salemi Drive, just off Ansonia's Main Street. It was founded back in 1908 and consisted of a huge, round cathedral and a spacious Italian Hall, which is where Dad and Uncle Gary fought at my sister's wedding. In the basement of the Italian Hall was the St. Sebastian Men's Club, where my dad would take me. He not only drank there with his buddies and brothers but also sat on the board and did the books.

Mom really loved the church. When Chas and I were kids,

Mom bought us cross rings. All through my teenage years, to when I first came to California, to when I was doing commentator work for ESPN, and up to the present day, I've always worn a cross ring. Wearing it makes me feel connected to Mom and Dad.

After going to Mass, we'd head home, and as soon as we would walk in the door, our mouths would start watering because it smelled so damn good. My mom would add meatballs or chicken to the sauce to bring it all together. Then, as if summoned by the wafting smells of the stove, relatives would start to show up.

My family lived by the unspoken rule that when you went to someone's house for a get-together, you "knocked with your elbows." That meant you showed up carrying a dish, drinks, or dessert, and didn't have any free hands. My family took this rule to the extreme, and everyone arrived with more food and drinks than would fit in the kitchen.

We were lucky to have so much of our family living near us, and for me, so many cousins to play with. It was usually one of Dad's brothers and their families, like Uncle Nelson and Auntie Millie and their kids, Scott and Richie; Uncle George and Auntie Anne and their kids, Connie, Terry, and Donna; Uncle Norman with his wife and kids; Uncle Pucci with his wife and kids; or Uncle Mike (my mom's brother), who would show up with Auntie Teresa and their four kids, Mark, Mary Ann, Michelle, and Michael Junior—the four "M"s.

Mark and I had formed a special bond. He was ten years younger than me, so having him around was like having a kid brother. Our bond became even stronger when he later helped me with my aging parents. Once everyone would arrive at our house in the afternoon, Italian chaos ensued. The guys would head into the parlor to watch sports, and then the razzing would begin. You know how Italians are.

"That player's a bum!"

"I got ten bucks riding on this!"

"They'll never make the playoffs!"

The guys bet all sorts of ways on all the games. My grandma Nonni even used to run a numbers game.

If you aren't familiar, "running numbers" was basically like a lotto. We'd all pick three numbers and give them to Nonni, along with some cash. Everyone got in on the action. When she'd draw numbers, everyone would gather around and hold their breath. After she'd announce the winning digits, one person would go crazy, and everyone else would mutter:

"They always win."

"Must be rigged."

"I better say more Hail Marys."

After that, the ladies would head into the kitchen to finish up the meal and set the table. When Mom would declare, "Dinner is ready," everyone would swarm in. What followed was a rumbling mix of laughter and conversations, with everyone talking a little bit louder than the person next to them. Despite the competition for airtime, it all worked out. I miss the banter, laughter, and love that filled that room.

Italians and their cooking, the family together, and the joy it brings—I think that's why Italian food is the best. It's a family thing. We'd eat for hours, finishing with dessert and coffee (and the adults with sambuca and brandy). Everyone would pitch in to clean up, and we would do it all over again the next Sunday. It was such a gift to grow up like that.

The serenity of those Sundays—if only life could be like that all the time. If only childhood could last forever, like the summers seemed to back then. Carefree. Safe. Innocent.

Unfortunately, my neighborhood wouldn't let that continue for long. We all grew up pretty quickly.

When I started school at Prendergast Elementary, I saw exactly what the neighborhood had to offer. I got tossed into a melting pot with kids of all races, backgrounds, and upbringings. That opened my eyes. Instead of picking up book smarts, I learned street smarts. And thanks to my flag football coaches, Jose Neves and Anthony Bruciata, I also got my first taste of athletic competition. We won the peewee flag football championship that year.

My big Italian family

At Prendergast, I saw how melting pots expose differences, how those differences lead to disagreements, and how those disagreements lead to fights. But thank God for that dysfunctional environment. It's where I met my best friend.

One day, out in the schoolyard, I was minding my own business when, all of a sudden, a basketball hit me in the back of my head. I whipped around to confront the punk who was laughing at me when I noticed his buddy coming up from behind. Here I was, a skinny little kid about to get into my first real fistfight, and it was me against two kids from another neighborhood.

"Shit, it's bound to happen sometime, so let's do this," I thought.

I balled up my fists, but before I could do anything, this other kid flew past me, screaming like a banshee. He started kicking their asses, and then I jumped in, and we taught those suckers a lesson. All four of us got suspended, and we were all cooler for it.

That kid turned out to be Jimmy Vane. Another Italian kid! And just like that, the Vane and Valente show was up and running. We were inseparable all the way through high school.

The fights in elementary school weren't just limited to the guys. The girls threw down with some serious brutality, too. Every time there was going to be a catfight, Jimmy and I would run to the corner as quickly as possible to get a good spot for the show. When the fight would start, we'd cheer them on like a bunch of crazed savages:

"Kick her ass!"

"Rip her hair out!"

And they would. It was fucking insane.

It was all so twisted and crazy, but to us, it seemed normal. And no one dared stop them because, if you tried, they'd fight your ass, too. You couldn't tell teachers, either, because then you'd be labeled a rat or a snitch, and that was the low of all lows, a surefire way to get blackballed by all the cool kids.

After cheering on a catfight like that, it always felt weird to go home and see Mom. I'd walk in and she would greet me with a big kiss and hug.

"How was school today? Learn anything interesting?" she'd ask.

I'd give her the standard response: "School was good, and yes, I learned a lot," but in my mind, I'd think, "I learned who could fight and who couldn't. Who had big balls and who was a pussy. That if you were in a fight and got someone on the ground, the first thing you were supposed to do was stomp on his fucking face."

I'm sure there are a lot of kids my age who grew up in Ansonia and didn't deal with any of this shit because they hung out with a totally different crowd. You are who you surround yourself with, and I ended up hanging out with the restless, more aggressive kids.

It seemed like our town had something to do with it, though. Grandpa Valente had seen it all unfold over decades and loved telling us kids the history of Ansonia. It went something like this:

Ansonia was a small industrial town located in a little nook on the fast-moving Naugatuck River, about ten miles west of New Haven. Industrialists needed a fast-moving river to power and cool their factories, and Ansonia was it. With the perfect location, Ansonia grew pretty quickly and got the title of "town," and then "city." With Ansonia's economy booming, it became known as the "Copper City" for its heavy manufacturing. Ah, the glory years.

Then "Black Friday" happened. On August 19, 1955, Hurricane Connie dropped tons of rain all over Connecticut. And before Ansonians knew it, the same river that kept all its factories up and running turned into a massive wall of water, tearing out bridges, factories, homes, and people. Imagine that. The same thing that created them destroyed them.

After the flood, downtown Ansonia never really recovered. Shops moved out and factories didn't rebuild. Fewer factories meant fewer jobs. Fewer jobs meant less hope. Once people lost hope, they looked for an escape. That escape came in the form of drugs and alcohol. And once those new forces took over, crime and violence followed. The cycle was born. Sounds like Italy a century earlier, huh?

It wasn't long before it all came to a head one day, when the combination of the neighborhood, family, and food showed me the path I was going take in my life. Funny how you look back and wonder if the universe lined these things up for you.

It was 1968. Mom and I were volunteering at the Holy Rosary Italian Festival to raise money for the church. There were all sorts of Italian food booths mixed in with carnival games and rides.

Mom and I worked at the pizza booth. The crowd was thick as Mom and I dished out slices left and right. I was having a blast working with her at the busiest booth in the festival. Then everything changed when someone yelled, "Catch that motherfucker!"

The crowd in front of us parted like the fucking Red Sea, and then two dudes tackled another guy from behind. They all jumped up and squared off right in front of me. I could hear them huffing and puffing as they stared each other down. And before I knew it, one of the dudes sucker punched the other guy right in the face. I saw his eyes roll back as he fell and smacked his head on the concrete, making a dull, hollow thud.

With the guy knocked unconscious, you'd think it would have ended right then. But no, they started kicking him in the ribs and stomping on his face. Literally mashing his face into the concrete with each blow to the head. This was happening right in front of me as my mom is frantically trying to pull me away.

"Ricky! Get back!" she yelled.

But I didn't budge. I was totally mesmerized. There was blood pouring out of the guy's nose and shit oozing out of his ears. It was playing out like a slow-motion movie. I saw every detail so clearly, I couldn't look away, let alone blink. Every punch. Every kick. Every drop of blood spilling out and pooling onto the ground.

When the two dudes were done turning the guy's face into hamburger meat, they jacked his wallet, snagged his watch, ripped off his gold chains, and ran. My adrenaline pumped full throttle while my heart pounded out of my chest. The sound of sirens filled the air, and I just stood there, struggling to understand what just happened.

When the cops finally showed up to investigate, they started questioning everyone.

"What happened?"

"Who was it?

"See anything?"

People looked the cops dead in the eye and answered:

"Don't know, was too busy eating."

"See what?"

"I didn't see anything."

Cops weren't our friends back then. Plus, getting involved might have put a big target on your back. Because if those guys were to find out you had snitched on them, it would be your ass getting the next beatdown.

The ambulance eventually took the guy away. To this day, I have no clue if he lived or died.

At the age of ten, I had never seen anything so raw and vicious. Sure, the elementary school fights were pretty intense, but this was fucking crazy. I had no idea what the guy had done to deserve that beatdown, and that scared the shit out of me. But, truthfully, watching those dudes beat that guy's ass made my adrenaline pump like nothing before. It's probably why I'm a huge boxing and MMA fan to this day.

That night, I replayed the fight over and over in my head. As I laid in bed, I made a promise to myself that I would do everything in my power to never be the guy on the bottom. No way. Fuck that.

The next day, I asked my parents if I could start taking a karate class. I also ordered the Charles Atlas workout program. The fire in my belly was lit. I wanted to get bigger, stronger, and be able to fight. When my Charles Atlas program arrived two weeks later, it was on.

CHAPTER THREE

THE GYM IN MY BASEMENT

"Nothing is as important as passion. No matter what you want to do with your life, be passionate."
—Jon Bon Jovi

FEAR AND EGO ARE TWO POWERFUL FORCES. They are at the root of so many of our choices in life. At the ripe age of ten, the passion growing in my belly was all about fear. It would be a few years before ego would enter the equation. It would be many more years, after a lot of reading and getting older, before I could set both down and just be happy. But before we get into all that, let's first focus on passion.

Chuck Norris and Bruce Lee

True passion doesn't have to be explained. It isn't something that is taught.

Passion wakes you up before your alarm clock goes off. It keeps you up late at night because you're too excited thinking about it to fall asleep. You can't stop studying and learning. It gets inside of you, and nothing will hinder your pursuit of it.

A passion is the crush of all crushes. And I had it bad for two in particular: karate and bodybuilding.

Tom Laughlin in "Billy Jack"

Let's start with karate. I was obsessed with it. The way legends like Bruce Lee, Chuck Norris, and Tom Laughlin (see the great film *Billy Jack*) coiled their bodies to strike like snakes was so badass. I admired their balance, power, and confidence. I wanted to be just like them. I mean, come on, who didn't want to be Bruce Lee? Pound for pound, the most amazing martial artist ever!

I was so pumped up about karate, but the problem was, I couldn't find a teacher. I asked everyone, but it was my brother who came through, introducing me to his buddy Geech from the nearby town of Shelton. And just like that, I found my first sensei!

Geech gave me karate lessons in my basement twice a week during my eighth-grade year. In those sessions, I learned all the basics, like how to block, throw punches, and kick using my homemade heavy bag—an old laundry bag stuffed with sand and rubber material my dad had in his workroom.

Geech also showed me these things called "katas," which are patterns of movements. Like a dance, each kata has a unique choreography to it. Different steps, kicks, punches, and blocks. (Years later, I'd lean on the principle of katas for my posing routines in bodybuilding contests.)

Geech ingrained in me that balance is key, and that power comes from the hips and core. He also taught me philosophies, like how when I throw a punch, I should think about punching all the way through my target for maximum impact. I was so into karate that I would put on my karate gi and head into the basement to practice on my own every chance I got.

I didn't realize I was learning values that would stick with me forever—things like repetition, discipline, focus, and the value of a good work ethic.

Karate also introduced me to the mind-body-spirit connection. To perform optimally, all three must function in harmony. If your head is somewhere else, your body can't perform, and if your body can't perform, then your spirit suffers. I had to learn to balance all three. And speaking of balance, physical balance was another huge component of martial arts, and something necessary to all sports, including bodybuilding.

I'm grateful my parents gave me the space—our basement and time—to pursue my dreams. They never hassled me about taking over downstairs, and I'm sure they let me slide on doing some chores as long as I was working on my passion. I have no idea if they planned that or if it just happened, but either way, it was genius.

In that basement, I learned that if I worked hard, I would get results, and with those results, my confidence grew. Looking back, I see how it created a deep-seated faith and trust in myself and the process.

In addition to training, I made my own karate weapons in Dad's woodshop. My favorite was the nunchucks. The only problem was that I'd be swinging them around trying to be like Bruce Lee and then—whack!—I would smack myself in the head or shin with them, or even worse, my balls. It fucking hurt like hell! Talk about getting knocked back down to earth. Things have a way of doing that when you get too full of yourself.

Passion makes you get your hands on everything related to it that you can. Back in those days, way before the internet, I read all the karate magazines and saw all the martial arts movies I could. I cut out the pictures of all the martial arts superstars and hung them on the wall in my basement, making the first version of my very own vision board. And we're not talking about a small corkboard. Oh, no, I took over a whole wall in our basement, making a six-by-six visual of the martial artist I wanted to be like.

Now, you have to keep in mind that this was the late '60s. I'm not even sure the term "vision board" existed yet. That's another thing about having a true passion. It makes you do things without anyone first telling you to do them—the things that will motivate and inspire you.

At the same time I was learning karate, I was also digging into my Charles Atlas book. That book soon became my bible. I followed the workouts religiously. To begin with, I didn't need much to challenge my scrawny physique. A couple of chairs, a towel, and a broomstick would do just fine for a full-body workout, according to Mr. Atlas.

For those first workouts, I'd put two chairs back to back, about shoulder-width apart, and practice dips, working my shoulders, chest, and triceps. Then, for my back and biceps, I'd move the chairs farther apart and put the broomstick across the tops of the chairs. I'd then lie on the ground, grab the broomstick, and do plank-style pull-ups. I'd do them overhand, with a wide grip to give my back width for that V-shape look. And then I'd do them underhand, with a narrow grip for thickness and depth.

Now, a word of warning—and trust me, I know from the painful experience of doing this: If you do too many dips or pull-ups, you start shaking. And once you start shaking, the chairs get a little unsteady, and that's when—boom!—a chair slips out and you bust your ass on the ground. But I guess what doesn't kill you only makes you stronger, right?

After doing dips and pull-ups, I'd take the broomstick off and face the chairs toward each other, about five feet apart, to do triceps dips, with my feet on one chair and my palms on the other. I'd focus on keeping my elbows in tight and facing straight back, keeping the weight on my triceps rather than my chest. I'd then use the towel to do overhead triceps extensions while using my other hand to provide resistance. Same for biceps curls. I'd then do standard military push-ups and inverted push-ups with my feet on a chair, doing both types with hands narrow and wide.

I'd wrap up my upper body workout by doing an ab routine. After that, I'd do my legs, which consisted of lunges, one-legged squats, and one-legged calf raises.

In terms of sets and reps, I'd start with three to four sets of each movement, doing at least ten to fifteen reps per set. My goal was to keep increasing my rep count until I hit twenty-five to fifty reps. It's amazing what you can do with so little. That workout created results.

For anyone starting a weight training program, your body weight is all you need. This lets your joints and body get used to the new stress you're putting on them. Once you get to the point when you're doing twenty-five to fifty reps on every movement, you're ready to start using weights.

At that time, I had no idea lifting weights would save my life. I know that sounds dramatic, but it kept me from going down some seriously dark paths. I can say this wholeheartedly because I had so many friends who went down those paths and died, became addicted to drugs, or went to prison. It was so fucking sad. My brother Chas fell into all these groups.

You see, at about the same time I got my Charles Atlas book and started my bodybuilding journey, Chas was packing our attic full of marijuana. It's a funny story, actually—at least the part when Dad came home from work and said to Mom, "I think there's a dead skunk in the attic."

No shit, that's how bad it smelled.

Dad followed the smell up into the attic and was shocked to find two huge garbage bags full of pot. He brought them down and immediately confronted Chas.

"What the fuck is this shit doing in my attic?" Dad asked.

Chas, of course, gave my dad that famous standard excuse: "It's not mine. I'm holding it for someone else."

I had to hold my breath so I wouldn't bust out laughing. It turns out "someone else" was a biker guy, and Dad knew biker guys didn't fuck around when it came to their drugs or their money. So, he told Chas to get it out of the house and give it back.

I'm pretty sure Chas stashed his weed somewhere else and then sold it. That was the beginning of Chas's journey selling drugs.

We were two brothers from the same parents who grew up in the same house, and we were headed in totally different directions. In my crazy neighborhood, temptation and peer pressure were powerful. We were a bunch of restless kids trying to channel our endless energy. We looked up to the older guys around us so much, and since they were doing drugs, my group of friends inevitably got involved with drugs, too. We all tried mushrooms, quaaludes, pot, acid, MDMA, speed, cocaine, LSD, peyote, and mescaline.

My first experience with drugs was in the sixth grade. I was at home when my brother came in with a girl on his arm. They were laughing like crazy and seemed to be having the time of their lives.

My brother walked up to me, handed me a few pieces of mushrooms, and said, "Hey, try this."

So, I did. Turned out they were psychedelic mushrooms. About thirty minutes later, I was sitting on the couch in our parlor smiling and laughing out of control.

Mom came into the room. "What are you laughing at?" she asked.

I stared at her, totally tripping my ass off, and all I could say was, "Chas."

Now, to tell you the truth, I kind of liked the feeling. That would begin my journey with drugs.

As a kid, I idolized Elvis Presley. I watched every one of his movies. To me, you couldn't get any cooler than Elvis—he could sing, he could dance, he could fight, and he was always with beautiful women. I wanted to be like Elvis.

Well, I couldn't sing or dance like Elvis, but I was about to get an education on what it's like to get a woman's attention.

My neighbor Barbara, who was a few years older than me, taught me how to French kiss. That was a moment I will never forget. In fact, thinking about it puts a big smile on my face.

Elvis Presley

We were sitting on her porch in the summertime. The sun was setting, and she had snuck some of her parents' wine. We were talking for a while, and out of the blue, she leaned over and kissed me. And then she did something I had never experienced: She shoved her tongue down my throat. At first, it was shocking, but then a second later, I thought, "Wow, this is fun."

We made out for a while, and before I knew it, I had a baseball bat in my pants.

From that day on, I was always looking to see if Barbara was out on her porch. What a great first kiss! Thank you, Barbara!

By the time I was in middle school, my friends and I were smoking pot regularly and dating girls every chance we got. A lot of my friends got into drinking, too, but that never stuck with me. Not sure why. I guess the hangovers didn't jibe well with working out the next day.

My two-chair, towel, and broomstick exercises had served their purpose. Between those workouts and karate, I was getting a lot stronger and ready to take the next step and start weight training. But here's the thing: Back then, you couldn't just join a gym down the street and hit the weights. There weren't any.

So, what did I do? Remember the newspaper route and all the yard work I did to buy my first minibike? Those same jobs paid for my own gym, built in my basement.

To make my own weight room, I searched flea markets and garage sales for a bench, a bar, and a set of weights. I scored a bench and bar pretty quickly, but I had to go down the street to

Bradley's Sporting Goods to buy a complete set of those cement-filled, plastic weights. I really liked the gym I put together, but I noticed that all the big boys in the magazines were using triceps pushdown machines to work their arms. So, guess what I did? I made one.

I got up on a ladder with one of Dad's drills and drilled a small hole in a wood beam in the ceiling. I screwed an eye hook into the hole and put a pulley up. Next, I sawed off a fourteen-inch piece of broomstick for the handle and drilled a hole all the way through it. I then ran a piece of rope through the hole and tied a big knot at the end to secure the handle. Next, I ran the rope through the pulley and down to the floor where I tied it around weights. With that, I had myself a triceps pushdown machine. Little did I know, I was on my way to my trademark horseshoe triceps and twenty-one-inch arms.

But I still needed one more thing to complete my basement gym: a full-length mirror to keep an eye on my form, which is the foundation of any sport, but especially bodybuilding. When your muscles are under great stress, poor form can easily lead to an injury. I also needed the mirror to make sure I was getting a full range of motion during my movements. And of course, I needed a mirror to keep track of my progress.

At that time, my vision board started to shift from martial artists to bodybuilders. All the top guys were on it: Steve Reeves, Bill Pearl, Arnold Schwarzenegger, Robbie Robinson, Lou Ferrigno, Boyer Coe, Roger Callard, Ken Waller, Franco Columbu, Casey Viator, Mike Mentzer, Ed Corney, Manuel Perry, Serge Nubret, Danny Padilla, Frank Zane, Albert Beckles, Chris Dickerson, Rick Wayne, and Mike Katz (a Connecticut legend).

There they were, on my wall, staring right back at me. I'd look at their supersized muscles and envision myself looking like that. I saw myself on the covers of magazines and in advertisements, just like they were. After all, isn't that what a vision board is for?

My vision board

I had a long way to go, of course, but I was on my way. In my mind, I saw it all so clearly.

The more I looked at that wall, the more I wanted to work out. I was pushing myself as hard as I could, which meant that a lot of times, I would lift to failure. I'd be bench pressing and thinking I could do just one more rep, even though my arms and chest were totally fried, and then—thump!—the bar would crash down on my chest. I would be totally stuck under its weight and have to roll the bar down off my chest and onto my stomach. I'd then lean to one side to dump the weights, and most of the time, the whole bench would tip over.

"Everything okay down there?" Mom would yell down the steps.

"Yeah, Mom, no problem!" I'd yell back.

I'm sure a lot of kids went through this because, if you're truly lifting to failure, it's inevitable.

It wasn't long until people in the neighborhood started

noticing my physique. They would throw me compliments about how I was looking bigger and stronger. It felt good to hear that, and it built up my confidence. I felt like I was getting some respect.

My brother taught me at a young age that in our neighborhood, respect was everything. You got respect by either being crazy or being able to fight. In a lot of cases, being crazy and being able to fight went hand in hand.

One day, I saw how Chas got his respect when he took me to the bowling alley. We walked in, and right off the bat, my brother spotted a group of tough-looking guys hanging out by the arcade.

"Stay here," Chas told me. I then watched him go over to the guys, put a finger in one dude's face, and ask, "You got my money?"

"Give me another week," the dude said.

My brother turned, looked at me, and then punched that punk right in the jaw. The dude went down and his buddies backed up. Next thing I knew, that guy was paying Chas the money he owed.

My brother walked back toward me, all jacked up. I could see the adrenaline in his eyes, totally on cloud nine. He wasn't going to let that guy rip him off. If Chas hadn't forced the issue, that dude would have never paid. No one was going to burn my brother.

Seeing what Chas did and how he felt after doing it was something I would never forget. I could barely focus on bowling. I kept thinking how my brother was crazy and scrappy. Needless to say, he was well respected in the neighborhood.

There's a common denominator between fighting, drugs, and weightlifting. It's called endorphins—those chemicals in the brain that give us a feeling of euphoria.

Throughout middle school, I kept hitting my basement gym every single day. I was reading and learning as much as I could about bodybuilding and its various techniques. I was also getting better at karate, steadily developing balance, flexibility, and speed.

Puberty was in full swing, and my shoulders were broadening. I was eating whatever I could get my hands on and was noticeably growing taller and thicker. High school was right around the corner, and my goal was to make the wrestling and football teams. A lot of great athletes came from Ansonia and Connecticut in general. I wanted to be one of them.

Before playing sports in high school, though, I had to pass my first test: the bus stop.

I had my fair share of fights in middle school, but nothing too crazy. I didn't think it was in me to be that ultraviolent animal like those I had seen out on the streets so many times. Maybe I just didn't know that I had it in me. It always takes a test, though. Someone or something that pushes your buttons just enough to see how far you'll go before snapping.

It was the first week of high school, and I was at the bus stop waiting to go to school. There was a handful of other kids also waiting, and one of those kids was a six-foot, two-inch-tall junior with a bad attitude.

I was minding my own business when the kid walked up, muttered something, and then sucker punched me with a right hook. My head snapped back, and I spun to the ground. It was my time to experience the real deal. It's one thing to see it happen to someone else, and an entirely different thing when it's you on the ground.

As I laid there, I heard the other kids laughing at me. The kid hawked a loogie at me and said something about my mom. I was so embarrassed, but more than anything, I was fucking pissed. Before I could react or do anything to retaliate, the bus pulled up and he got on with the other kids. As the bus drove away, I started to walk my sorry ass home.

The only thing I thought about for the rest of the day was how I was going to get my revenge. I knew that if I didn't stand up for myself, word would travel fast around town that I was a punk. I had to retaliate in a big way, or I would have a target on my back and my life would be fucking miserable.

Later that day, my brother confronted me. "I heard what happened. What are you gonna do about it?" he asked.

"I'm gonna get him tomorrow at the bus stop," I said.

I barely slept. My heart raced and my palms sweated as I kept thinking about what the kid had done and said. That night, I came up with a game plan and went over it again and again in my head. I was going to teach him a fucking lesson.

The next morning, I went into my gym to get my nunchucks. Problem was, I had lent them to my neighbor, Stevie, so I had to come up with a backup plan. I grabbed a dumbbell and took the weights off it. What was left was a twelve-inch, cast-iron bar. I slid the bar up my shirt sleeve and walked the two blocks to the bus stop.

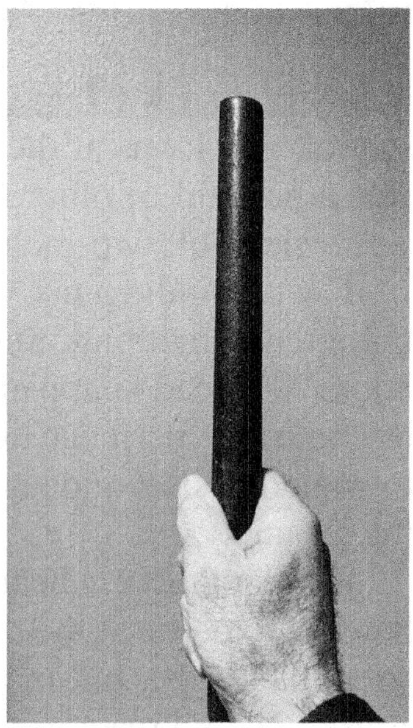

The cast-iron bar

When I got there and saw the kid, I made a beeline for him. My heart was pounding. The plan was in motion. There was no turning back.

"What did you say about my mom?" I yelled as I approached him.

Before he could say anything, I slid the iron bar into my hand and clocked that motherfucker as hard as I could, right in the fucking temple. I wasn't worried about anything except making him pay.

The sound of that bar against the kid's head was worse than the sound of that guy's head hitting the sidewalk at the Italian Festival.

The kid went down like a ton of bricks. As I stood over him, so many thoughts raced through my head. On the one hand, I felt like a fucking badass, while on the other, I thought, "Holy shit! What the fuck did I just do?"

I didn't know if I had killed or seriously injured him. I didn't know if I was going to get in trouble and sent off to prison. Luckily, none of those things happened. It was a fucking miracle.

As all this was going through my head, I noticed the other kids weren't laughing, like they did when I was down. I guess it was normal to sucker punch someone, like the kid had done to me, but absolutely nuts to whack someone in the head with an iron bar.

From that day on, I got all the respect in the world whenever I would go to the bus stop. Kids would ask me how I was doing and how my mom was doing, too. It was crazy that I felt like I had to do that to get respect. But that's just how it was in our neighborhood back then.

To this day, I feel like I owe the kid an apology for what I did. Even though he had hit me first, I know now that in life, it's not what happens to you; it's how you react to it. Responding the way I did was stupid. I'm a momma's boy, and I could have taken the kid away from his own mom if I'd killed him that day. That's the kind of shit you don't think about when you're a kid or when you're in the heat of the moment. Sorry, dude.

But shit, what a welcome to high school, right? I guess that was my initiation to the next phase of life. A life where bigger, stronger, and more violent kids roamed the halls. If grammar school was a melting pot, high school was more like a powder keg in a much tougher part of town.

From Geech and my basement, I moved on to the guys down at West Haven Academy of Karate. My senseis there were Charlie Ferraro, Roger Petra, and a judo expert named Patrick.

I remember we would all go out to a local park and practice catching raw eggs without breaking them. Imagine the challenge of an egg being hurled at your face, and you have to catch it with enough power so as to stop it, but also with enough care so as to not break it. It was one of the ultimate tests of determining how you respond to what life throws at you.

After a few months, I really got into it and learned so much from all those guys, especially when it came to routine and discipline. Such nice, respectful, classy guys. Thank you, gentlemen, I am forever grateful!

The next four years would test me every which way imaginable, and you know I'm not talking about in the classroom.

CHAPTER FOUR

MY HIGH SCHOOL YEARS

"I've seen the needle and the damage done."
—Neil Young

IN HIGH SCHOOL, MY CREW WAS MOSTLY INTO PARTYING, scoring drugs, and getting in fights, pretty much in that order. Did I mention girls? Our lives revolved around them. And I'm sure the girls would have said the same thing about us boys.

High school was crazy. Mix in all these kids of different ages, genders, and backgrounds with a bunch of raging hormones and—boom!

Sounds like high school should have been a great time, right? Well, I don't know about you, but my high school years were some of the most conflicted of my life. I felt torn in half searching for my identity. Part of me wanted to be a leather jacket-wearing badass biker, cruising the neighborhood, doing drugs, raising hell, and getting with girls. The other part of me wanted to be an elite athlete who trained like an animal and looked like one of the bodybuilders on my vision board.

I knew I couldn't do both, but I sure as hell tried. Doing my best to live in both worlds built up this struggle inside of me. I'm sure a lot of kids deal with this kind of stuff in high schools all around the world, trying to get a handle on their own issues, insecurities, and peer pressures.

My love affair with motorcycles and muscle cars goes way back. Young kids love what is loud, fast, and cool. When I was ten years old, Stevie Picard (one of my best friends who lived across the street from me) and I were in his front yard washing our minibikes when we heard a deep, rumbling *vrrrr, vrrrr, vrrrr*. Then the ground shook beneath our feet. We looked up, dropped our sponges, ran to the edge of his driveway, and froze with anticipation. And sure enough, there they were—ten bikers on their choppers with straight pipes. The sound was deafening, but it was awesome. All that leather and steel cruising past us like a slow-motion scene straight out of a movie. We just stared, hypnotized.

As a kid, it seemed to me that in my neighborhood, you could either grow up and work in a factory, or you could join a bike club. The bikers' non-conforming, rebellious attitude made them seem cool.

Our neighborhood was full of motorcycles and muscle cars. This was way before the environmental movement, not to mention smog checks. Every chopper and muscle car builder tried to outdo the other with bigger, more powerful, and faster engines. The guys would take those stock engines and tweak them out. I'm talking about a 427 big block with a racing cam, a blower, and open headers.

When we would hear an engine like that coming down the street, we would run outside and gather around to watch the show. The muscle car would stop right in front of us and rev the RPMs into a loud roar. It was music to our ears. And then, the driver would pop the clutch and burn the rubber off the tires. We'd be cheering like it was the Super Bowl as the smoke and burnt tire smell hit our noses. The muscle car would tear off down the street, and behind it would be twenty yards of Positraction rubber tattooed on the street. We would all run out and touch the burnt rubber and laugh our asses off.

My passion for motorcycles increased tenfold when Stevie and I watched his dad build a Harley from a box of rusty parts. Back then, it was called a basket case. Every night, Stevie and I would excitedly wait for his dad to finish dinner and then go into his garage to work on his bike. We'd watch and help when he would let us. His attention to detail was insane. He had to clean the rust off every part, rebuild the motor, and rewire the entire bike from scratch.

Piece by piece, he put that bike together, and before we knew it, it was done and ready for a paint job. By the time he finished, it looked like it had come off the showroom floor.

Mr. Picard would take it on a test ride. Then, he would take Stevie out for a ride. And after that, it was my turn. Feeling that power and hearing that thunder underneath me was like nothing I had experienced before. I had only ridden minibikes. This was a whole different beast. And that was it—I was hooked. The love affair was on.

Mr. Picard, like my dad, was a man's man. He was a heavy equipment welder. Bulldozers, dump trucks—you name it, he could fix it. Most afternoons when he'd come home, if he wasn't working on a project in his garage, he would strip off his greasy work clothes down to his boxer shorts and Guinea tank top, then sit on the porch with a Scotch in one hand and a cigar in the other. When I'd see him out there, I'd run over and talk to him and listen to all his stories.

He was one of the toughest dads from the neighborhood I've ever known. I mean, who goes bear hunting in Canada with nothing but a bow and arrow and a buck knife? I am so grateful we were neighbors, and when I was old enough, he gave me a part-time job helping him with his construction work.

When we were teenagers, I helped Stevie rebuild the engine in his 1969 Chevy Chevelle SS 396. Stevie was super smart when it came to engines and could fix almost anything mechanical, just like his dad. Learning how the insides of an engine worked blew my mind. The sense of accomplishment we felt from doing it ourselves was empowering. We loved the wrenches, grease, and grit.

'69 Chevy Chevelle SS 396

When we started it up for the first time and heard that engine purr, we laughed and high-fived each other. We then jumped in and peeled off down the street. Now we were the ones laying down the rubber! We cruised down to Persian Drive, where all the other kids cruised the diners in their muscle cars and choppers, showing off our handiwork.

That's the kind of shit that turned me on when it came to muscle cars—the power, the speed, the image. A few years later, Stevie got a '68 Camaro.

Stevie's '68 Camaro

My buddy Joe Cardella said it best: "Where we grew up, we idolized the guys with the muscle cars and the choppers. And shit, I guess we also looked up to the gangsters and drug dealers who had the Cadillacs, nice clothes, and hot women on their arms."

All the incredible athletes who played at Ansonia High School also inspired me. Joe was one of those guys. As a freshman, I looked up to him because he played the same position as me—linebacker. I loved the way he flew around the field, taking people's heads off. I really respected that and wanted to play the game just like he did—fearless and ferocious.

Joe played with other amazing athletes, like Roger Ings, an All-Star running back, and Gary Taylor, an All-Star lineman. Roger was a beast who had a great physique and could bench press four hundred pounds in high school. He went on to play for the University of Connecticut and was considered the strongest guy on the team.

Gary was a door jamb of a guy—tall, thick, and impossible for pass rushers to get past. He lived a few blocks away from my house. His older brother, Custard, who has since passed away, was a high-ranking member of a bike club who we all looked up to and respected.

I'll never forget when Custard came by my house on his

chopper and saw me in the yard with my Doberman Pinscher, Damien. He parked his bike in my driveway and watched Damien and I play. He could see that the dog needed some training, so he offered to help.

Damien

Damien would not have had discipline and stamina had it not been for Custard. When I would take Damien on walks, everyone would smile and wave at us and show us so much respect. You should have seen him run when we would go to the baseball fields and play catch. He would run like a fucking deer. That dog might have been my first love. So powerful, big, loyal, and disciplined. Thank you, Custard. Rest in peace, brother.

Custard

Now, when I was a freshman in the fall of 1973, Joe, Gary, and Roger were co-captains of our varsity football team. I loved going to the games on Friday nights and watching those guys fly around the field making great plays. Ansonia's varsity football went 7-3 that year and was ranked seventh in the state, having suffered those three losses to the first-, second-, and third-ranked teams.

People in Ansonia were so passionate and proud of their high school sports. Total fanatics. Ansonia High, for being such a small high school, kicked ass in so many sports including basketball and baseball, and, of course, football. In fact, last time I checked, the school had something like twenty state football championships. So many athletes went on to play at local colleges like UConn, Central Connecticut, Fairfield College, and others.

Roger, Joe, and Gary

When people would see their local high school heroes in town, they would go out of their way to pat them on the back or pick up the tab for their meals. They'd tell them, "Great job, way to go!"

I admired that big time, and I wanted to feel what that felt like—the pride of a small town backing you as you pushed your limits.

My main man, Jimmy Vane, and my other friends, Clarence Adams and Jeff Bailey, and I were on the freshman football team, which got some attention, but not like the varsity team. We started the year off with a win, and then another and another. And before we knew it, we almost put together an undefeated season but lost our last game.

It was a beautiful thing to be a part of. We did the day-to-day work in practice, and during games, we trusted each other. Everyone had a role and a responsibility. I learned discipline, teamwork, and dedication. A big thanks to our coach, Mr. Sponheimer, for showing us the way.

Jimmy Vane and I were already great friends, but that freshman football season strengthened our bond even more. I played middle linebacker, and Jimmy played free safety. If anyone got past me, Jimmy would lay them out. Sometimes, we'd be lined up for a play and I'd feel a *tink!* on my helmet. I'd turn around and Jimmy would have a shit-eating grin on his face. That crazy bastard would be throwing rocks at my head so he could point out which way he thought the ball was going.

Jimmy Vane

Off the field, Jimmy and I were pretty much inseparable, which is why people called us the Vane and Valente Show. Like a lot of kids, we were restless, so we used that energy to get ourselves into a fair amount of trouble. If we weren't instigating it, then trouble always had a way of finding us.

One day after practice, Jimmy and I were cutting through the projects on our way to the mall just off Main Street when I spotted a dude heading toward us. This guy must have been six feet, four inches tall, two hundred and fifty pounds, and at least thirty years old. Something about him didn't feel right to me. I guess he triggered that sixth sense you develop when you grow up hanging out on the streets.

Sure as shit, when the guy was just about to pass us, he turned and sucker punched Jimmy right in the fucking face! Jimmy, who had a steel jaw, jumped on the dude's back and started choking his ass out, while I punched and kicked the guy in his stomach.

Next thing we knew, a squad car pulled up, and all we heard was, "Get the fuck off him! Put your hands up where we can see them!"

What the cops had seen was two kids fighting one dude. Despite our self-defense claims, they hauled all three of us into the small jail on Main Street. They threw Jimmy and me in one cell, and the other dude into the cell next to us.

After being locked up for a few hours, the other guy started yelling, "Help me! Help me! Help me!" He then started slamming his forehead against the metal bars. *Thud. Thud. Thud.* With each slam, blood squirted all over the place, but the cops couldn't give two shits about it. Instead, they snickered and laughed, taking bets on how many hits it would take for the guy to knock himself out. With that, they saw how crazy the guy was and finally believed our self-defense story and let us go.

Things like that created this great bond between Jimmy and me. We always had each other's backs. He was just a cool-ass dude who could do anything, like when we'd go skiing and he'd hit the moguls and do backflips off jumps. And it wasn't just sports. He was a very talented photographer, too, and had a real passion for it. He used to take pictures of my motorcycles and come with me to the YMCA to take pictures of me doing katas and kicks.

That's the kind of guy Jimmy was. He'd give you the shirt off his back. He was my goombah.

Me and Jimmy's sisters

Jimmy had a beautiful Italian family like mine that I loved—two sisters, a hardworking dad, and a really sweet mom. Our high school was close to Jimmy's house, so during our lunch hour, we'd head there, go straight into his room, crank up

Aerosmith, and take hits off his Richard Nixon bong. We'd come out smiling and giggling. His mom would feed us lunch, but she either didn't know what we were doing or decided to look the other way. She was probably just happy to have us in her house instead of out on the streets.

Jimmy's Richard Nixon bong

Jimmy's mom worked nights as a nurse at the Griffin Hospital emergency room. She'd tell us about all the overdoses and people who'd died from drugs the night before. She made us swear up and down that we'd never do heroin. Of course, we both promised that we wouldn't. We hadn't ever tried it, and neither of us had plans to. It was the one drug we knew to stay away from.

Sadly, only one of us would keep that promise.

As high school went on, I kept trying to balance my two lives. It always seemed that if partying was taking over, then my passion for working out would attract someone positive into my life, and that person would get me back on track.

Take, for example, Mr. Germe, my physical education teacher in high school. He knew I had a burning passion to work out, so most days at the start of his class, he'd say, "All right, today we're going to play baseball, and anyone who wants to work out with Valente, go ahead."

He'd then head out with the class, and I'd take a small group of kids to the weight room. Talk about a confidence boost. This person of responsibility trusted me to train my fellow students the right way, to stay on point, and not fuck around. I was so pumped about lifting and had studied it so much in books and magazines that I was bursting with information to share. Things like correct form, the order of muscle groups to train, how many sets and reps to do, when and how to stretch, and on and on.

I got a big-time buzz when people listened to me and were

eager to learn about what I was passionate about. I got an even bigger buzz when I saw them get results. I watched their confidence build and their energy turn way more positive. They also seemed to stand taller with better posture. It's amazing how working out can change your life.

Of course, at that time, I had no idea that one day I'd train A-list actors, athletes, and musicians, as well as business titans, entrepreneurs, doctors, lawyers, and everyone else in between at Gold's Gym Venice. I had no clue that I'd cohost a number one-rated fitness show on ESPN and help so many people around the world achieve their fitness goals. Thank you, thank you, thank you, Mr. Germe! Much love and respect!

But even stuff like that couldn't keep me from swinging back the other way where I'd get involved in more trouble, like the time Jimmy and I went to a party in nearby Derby, hosted by the guys from our rival football team. We ended up hitting on the quarterback's girlfriend, and it seemed like the whole team took us out back and kicked our asses.

Or the time one of my good friends, Ray, who lived a few blocks from me, and I were at this wild party, and when I came out of the bathroom, I saw two state troopers standing in the doorway. Right then and there, I grabbed Ray, and we ran into an upstairs bedroom and hid under the bed. The funny thing was, not only did the cops not look under the bed, but they used the room as their headquarters to store all the drugs and weapons that they confiscated. They sat their asses on the bed above us and talked shit about how they busted the party and arrested all "us punks."

They didn't get Ray or me. We laid under that bed until we heard the last cop leave. And then we laid under there for another half hour. Too scared to use the front door, we climbed out the window. The next time we saw everyone at school, they gave us high fives for getting away with it.

Ray is one of my friends who died way too young. RIP, my friend.

Staying out late and getting in trouble was cool, but when I would go into my basement after a night of partying to work out, I'd feel weak and lazy. It sucked. It was as if the drugs, drinking, and goofing off were putting out the fire in my belly for working out.

I'd look in the mirror and see this flat, skinny guy with no energy. I felt like shit. I would look at all the bodybuilders on my vision board and ask myself, "What the fuck are you doing?"

While all of this was going on, we all had part-time jobs, me included. My personal goal was to earn enough money to buy myself a real deal motorcycle and a muscle car by my sixteenth birthday. That's one thing about us kids from Ansonia; we weren't afraid to work. We all came from blue-collar families and didn't mind getting our hands dirty.

My list of jobs during those years included the following: landscaping; construction; working the flea markets; loading trucks with hundred-pound bags of feed; delivering furniture; working at a convalescent home as a maintenance man; and collecting carts at the grocery store. When one job ended, I went right to the next.

My first set of wheels was a used, beat-up '67 Mustang with a six-cylinder engine. Not the big block I wanted, but it only cost $500. Every so often, I'd sell the car I had and buy something else. I never had anything new or expensive, but I loved each just the same. I went on to own a '67 Chevy Malibu (yellow with black mags) and a blue Chevy van. I put carpet all inside the van—on the ceiling, walls, and floor. Then, I put a mattress in the back and speakers on the wall. Now, this thing had no windows in the back, so let's just say it offered a lot of privacy when I'd be with that special person.

Now, my buddy Tony Palmero always wanted to borrow the van. So, we made an arrangement—he could use the van whenever he wanted, provided that he loaned me his 1970 LT-1 Corvette. This Corvette had side pipes, making it sound incredible. It was a rocket! At seventeen years of age, driving a beast like this was a total rush.

1970 LT-1 Corvette

I did the same with bikes, buying and selling them when I could, never owning two at the same time. From my minibike, I got a BSA 650, a custom chopper. After about six months, I sold it because I wanted to replace it with a Harley Sportster. So with Tony's help, I was able to find one.

Once I brought it home, Tony did some work on it, replacing the mufflers with straight pipes. That made the bike sound amazing.

BSA 650

Tony was a great guy. Sadly, like so many others from my neighborhood, Tony left us way too soon. Rest in peace, Tony.

After I sold the Sportster, I had a '47 Harley Knucklehead suicide shifter, a Harley Shovelhead, and a '47 Harley Knucklehead chopper.

Harley Sportster

I'd bought a few of my bikes from a friend of mine named Breeze. He had a small motorcycle shop on Route 34, right next to Barry Toolie's father's gas station. Breeze was such a cool guy, and his bikes were great-looking and dependable. He treated us fairly, and his price was always right. Thank you, Breeze.

Harley Shovelhead

'47 Harley Knucklehead chopper

With my license and a way to get around, I started spending less time in my basement gym and ventured out to lift at places like Bubba Green's Knock-Out Boy's Club.

Bubba was a legend in town. He was all about helping kids, giving them a place to hit the weights and play pool, instead of hanging out on the streets and getting in trouble.

Later, I started going to my local YMCA. Now, to be straight up, the Y's weight room was a total afterthought. It was down in the basement, inside the boiler room. No windows. No ventilation. And definitely no girls. We nicknamed it "the Dungeon." But don't get me wrong, we still loved it. Back then, the Y and the Dungeon were nothing like the YMCAs you see these days, which seem more like country clubs. This place was bare bones. But it had all the weights we could handle, even if they were covered in rust from the musty air.

The Y is the first place I worked out while using a training partner. Jimmy would lift with me, along with another friend, Alfie Baranek. I relied on them, and they relied on me. A good training partner is very important when you need to stoke that competitive fire inside of you. They push you to lift more weight, to do more reps, and are there to give you a spot if you need it.

Even in an individual sport like bodybuilding, you still need a good team around you to be your best. The sooner I realized that, the better off I became inside and outside of the weight room. The same goes for everything in life. You need a good team to achieve whatever passions you're chasing.

Also, around that time, I heard about pro bodybuilder Mike Katz, who lifted at a gym in nearby Hamden. Turns out Mike owned the gym, which was called World Gym East, along with two other bodybuilders, Jerry Mastrangelo and Ken Passariello.

It was amazing to see these guys working out, as well as seeing some of the top amateurs in the area, like Joe Eukilic, Pete Leonitti, and Ronnie Magnum. Seeing them in the flesh and blood, and how big they were, was super inspiring. It took the dream of the vision board and made it seem attainable. I mean, here were guys right in front me, doing what I wanted to be doing, just a few miles from my house.

A few years after I moved to California, I heard through the grapevine that someone had tried to whack Jerry. Apparently, Jerry was coming out of his house when someone ran up and shot him four times in the chest. Luckily, he survived, and it would be ten years of hell for him trying to find out exactly who did it. Ultimately, the cops arrested a couple of guys in a Mafia sting operation. It made all the newspapers, and all sorts of rumors were flying around about who was responsible, but nothing ever stuck.

Despite all that, Jerry grew World Gym East and ended up owning five other locations, which he eventually sold to Planet Fitness, the major player in the gym world, with hundreds of locations all over.

Jerry getting shot was the kind of crazy stuff that happened in and near my hometown way too often. Everyone had a gangster mentality. As much as I loved to work out, I still hung out with my same crew, who was mostly up to no good.

The pressure to fit in during high school was some of the most intense I've ever felt. As I was still searching for my true identity, the partying started to bore me. But the thing is, I didn't feel like I could pull my friends aside and tell them how I really felt, so I went along with it. I didn't know how to put it into words that I wanted to do more and be more.

This was way before the internet, and way before I'd even think about reading a self-help book. I didn't fully understand the mind-body-spirit connection. That to be the best version of myself, there needed to be a harmony between those three things. I couldn't comprehend that I had choices. It seemed impossible to break the mold that our town cast on so many guys before and around me. It was like I needed something else to wake me up, and I got it from an unusual source—my brother, who was making his own choices in life.

Chas was four years older than me and got out of high school just as I was going into it. He had already made a name for himself from fighting and dealing drugs. He'd pick up a job here and there, probably to make himself look like he was a law-abiding citizen. But while he was working one factory job, a huge piece of machinery fell and crushed his leg. And that's when things took a turn for the worse.

After the accident, Chas needed surgery to fix his leg, and that put him out of commission for a while. And guess what the doctors gave him for the pain? Yup, opioid-based painkillers.

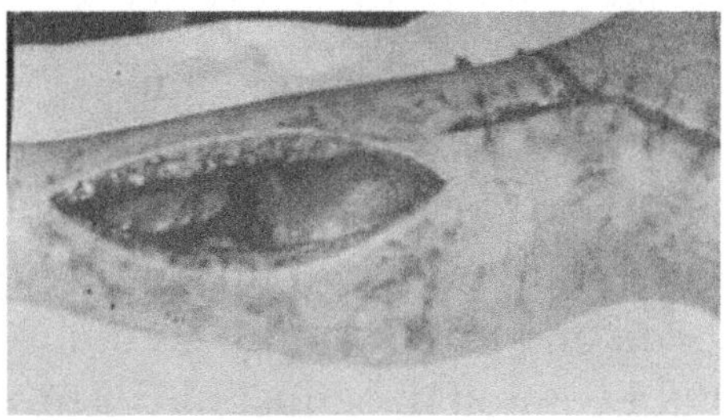

Chas's leg injury

My brother was never the same after that. He walked with a limp and relied on his prescription drugs to deal with the physical and emotional challenge of his injury. That machine crushed his leg, but it might as well have crushed his spirit because, when the prescriptions ran out, he turned to quaaludes.

Things took another turn for the worse when a good friend of his, who was a good-looking lead singer in a rock-'n'-roll band, hanged himself in his parents' garage. This pushed Chas over the edge, and he moved on to heroin to self-medicate.

Look, it's no secret that heroin is a nasty, powerful drug. It takes over your character, your morals, your soul, and every inch of your body. My brother withered away physically and mentally. He became a totally different person right in front of my eyes. He went from this handsome, athletic Italian kid to this skinny, unhealthy-looking drug addict. He also turned into an incredible con artist who would lie, cheat, steal, and do anything necessary to get his next fix.

Chas would leave the house for days on a drug binge, and that would torture Mom. She'd sit and stare out the front parlor window at night, crying, hoping, and praying that she'd see him walk up the sidewalk. That's when I really started to resent drugs and what they had done to my brother. But my mom was such an angel that she never said a cross word about Chas. No matter what he did, no matter how fucked up his actions were, how illegal or dangerous they were, it didn't matter to her. Mom would always say, "It's not Chas; it's the drugs."

Watching my mom cry and be in so much pain was one of the toughest things I've ever had to witness. I also saw how Dad silently dealt with the pain in his own way. Seeing Mom and Dad like that made me realize that I never wanted to cause them that kind of heartache and pain.

It just seemed like it was one thing after another with Chas, and I had started to lose hope and respect for him. It killed me to watch him go down this path, putting my parents through hell. I loved and idolized him so much. He was one of my first heroes, and I wanted to be just like him, so witnessing this hurt me really bad.

I wish I could have done something back then to help him out, but all I can do now is share his story to show people that they're not alone, that families and addicts can beat the addiction if they handle it straight on.

My parents put Chas in rehab, but rehab alone wasn't enough to get that gorilla off his back. After a few days, he'd simply walk out. It got out of control pretty fast. I remember three incidents in particular that highlight just how bad it got.

The first one happened when Chas was nineteen and just out of high school. He was driving one night while high when a couple of cops pulled him over. Chas freaked the fuck out and hit the gas, running over one of the cops. He was lucky he didn't kill the guy. After they arrested him, they charged him with possession of marijuana, second-degree assault, carrying a deadly weapon, and interfering with a police search. And just like that, Chas got himself a few years in prison.

Mom and Dad, being the loving parents they were, would load me up in the car every other weekend to drive the two hours to visit Chas in prison. We'd all sit there, looking at him through a thick plate of glass as we took turns talking to him on the phone. When it was my turn to talk to Chas, I'd look across at him, not sure what to say. Sometimes the glass would reflect my face over his, making it seem like I was the one doing time. It felt like a wake-up call because I knew full well in my gut that some of the shit I was doing could land me in jail, too.

After doing his time, Chas finally got released. We all hoped he'd get himself on track, but that never happened. Drugs reentered his life, and little did I know, things were about to get worse.

I remember walking up to the house and seeing a police cruiser parked out front. I thought, the cops were there for some stupid shit I'd done. But when I walked inside, my dad called for me from the basement. I went downstairs, and there they were, two cops doing a full-on burglary investigation. Turns out, someone had stolen twenty-two of my dad's guns from the gun cabinet he had built. My pops looked like someone had ripped his guts out.

"Look, Mr. Valente, you got two Dobermans down here who didn't bark or attack. There are no signs of breaking and entering. This was an inside job. I'm sorry, sir," one of the cops told my dad in a low, heartfelt voice.

Dad and I shared a look, knowing exactly who had done it—Chas.

And as if it couldn't get any worse, my mom ran down into the basement, yelling, "My wedding band and engagement rings are gone!"

Dad's face dropped even more. He held it together while the cops were there, but once they left, he sat on the floor right in front of his gun cabinet and started to weep.

Dad couldn't hold his tears back. It was the first time in my life I had seen him cry, and it hit me hard. How could Chas do this to our parents, who did nothing but love and support him? Fucking heroin.

Fortunately, because Dad knew everyone in town, he was lucky to get most of his guns back. Apparently, Chas had sold them to a few biker clubs and pawn shops, and the guys actually respected my dad enough to sell them back to him. Sadly, Mom never got her rings back.

Eventually, the police found Chas, and he was arrested. My parents couldn't bear to press charges against their own son, so Chas didn't end up doing any time. But my folks did put him into rehab. This whole incident became one of those family things no one ever talked about.

Rehab didn't work for Chas. We walked on eggshells every day, waiting for something crazy to happen. Chas was so far gone that he'd actually had a conversation with me about how he thought he could shoot heroin two or three times a week and control it. I knew he was out of his mind, and sure enough, he proved me right.

Six months later, I was out with friends and got home pretty late. As I walked up to my house, I noticed the lights were on, which wasn't normal because it was 1 a.m. I then heard screaming and ran inside to see what the fuck was going on. What I saw, I never forgot.

In the kitchen, Dad held Chas by the throat, pinning him up against the wall—a wall Dad had just wallpapered.

"You son of a bitch, I'll blackball you!" he yelled as he wailed on Chas. "You're not disrespecting our family like this!

How could you stumble in here high as a kite in the middle of the night with two girls?!"

That was about the time I noticed the two girls Dad was talking about sneaking out of the house.

Dad kept punching Chas, and Chas's blood splattered all over the wallpaper. Then, suddenly, Dad stopped, grabbed his chest, and fell backward. He was out cold and looked like he had just died.

"Sonny! Sonny!" Mom yelled.

I freaked out, and for whatever reason, I ran to our neighbors, the Skermanties, screaming, "Call an ambulance! Call an ambulance!"

It didn't take long for the ambulance to arrive. The paramedics loaded my dad onto a stretcher and took him to the hospital.

As Mom and I walked back to the house, Chas and the two girls were stumbling down the sidewalk toward us. I got a sudden rush of rage, and just as Chas was about to pass us, I punched him right in the fucking face. He fell back into a pricker bush and didn't get up. And for the first time ever, I heard my mom say something mean-spirited about him.

"Just leave him there," she said.

Once my mom and I arrived at the hospital, we waited for the doctor to give us an update. Each minute felt like an hour. Finally, the doctor came out and reported that Dad had suffered a heart attack, but he was stable and he'd recover in time with some rest.

On the drive home, Mom and I talked about how crazy everything had gotten with Chas. Dad had nearly died, and all I wanted to do was wake up from this nightmare that Chas's drug addiction had created for my family.

When my mom and I got back to the house at about five in the morning, we pulled into the driveway and noticed right away that Dad's brand-new Ford Bronco was missing. A week or so later, they found Chas in Florida with the two girls in Dad's

Bronco, of course. When Chas and the Bronco got back home, once again, my parents didn't press charges.

You have to remember that Chas was my parents' firstborn son. They loved him and wanted nothing more than for him to get the help he needed. They didn't want him to go to jail. They wanted him to go back to rehab.

Seeing Chas like this confirmed that the last thing I'd ever do in my life was try heroin. I asked myself, "Is this what drugs and the neighborhood do to people? Turn them into evil, twisted animals?"

Dad and his Ford Bronco

The reason I'm telling these stories about Chas and his addiction isn't because I want to trash my brother. That couldn't be farther from the truth. My aim in relating these stories is that I know the toll that addiction takes on not just the addict but the family as well. I hope that if my stories about Chas help even just one person stay away from drugs, then some good will have come from all the misery my parents and I endured.

When I was a junior in high school, I worked at a small grocery store stocking shelves and gathering carts in the parking lot. That job came with a few perks, namely a cashier named Marlene, who became my first real girlfriend. I'd take her on motorcycle rides, and we hung out as much as we could. When we were working together, we'd make sure to take our lunch breaks at the same time so we could spend an hour in my van. And that, my friends, is what we called an afternoon delight.

At that time, because my grades were shitty and I had gotten in enough small-time trouble, I made it to what I thought was the Shangri-la of high school—the work diversion program. What that meant was that I went to school for a few hours in the morning, then got out at noon to clean up the streets with drug addicts and convicted criminals who were doing their community service.

Marlene

While I loved getting out of the classroom, the work diversion program also reinforced what I didn't want to become. This one time, we were feeding tree branches into a high-powered wood chipper. The guys were extra chatty that day, trading stories about how tough they were and what crimes they had committed. And that's about the time a cat walked up to us. One guy bent over, and I thought he was going to pet it, but instead, this crazy motherfucker grabbed it by its tail and threw it into the wood chipper. I flipped out and snapped on him, but the other guys kept us apart. I went home that night sick to my stomach.

On another day, I was raking leaves next to this guy who was telling me that he had been on a coke bender and hadn't slept in three days. And then, all of a sudden, he fell backward, smacked his head on the concrete, and had a full-on seizure. He was convulsing on the ground, and everyone just walked away and left him there. No one wanted to get involved.

Witnessing shit like that scared me to death. Was this my future? Being a soulless, heartless street thug? I really had to take a long, hard look at who I was surrounding myself with and what I was doing. My group of friends was usually up to no good, and this work diversion program was definitely not what I had expected.

As torn as I was, I was still doing dumb stuff, like getting jailhouse-style tattoos in my friend's basement just to try to fit in. When I got home and Dad saw a Harley Davidson number "1" logo tattooed on the top of my left hand and the Zig-Zag rolling paper man tattooed on my forearm, he was pissed.

"You stupid bastard, you're gonna fucking regret doing that!" he shouted.

The very next day, while I was working at my grocery store job, I was in the parking lot collecting carts, thinking my dad was probably right. I then heard the deep rumble of a supercharged Plymouth Roadrunner with a big 383 under the hood. When I looked up, I saw Sherman Backus, a badass, dedicated powerlifter, drive by me very slowly with his window rolled down. He then flexed his huge biceps and gave me a smile. That put me in a better mood as it got me thinking about the gym, a positive thing in my life, instead of the tattoos and how I pissed off Dad.

Sherman Backus

Sherman Backus

Sherman had a V-shaped back just like Franco Columbu, but even more massive. Every chance I got, I talked to him about working out. Whenever I'd run into Sherman at the Y, he'd always coach me on my form and push me to go heavier. He was another positive force, and I don't even know if he realizes how much he impacted my life. A big thank you, Sherman!

The Y always had a lot of interesting characters who worked out there. One day, I noticed a beautiful, brand-new Corvette pull up and park. I watched a guy get out who had long hair and was dressed in a three-piece suit. The whole scene was a little unusual because no one drove fancy cars like that to the Y, and the only time people wore suits in my neighborhood was when they were going to court.

I went down into the Dungeon and was surprised to see the guy come down in workout clothes. He was about ten years older than me, and on his very first day down there, he busted out a tube of Icy Hot and lathered his elbows and knees up. When the nasty ass smell of that cream hit everyone's noses, they all thought, "What the fuck is this dude doing?!"

They wanted to kick his ass and throw him in the dumpster, but before they could, I jumped between them and said, "Hey, let me talk to him."

I then introduced myself.

"Look, man, you can't put that smelly shit on down here," I told him. There are no windows, and these guys will kick your ass."

He understood and wiped it off with a towel, but the damage had been done. The place stunk!

Meet Bobby LeVine.

After that, we kind of hit it off, and each time I'd see him at the Y, we'd talk about cars and train together. He'd told me how he was the sales manager down at the new Dworkin Chevrolet dealership off Main Street. He had grown up with Carl Dworkin and had fallen in love with cars as a kid. He got an English degree at the University of Connecticut and moved down to Fort Lauderdale in 1972, to take a break from Connecticut. He moved back and forth a few times, and it was in 1976 that I met him at the Y. He was the only person I knew who had moved away from our hometown.

Bobby LeVine

In early to mid-1977, Bobby had had enough with Ansonia and decided to move back to Fort Lauderdale for good. On his

Bobby LeVine's Corvette

last day at the Y, he scribbled a phone number on his business card and then handed it to me.

"If you ever want to get out of here, give me a call," he said.

I didn't think much of his offer at the time. Moving away from my family and friends had never crossed my mind, so I went home and threw Bobby's card in my junk drawer.

Graduation was approaching, and I couldn't have been more clueless about the future. I was barely squeaking by in most of my classes. I had a lot of girlfriends, but none of them lasted for whatever reason. In those four years, I hadn't figured out any type of long-term game plan. I hadn't gotten any closer to answering the question about what the fuck I was going to do with my life. I mean, what was my career going to be? My profession? How was I going to make a living and support myself?

For a minute, I thought about joining the Marine Corps. The Marines had a fitness test consisting of push-ups, pull-ups, and running. I took the test and ended up getting the highest score. This gave me a rush, reminding me how much I enjoyed competing. But as good as that felt, I still didn't have a plan for the future.

It would take a wild night at a Clint Eastwood movie, a friend's suicide, and a sit-down conversation with my dad to help me figure out my next move.

CHAPTER FIVE

GOTTA GET OUT

"If you can't figure out your purpose, figure out your passion. For your passion will lead you right into your purpose."
—Bishop T.D. Jakes

THE DAY ARRIVED WHEN I WALKED across the stage in my cap and gown, shook the principal's hand, and got my high school diploma. And I couldn't have given two shits about it. Graduation felt more like something I had to do for my mom and dad than for myself. Other kids had their plans to go into the military, college, or a trade. And here I was living day by day, with no real strategy except that I knew I really loved my motorcycles and working out.

About a year after graduation, Dad sat me down for a man-to-man talk. What he said to me was straightforward and to the point:

"Ricky, look, you graduated high school, you're a grown man now, and so it's time for you to go out into the world and do something with your life."

He didn't say I had to move out of the house, or leave town for that matter, but I think that's what he meant—at least that's how I took it. He probably feared I was heading down the wrong path, on my way to jail, becoming a drug addict, or for that matter, winding up dead.

A few weeks later, on a Saturday night, Joey Cardella, Wojo (another football player), and I had made plans to see *The Outlaw Josey Wales*, starring one of the biggest action heroes of our time, Clint Eastwood. When we went out, the first order of business was to get high. So, we smoked a joint, dropped some acid, and went into the theater tripping our brains out.

We took our seats, and to tell you the truth, I had no idea what I was watching. I sat back, trying to focus, and when I put my feet up on the chair in front me, I put them on some lady's shoulders. She turned around and ripped me a new ass—as she had a right to—and that got the attention of the usher.

The usher tried to diffuse the situation, but it got out of hand pretty quick. The manager showed up, and then we all got thrown out. We left defiantly and went to a local pub off Main Street. After popping back a few beers, the boys dropped me off at home in the middle of the night.

I got out of Joey's car and snuck into the basement, hoping I wouldn't wake up Mom and Dad. Once inside, I had to navigate past my motorcycle. (Because of the weather and the threat that someone might steal it, everyone parked their motorcycles inside their basements, if they didn't have a garage.) I then made it past the minefield of my weights, tried not to trip over my dog, and finally landed on my bed. That's right, I had moved my bedroom downstairs so I could come and go as I pleased. It was like I had my own little apartment down there.

Early the next morning, I woke up to my mom yelling at me from the top of the stairs.

"Ricky! Stevie is on the phone. He has to talk to you."

"Has to talk to me?" I thought, my head pounding. This ain't gonna be good. I forced myself out of bed and over to the phone.

"Hey, Stevie, man, what's up?"

"Did you hear what happened?" Stevie asked. He seemed choked up.

"Naw, what?"

"Timmy Rose killed himself with a shotgun last night."

All I could say was a heavy-hearted, "What the fuck, why?"

Hearing about someone's death, especially when it was unexpected, has a way of fucking you up. I couldn't believe another person I knew was dead at such a young age.

Timmy lived about five houses down from me. He seemed fine a few days earlier. I guess you never really know what someone is going through.

After the call, I climbed back in bed and stared at the ceiling. I thought about the night before, how it was just wasted time. You add up a bunch of those nights and you get a big, fat nothing to show for it.

Look, I know that partying, drinking, and doing drugs seems like it's the fun thing to do as a restless kid. But I'm telling you right now, when you look back on your life, you're going to wish you had used at least some of that time more productively. I'm not saying you have to be a perfect angel. God knows I wasn't. But with even just a little focus, you will achieve anything you're passionate about. Time is something you will never get back.

There's nothing like death to make you think about life. Even as a nineteen-year-old kid, I knew there had to be more to life than what I was doing. I knew I had to create something for myself, but I didn't know if my hometown would let me.

Still lying in bed, I took stock of my life and my neighborhood. Things had been getting crazier by the day, yet we still considered it to be our norm. I started reliving some of the craziness in my head, like the time Gary Taylor walked out of a bar on Route 34 and some guy shot him five times. I found out later on from Joey that the kid who shot up Gary did so because he and Gary had gotten into a fight a few days earlier, and Gary had busted a bottle over the guy's head.

Thank God Gary was a big dude and that guy only had a .22.

If it were a .357, Gary would have been dead.

Or the time my neighbor down the street thought it would be a good idea to set up a coke deal and then have his friends come rob it for the coke and the cash, just as the deal was going down. It worked, but a few days later, the dudes they robbed came back and sprayed my neighbor's house with machine gunfire.

Then, there was this kid I knew who worked at one of the gas stations on Persian Drive, where we all cruised the strip. He stole nice cars and sold them down in New York City. He had gone missing for a few days, and the cops had finally found him in West Rock, a park we partied in near New Haven. The only problem was that they found him slumped over the steering wheel of a Corvette, with a single gunshot wound to the back of his head, execution style.

I don't know if it was the power of the universe or whatever, but right then and there, I turned my head to the right and looked over at my vision board. It reminded me of what was possible if I stayed dedicated and focused on my passion.

And then something clicked in my head. "That can be me," I thought.

In the weight room, I could control everything. It was black and white. It had a logic to it, a cause and effect. Bodybuilding was my passion. The gym was my sweet spot, the place I felt most at home. In the gym, I was in charge of my choices, but I wasn't using these same principles in my life outside of it.

A big part of bodybuilding is shocking the muscle, meaning switching up the routine so you can keep your muscles guessing, forcing them to work harder. Same goes for life. I had to shock my routine. Change things up. For me to find what more was in store for my life, I had to be willing to be fearless, take a risk, and go out and pursue my passion.

So, that afternoon, I went to see the documentary *Pumping Iron* with my friend Mark Dzvileski. Only this time, we didn't get high. It was so powerful and inspiring to see a movie about bodybuilders competing at the highest levels, to see their lifestyles and how they trained. It was set mostly at Gold's Gym in Venice Beach, on the Westside of Los Angeles. Watching the film reinforced the fire in my belly. It showed me what was possible.

Me and Mark Dzvileski

And so, as I walked out of the theater, a light bulb went off in my head. The guy who stunk up the Y with all that Icy Hot! The dude who managed the Chevrolet dealership! Bobby LeVine! I had to call him.

I ran home and dug around in my junk drawer and found it—Bobby's business card, the one he had given me the year before. I grabbed the phone and gave him a call. It rang and rang, and then he answered.

"Hey, Bobby! This is Rick Valente, up in Ansonia. Remember me?"

"Hey, Rick! Of course! Great to hear from you, man. What's happening?"

"So, hey, I was wondering if your offer was still open?"

"One hundred percent it is!" he said without hesitation. "I just never thought you would call!"

We talked for a while, and I must have said, "Thank you" fifty times.

Later that same day, I called my parents into the kitchen to make my big announcement. We all sat down at the kitchen table.

"Mom, Dad, I'm moving to Fort Lauderdale," I confidently told them.

My mom's face dropped. It was obvious she didn't want me to go.

She had so many questions. How? Why? Who? When? What?

My dad just busted out a little smirk. "Good. Good for you," he said.

Once it had sunk in that I was taking control, adrenaline and excitement coursed through my body. I told all my friends, including Jimmy Vane, who promised me that he'd come down and visit me once I got settled in.

It's funny how fearless you can be when you follow your passion. Within a week of making that phone call, I sold my car and Harley. I took that cash and paid off some debts and bought a one-way plane ticket to Florida. I had less than a thousand bucks to my name to make the big move.

Over the next week, I stopped doing drugs and went around and said my goodbyes to my friends. I felt lighter and freer than I had felt in a long time, maybe ever. As I looked around through this new set of eyes, I started to realize that my life was my life, and that my Ansonia experience was mine and mine alone. I knew a lot of great families and kids in Ansonia who never touched drugs and never resorted to violence or brushed up against it. The town itself was filled with so many good people who walked on the right side of the law.

But I wanted more.

I packed one gym bag full of the essentials—sweatpants, T-shirts, underwear, jeans, one dress shirt, and Bill Pearl's *Keys to the Inner Universe*, a 600-page instructional manual dedicated to bodybuilding. To this day, I refer to it when I need to tweak my routine or need a shot of inspiration. In my opinion, this book is the best on the subject. In the forty-five years since it's been published, it's never been topped.

Oh, and there's one other thing I put in that gym bag—the twelve-inch steel bar that I hit that kid in the head with at the bus stop. Don't ask me why, but it was coming with me. And it's come with me everywhere I've been since. I guess some kids had security blankets. I had a steel bar. Crazy, because these days, I wouldn't even make it past TSA with it.

Before I left, I spent a solid half-hour hugging and talking with my dog. It's amazing how attached we become to our pets. Saying goodbye to that dog was way harder than I could have imagined.

My parents drove me down to JFK to see me off. At the airport, I hugged and kissed Mom and Dad goodbye, told them I'd call them every Sunday, and that I'd be back for Christmas. I checked in, made my way to the gate, and as I waited, I observed all these people coming and going. I hadn't really seen this before or felt it. The buzz and excitement of life and traveling. I loved it.

They eventually announced my flight, and I boarded the plane. As I took my seat and buckled up, my adrenaline was off the charts. My brain was spinning with the anticipation of the adventures yet to come.

The flight attendants did their safety spiel as the plane backed out and taxied to the runway. The captain then revved up those big jet engines and said matter-of-factly over the loudspeaker, "We are cleared for takeoff."

"Hell yeah, I am!" I thought.

CHAPTER SIX

ENJOYING "SUMMERS" IN THE SUNSHINE STATE

"Challenge yourself; it's the only path that leads to growth."
—Morgan Freeman

THE WORLD LOOKED A WHOLE LOT DIFFERENT from 36,000 feet up. I stared down at all the patterns, some man-made, like highways and cities, and others God-made, like waterways and mountains. This was only my second flight ever, and it tripped me out that this massive tube of metal could actually get up in the air and transport hundreds of people to an entirely different place.

As we got closer to Florida and farther from Connecticut, I felt a wave of relief knowing that I didn't have to live up to anyone's expectations anymore. All the peer pressure to do drugs and be violent was completely gone. I had a blank slate to be anything I wanted. To put it mildly, I was super excited about this new chapter in my life.

Lost in my thoughts and filled with anticipation, the two-and-a-half-hour flight was over before I knew it. We safely touched down and pulled into the gate right on time. I exited the plane onto the jetway, and the hot, humid, sweet Florida air hit my skin. I walked up the ramp and headed toward the baggage claim with a bounce in my step.

As I strutted through the airport, I spotted one of those tourism signs that said, "Welcome to the Sunshine State!" It had a scene of a beach, complete with palm trees, happy people, blue sky, and beautiful ocean. I got my bag and walked outside, right into the Sunshine State.

Bobby was easy to pick out. He was the only guy leaning up against a '67 Marlboro Maroon convertible Corvette. He had long hair and flashed a big smile. We hugged hello.

"About time you decided to get out of that shit hole!" Bobby said.

I laughed and reminded him that Ansonia had brought us together, so it couldn't have been that bad. I then tried not to bombard him with all the questions that were running through my mind.

As I threw my bag behind the passenger seat, Bobby noticed the Harley number "1" tattooed on the top of my left hand, and the Zig-Zag man on my forearm.

"What the hell are those?" he asked.

I knew it wasn't really a question. Bobby didn't sugarcoat shit, and his obvious displeasure took me right back to when my dad ripped me a new ass after I came home with those tattoos.

Bobby's Corvette had side pipes, and it purred that deep, throaty sound as we took off out of the airport. Music to my ears. We hit the open road with the wind blowing through our hair as he blasted some surf music. I think it was the Beach Boys. It fit the mood perfectly.

We drove twenty miles into the heart of Fort Lauderdale and through its famous canals that were lined with high-end shops, upscale restaurants, bars, and clubs. I definitely hadn't seen anything like that before. Not to mention all the huge boats and yachts that were docked on the Intracoastal Waterway. Bobby explained that the Navy moved into Fort Lauderdale in 1920 and built the system of canals. There are so many of them that the city's seal proclaims that it is the "Venice of America."

As we drove, Bobby summed up the people when he said, "The attitude in Fort Lauderdale is easy like Sunday morning. People here just want to look beautiful, hit the beach, and have a good time. It's a dreamland."

It sounded too good to be true, and as we drove around, I took in the palm trees and saw what he was talking about. The streets were wider and cleaner. The buildings were shinier and taller. And the people seemed happier and in better shape. I felt the air of money the moment we rolled into town. We then pulled up to a huge stretch of beach.

"You've heard of spring break down here, right?" Bobby asked.

Actually, I hadn't. We never took vacations, and I didn't know what other people did outside of Ansonia. He couldn't believe how small-town-minded I was and told me all about spring break. That it was so big that over a few weeks, the population increased by 350,000 college kids looking to party, get drunk, act crazy, and get lucky.

That got my attention! "Oh?! Really?!" I thought.

Partygoers had been flocking there since the 1950s, and half of the time they had to call in the National Guard to control the crowds. They even made movies about it, such as *Where the Boys Are* in 1960 (and a reboot in 1984) and *Spring Break* in 1983, among others.

Spring break was six months away and I already couldn't wait to experience the madness, but I had to ask, "If it's only part of the year, what else do people do down here?"

"They wheel and deal real estate and cater to the super wealthy," Bobby replied. "So, of course, you got your boutiques and nice restaurants, and you also got a lot of health and beauty stuff, not to mention tons of gyms. Everyone's looking for that fountain of youth down here."

Miami was just south of Fort Lauderdale, and beyond it was Cuba and South America. That meant a lot of cocaine flowed through South Florida, making it another big industry in the area. In the '80s, cocaine was the drug of choice, not only for the rich and famous but for everyone. And there was no shortage of people willing to risk jail time to cash in on the white powder. (Check out the documentary *Cocaine Cowboys* for a better understanding of what it was like back then.)

We then drove up the famous State Road A1A to an area called Galt Ocean Mile, where some of the most luxurious hotels and restaurants were. The best, according to Bobby, was the Galt Ocean Mile Hotel. It was one of the originals, and not a penny was spared in designing and decking it out. Apparently, a bunch of famous people lived in that area, including the inspirational book author Wayne Dyer.

After that, we then headed south a few miles and pulled up to a big, beautiful building, with a sign out front that read "White Egret Condominiums." The only thing between it and the beach was North Ocean Boulevard.

When Bobby said, "Home sweet home," my jaw dropped.

"This is where you live?"

"Hell yeah! And now, so do you!"

I high-fived him and grabbed my bag.

We walked into the ritzy foyer, and then a voice from somewhere said, "Good afternoon, Mr. LeVine."

It took me a second to find the source of those words, but then I spotted a doorman. A doorman?! Are you kidding me?

We got on the elevator and Bobby pressed the "8" button. We went up and up until it dinged, then went down the hall to his condo. He had just bought it and warned me he didn't have much furniture. We walked in, and to tell you the truth, even if it had furniture, I wouldn't have noticed. The entire back wall was glass and overlooked the Atlantic. I ran out to the patio and checked out the view, and it looked just like that tourism sign in the airport. I took a big breath of that ocean air and, damn, it felt good.

Bobby gave me a pillow and a sleeping bag, and I made my "room" in a corner on the floor. I couldn't have been happier. This one-bedroom, mostly empty condo felt like the Taj Mahal to me.

It turned out that Bobby managed a high-end gym called European Health Spa and could get me a job helping and training clients. When he asked me if I had any experience as a personal trainer, I laughed and launched into all the times I trained my fellow students during Mr. Germe's gym class. That was enough for Bobby, and I was hired.

If I needed any certificates or licenses to be a personal trainer, I didn't know about it. My certification was in my passion, having read all the bodybuilding books and magazines I could get my hands on, not to mention that I watched *The Jack LaLanne Show* as much as I could.

If you're not familiar with Jack LaLanne, he was widely known for being the "Godfather" of the fitness world and fitness television shows. He was the trainer of all trainers. He had a high-energy delivery that resulted in him having a thirty-plus-year run on ABC from the early 1950s into the '80s. When I'd get the chance, I'd tune in for the latest fitness tips, encouragement, and inspiration.

More than that, though, Jack was just flat-out entertaining. His upbeat attitude was contagious. He even brought his dog, Happy, on the show. Check Jack out sometime. Full episodes of his show have been released on Amazon and are just as relevant today as back then. Thank God for you, Jack! You were the real guru of fitness. Rest in peace, my man.

Bobby landed the European Health Spa job through a guy named Bill D'Addio (everyone called him Billy) who he'd met in Hamden, Connecticut, at a European Health Spa up there. In Hamden, Billy started off as the towel boy and locker room attendant but soon worked his way up to a sales consultant position. When he'd earned his next promotion, the company transferred Billy to Florida to manage the Fort Lauderdale location. Soon after, Billy became the regional manager, overseeing clubs in Florida, Georgia, and North Carolina, and that was when he offered Bobby the manager position in Fort Lauderdale. Lucky me!

The very next morning, I went with Bobby to European Health Spa to fill out some paperwork, and just like that, it was official. This place was about as far from the Ansonia YMCA as you could get. The machines looked brand spanking new, with shiny chrome and purple vinyl padding. The carpet matched the vinyl, and cold air blasted out of air conditioning vents. AC?! In a gym? It didn't feel right, but with it so hot and humid outside, I understood why.

Since I wasn't that familiar with these types of machines, I made sure to work out on them so I could figure out exactly what muscle groups they hit. It didn't take long for me to get my groove training the often older clientele. I'd start by getting to know them and learning about their health histories, injuries, and goals. I learned everyone worked out for a different reason, and sometimes people just wanted a trainer for someone to talk to and to get out of the house. I liked hearing their personal stories, and I learned pretty quickly that when you make people feel comfortable, they really open up. Turns out I was training some very successful people, including a guy named Roy Sklarin.

Roy was an interior designer who specialized in multimillion-dollar houses and yachts. He collected cars, so we hit it off right away, talking about engines, horsepower, tires, and everything else to do with them. I told him all about my first muscle car and motorcycle, and how I watched my neighbor, Mr. Picard, build his from a box of parts. I also told him how Stevie and I rebuilt the engine in his 396 Chevelle SS.

Because we had formed a bond over cars, Roy once asked me during one of our training sessions if I'd be interested in working for him as a bodyguard and chauffeur. Growing up with the work ethic I had and not being one to turn down a shot at earning extra money, I accepted his offer.

Roy was the first openly gay guy I had ever met. If you were gay in Ansonia, the last thing you'd want is for people to find out. Down here, though, things were a lot different. People were less hung up on stuff like that and more concerned with living life and letting others live theirs. Live and let live, right?

Roy introduced me to a whole world I didn't know anything

about—the high-end fashion, art, and interior design world. After his friends knew I was straight, they used to take cracks at me since I was the outsider. It was all in good fun, and we always had a great time hanging out and laughing.

Most of the time, I'd drive Roy to a hip gallery, an art opening, or a client's house. This one time, I took him to an art show, and as I waited around, I got to talking to a cute receptionist who was wearing glasses and a miniskirt. We hit it off, and when I told her I drove Mr. Sklarin's limo, she told me she'd love to see the inside of it. So, of course, I showed her, and let's just say we spent a few hours in there getting to know each other a bit better.

Roy had a super creative mind and was also a great businessman. I learned so much from him during our conversations and seeing how he handled himself in certain circles and with clients. Thank you, Roy!

I also trained an entrepreneur who owned and operated the cabanas at the Galt Ocean Mile Hotel. It turned out he needed someone to help run the day-to-day operations, so he offered me a job. Remembering what Bobby had told me about the hotel, I accepted the position on the spot.

Galt Ocean Mile Hotel opened in 1957, quickly becoming the place to stay for the "see and be seen." It was where the famous picture of Joe Namath was taken in 1969, the day after he was quoted saying, "I've got news for you. We're gonna win the game. I guarantee it."

Joe's bravado was in spite of the fact his New York Jets were an eighteen-point underdog in Super Bowl III. But guess what? He backed up his words and won it! Talk about a confident alpha male. Much respect, Joe.

When I would arrive at work each day, I loved walking through the hotel's huge open-air lobby. I felt a sense of pride waving hello to my co-workers in my lifeguard uniform. I would then exit out the back of the lobby, heading to the stunning pool area that led to the hotel's private beach. There were two dozen

My lifeguard uniform

cabanas out there, and I was responsible each morning for opening them up, wiping them down, and stocking each of them with towels and menus. I'd then settle in during the day, sharing my time between my lifeguard tower and getting towels for rich men and women. At the end of the day, I'd clean up and close down each cabana.

My favorite thing about the job was getting to be around all these incredibly good-looking women. And trust me, there was no shortage of them. Whether it was a group of pretty girls lying out in their skimpy bikinis right in front of my lifeguard tower, or rich older women parading around while their husbands played golf, it was always a sight to see.

Every once in a while, I'd get a call to deliver a towel to a room number, and when I'd knock on the door, it would open and there would be a woman standing there in a half-opened robe with nothing underneath. It doesn't take a genius to figure out what would happen next.

I was really starting to like Florida. I mean, come on, this was my job?! I would have paid the hotel to work there!

Another cool perk about being a cabana boy was that I got to see and meet a lot of talented and famous people, like pop-rockstar legend Tina Turner, who visited and stayed at the hotel. And sure enough, one day, I also met Wayne

Dyer, who liked to come in with some of the local big shots and hang out by the pool.

Wayne was always easy and nice to talk to, but what really impressed me about him was his curiosity and listening skills. One day, after I told him how I ended up in Fort Lauderdale, he brought me one of his latest books, *The Sky's the Limit*.

I don't think anyone had ever given me an inspirational self-help book before. I read it and found it to be super interesting, but I think I was just too young or brash to comprehend the message. Looking back, though, it was funny how my passion led me inherently to do the things he was talking about in his book, like making the vision board of the bodybuilders in my basement when I was a kid.

I had to stop now and then and pinch myself. One thing had led to another, and it seemed like doors were flying open faster than I could walk through them. It was like I was being rewarded for being fearless and staying true to my passion.

Even while juggling three part-time jobs, I still had plenty of energy to work out. I didn't stop partying completely, but my lifestyle was much healthier in Fort Lauderdale (not to mention way less stressful) than it ever was in Ansonia.

When I left Ansonia, I promised my parents I'd call them every Sunday afternoon. We'd talk for hours, and they'd ask me all about what I was up to. I loved filling them in on my week's events and all the new experiences and friends I had made.

Mom told me how she got a job at

the Harvey Hubbell corporate office, and that she loved cooking for the executives. I was so proud of her for stepping out of her comfort zone to get that job, and that she found a way to play in her passion, cooking. She also would tell me about all her church functions and social activities.

Dad would hop on the call and tell me about his latest project at work, and any hunting or fishing trips he had been on. At some point, Mom would fill me in about Chas's brushes with the law, people I knew who had been arrested, and people who had passed away from overdoses. This part of the weekly conversation served as a reality check, confirming that there was more to life than running around acting crazy and partying.

I talked to my friends less frequently than my parents, but the second I got into a rhythm down in Florida, I made sure to call my main man, Jimmy Vane, to tell him to get his ass down here. I was pumped to hear that he had gotten a job to earn some money for his trip to Florida. I couldn't wait to show him my new digs, my new friends, and my new life. I also couldn't wait to hit the strip with him and see what kind of fun we could have. In the back of my mind, I thought that I'd show him such a good time that he'd want to move down here and bring the Vane and

Valente show to Florida.

Six months into my Florida experience, I was loving life. I was meeting cool people, mixing it up with bodybuilders at the gym, and hanging out with beautiful women. I'm not one to kiss and tell, but it was Florida in the early '80s, before the HIV epidemic, and well, let's just say everyone had a little more of that "free love" attitude. I didn't have a care in the world, and I walked around every day feeling like a kid in a candy store.

Everything was cruising along smoothly until Bobby one day got into an argument with the brass over at European Health Spa. Up until then, Bobby had been working his ass off selling memberships like hotcakes, bringing in more money than any other club in the region. In return for that, Bobby thought he should be given a little more leeway and a few more perks. So, he did a lot of things he probably shouldn't have, like working out with his shirt off, parking his Corvette in the guest-only parking spots right up front, and working his own hours. After the bosses got done busting his balls, Bobby quit.

Little did I know that the universe was setting up something special for both of us.

Wanting a break from the gym sales world, Bobby got a job bartending at one of the biggest spring break spots in Fort Lauderdale—Summers on the Beach (previously known as the Ocean Mist). Pretty soon after he started working there, I'd go hang out at his bar, meet pretty girls, and have a blast.

One night, I got to talking with the owners, Suzanne and Allan Migdall, and the next thing I knew, they offered me a bouncer position.

Summers on the Beach had been a mainstay on the strip for a while, but when Suzanne and Allan bought it in 1980, it went up a few more notches into the stratosphere. Suzanne and Allan were a husband-wife team that had a nose for marketing and a love for a good time. This savvy dynamic duo knew just what to do to maximize the spring break experience and expand their business. One of their most ingenious moves was the simple act of giving away over 50,000 T-shirts every year. Soon, the Summers name was known all around the world.

Summers wasn't so much a bar or club as it was an institution. It was a huge, 10,000-square-foot warehouse-type of space about the size of a medium grocery store. It had several bars throughout, and of course, an outdoor pool and deck where it hosted its famous wet T-shirt, belly flop, best buns on the beach, and beer chugging contests, not to mention all sorts of other events that would attract spring breakers and locals alike. It was also known as "South Florida's Home of Rock 'n' Roll," and it seemed like every night it showcased the latest and greatest band. You name the group and they probably played there: Skid Row, War, Cheap Trick, The Marshall Tucker Band, Night Ranger, The Bangles, Midnight Oil, and dozens of other big names.

Allan and Suzanne Migdall

Because of its popularity, craziness, good times, and hot college kids willing to bare all, Summers was featured on MTV's *Spring Break* show. Playboy and its playmates also frequented Summers, which landed Summers in a six-page spread in *Playboy* magazine. Major corporations like Hawaiian Tropic, Ray-Ban, Coors, Budweiser, Miller, Smirnoff, Newport, and Jägermeister, to mention a few, would rent out Summers's pool and throw huge promotional parties to market their products. Every day was a scene, and with 5,000-plus heads per day, Summers was the place to be.

With all this going on, you can imagine why Summers needed at least fifteen bouncers on the clock on any given day or night and had seventy guys in total that they would schedule from. According to Suzanne, Summers always tried to hire personable, charming, good-looking staff members. As for the bouncers, Summers preferred to hire wrestlers, martial arts guys, and bodybuilders as opposed to boxers, who had a fight-first mentality. Suzanne's motto was, "Better to put them in a chokehold or an arm bar and walk them out instead of punching them out."

Allan and Suzanne with Mike Love of the Beach Boys

The funny part about bouncing was that, suddenly, I was the person enforcing the rules instead of breaking them. Each night, it never seemed to fail. Some college kids would come in, drink too much, and cross a line, whether it was grabbing a girl's ass or fighting over a bar stool.

When things would get out of hand, we had what we called "fight lights" on the ceiling that were color coordinated to let all of us bouncers know where to go when a fight broke out so we could restore the peace.

The group of guys I bounced with was a solid crew. David

Langworthy was a silver medalist wrestler in the Pan American Games and coached wrestling at a nearby college. He went on to be a strength and conditioning coach at Ohio State University.

James Sisco was a karate instructor who had a big-time competitive career in martial arts. He became a pastor, motivational speaker, all-around great guy, and my lifelong friend.

Another one of the bouncers, Charlie "Jelly Roll" Smith, taught karate at a nearby dojo.

There was also Eddie Hudak, who was a University of Miami football player. When we were shorthanded, he would bring his football player buddies to the bar to help us out. He ended up getting a job as a prison guard and went on to become the chief of police in Coral Gables.

We had one journeyman boxer on the staff, Tim Anderson, who had fought all sorts of pros, like George Foreman. Tim went on to get mixed up with a guy named Rick "Elvis" Parker, an allegedly corrupt boxing promoter. One thing led to another, and after a series of fixed fights and many disagreements, Tim shot and killed Rick in a hotel in 1996. Tim was sentenced to life for that and is still serving his sentence. There's way more to the crazy story. Check out the book *The Years of the Locust* by Jon Hotten.

There were also a few amateur bodybuilders in the group, including Chris Duffy, Mike Parsons, and Mike Ambrose.

Long story short, these were guys you didn't want to mess with, each making an extra buck on the side from their regular gigs.

Our team of bouncers felt like a family to me, and I was so grateful for the bond, loyalty, and friendships that we developed. We had each other's backs like a police, fire, or military unit. There's a certain trust you have to put in someone, and them in you, when you are confronted with violent and dangerous situations. Knowing that none of us had any hesitation about jumping in to help the other was an amazing feeling. We took great pride and honor in making sure Summers ran smoothly, and we usually went home unscathed.

Summers's famous pool

It didn't take long for the guys to know that I loved bodybuilding. Peter Potter was a bodybuilding contest promoter with the National Physique Committee (NPC). He was in the area looking for a venue to host his next contest. Suzanne and Allan got wind of this and hatched an idea to hold the first ever

Summers Bodybuilding Championship contest. They met with Peter, and the deal was sealed.

But there was more to Suzanne and Allan's plan than just providing a venue for the contest. They thought I should compete in it. They kept egging me on to sign up for it. The truth was, I didn't feel ready to compete, and frankly, I just didn't have the confidence. I didn't think I had a complete enough physique to get onstage, not to mention that I hadn't been dieting down for a show. So I told them, "Not this time," and didn't lose any sleep over it.

My buddy Jimmy was set to fly in from Ansonia in a week, and I had a list of things I couldn't wait to show him.

We'd go to the beach, hit Summers, and walk the main strip to meet girls and have a blast. I was on cloud nine as the day neared, but then I got a surprise call from my mom. She didn't know how to say it, except to just tell me flat out while choking back tears:

Jimmy and his niece

"Ricky, I'm so sorry, but Jimmy passed away."

I got a rush of rage. "What?! How?!"

"His mom found him in his bedroom with a needle in his arm."

I wanted to scream, "What the fuck?!" I was angry. I was sad. I was confused. I felt so heartbroken for him and his family. No one deserves that. We made a promise never to do heroin, and he broke it.

Jimmy's death took a long time for me to process. I realized that I had a choice to make—be bitter and angry, or try to honor Jimmy by focusing and doing more with my life.

By thinking of him every day, I started lifting harder and

harder. I felt like he had my back from way up above, just like in elementary school when he magically appeared out of nowhere and saved my ass when it was me against two.

Everyone is going to lose loved ones, and saying goodbye to certain people impacts you more than others. The tough ones never leave me and actually challenge me every single day to wake up with an enthusiasm for life. As for Jimmy, I have an eight-by-ten headshot of him in my home office that's always there to remind me of my best friend.

Life goes on and the world keeps on spinning. And before I knew it, the time had come for the first ever Bodybuilding Contest at Summers in 1981.

I was working that night and was excited to see the show and the guys' physiques. After I clocked in, I headed to the front door and started getting ready for the busy night. As the crowd kept growing, the other bouncers kept stopping by and breaking my balls to get in the show.

"You in this?"

"Go for it. Do this thing!"

"Get your ass up there!"

Even Suzanne was telling me to take the night off and give it a go. I kept saying no, but when the other athletes arrived, I started to get this burning desire to compete. I also thought about Jimmy and how he would have wanted me to get on the stage.

When Bobby told me to get my ass into the contest, it was on. I thought, "What the hell, at some point I'm going to have to get onstage. Fuck it, let's see what happens."

I ran home and got my posing trunks.

Now, because it was sanctioned by the NPC, the contest was run according to the strict rules of bodybuilding, even though it was set in a wild bar filled with partying kids. The panel of three judges consisted of Peter Potter, Rick Hall, and Raphael Guerrero, who coached the Cuban National Powerlifting Team. The contest was held on the same platform where the wet T-shirt and best buns contests were held. We had to hit the mandatory poses, walk back and forth, and do a little routine. I was scared as all hell, having never been onstage before, and so I just tried to do what the other guys were doing and what I had seen in magazines and in the movie *Pumping Iron*.

1981 Summers Bodybuilding Contest

To tell you the truth, being up there in the eyes of everyone and feeling the energy of the crowd was awesome. It was the ultimate high, better than any drug I had ever taken.

Each round went by, and I kept making it through. And then it was down to just me and one other guy who had a seriously fit physique. We had to hit our mandatory poses again and then wait for the judges to tally up the final scores.

When the announcer said, "The runner-up is…" and then paused to let the crowd get antsy, I got a huge lump in my throat. Here I was, a thousand miles from Ansonia, striking poses like the guys on my vision board. In what felt like a blink of an eye, I had transformed from this scrawny kid on his way to jail (or worse) to someone who could take care of himself and get through a few rounds of a contest.

All of this flooded my brain, so I barely heard the announcer when he said that the runner-up was the other guy. And that meant I had won. Holy shit, I won!

Lifting that trophy above my head was the single best feeling I had ever felt. My bouncer friends went crazy, carrying me off the stage on their shoulders. The only time a smile left my face was when I thought about telling Jimmy.

With that victory, my burning passion turned into a serious inferno. My brain raced a million miles a minute as I researched upcoming contests to enter. I also started studying the specific science about how to "peak" for a show. And just like that, I felt like I was on my true path. But there was one thing that kept gnawing at me that I wanted to take care of before I stepped back onstage again.

And so, I worked more shifts, saved up some extra money, and then made the appointment. When that day arrived, Bobby was all set to go the gym when I told him, "Hey, can't make it today."

"You got a contest to get ready for! What could be more important than that?" he shot back.

I held out my hand and arm to show him the two tattoos again. "I think it's time I get rid of these."

I had finally realized what Dad had told me about them, that they weren't as cool I thought they were. That back then, people saw tattoos and thought the person was a criminal or a thug. Nowadays, of course, tattoos are way more popular and accepted.

In Florida, I didn't have the biker gang mentality anymore, so the tattoos didn't fit my lifestyle or image. When I got onstage, I wanted the judges and crowd to notice my physique, not a tattoo of a number "1" on my hand, or the Zig-Zag man on my forearm that basically told the world I smoked pot. That stuff was in my past. I had bigger things ahead of me.

And so, I went to the doctor to get them removed. But back then, they didn't have lasers. Oh, no. Instead, the doctor took out a woodblock with medical sandpaper wrapped around it. What the hell?! And then he proceeded to sand my skin down until the ink was gone and my skin looked like bloody Swiss cheese. "Dermabrasion," they called it, and damn, it hurt like hell, but that's how bad I wanted to be a force in bodybuilding.

With the tattoos removed and my first contest victory under my belt, I couldn't wait to get on a bigger stage. The Mr. Gold Coast was three months away, and I was going to get primed up for it big time. Game on.

Allan and Suzanne are a couple who are super creative and productive. I found out that they created Summers Production Company and went on to produce several mainstream films that aired on HBO, Showtime, Cinemax, and TNT, as well as promote major concerts nationally.

If that wasn't enough, Allan had a famous T-shirt company called Altuf and was a high-end tax attorney for the wealthy.

Suzanne is a founding member of the Fort Lauderdale Film Festival, as well as a published poet. In 2017, she joined Lamborghini Luxury as a brand ambassador for Lamborghini Winery, which was founded by the legendary carmaker in 1960.

I was always inspired by Suzanne and Allan, and I respected them greatly. So, when working on this chapter, I wanted to get their perspective of me during the time I worked for them. Here's what they had to say:

We loved having Rick on staff and enjoyed the great energy he brought each and every night. We also loved having Rick because a lot of nights, he'd have to physically hold back surging crowds when they tried to storm through the doors to skip paying the cover charge. This good-looking Italian kid from the northeast had the muscles, the hair, and the right attitude. It always seemed like the guys wanted to hang out with him and the girls were always flirting with him. I think he had some fun times while he was here. I'll just leave it at that. Summers had a sweet run and we're thrilled that Rick, along with a lot of our staff, went on to make something of himself.

Much love, Rick!

—Suzanne and Allan

Allan and Suzanne

A huge thank you to Suzanne, Allan, and Summers for everything, and especially for jumpstarting my bodybuilding career. What an incredible time in my journey!

CHAPTER SEVEN

TAKING MY PASSION TO THE NEXT LEVEL

"Success is no accident. It is hard work, perseverance, learning, studying, sacrifice, and most of all, love of what you are doing or learning to do."
—Pelé

TO ME, BODYBUILDING IS MORE OF AN ART FORM, closer to sculpting, martial arts, and dance than a pure sport. No matter how you define or describe it, bodybuilding at its root is the pursuit of creating the most aesthetically pleasing, symmetrical physique, then putting on a posing routine that will tear the fucking house down. It's a discipline where you're chasing perfection that doesn't exist and loving every second of it. Unlike a cut-and-dried sport like powerlifting, where you either lift the weight or you don't, bodybuilding is an aesthetic, subjective event where judges have their own opinions about the perfect physique.

The body is constantly evolving, so you're constantly trying to solve the puzzle of what works for you and what doesn't. This starts with an honest self-assessment of what body parts are good and what body parts need to improve to have better shape. For me, it was always my small calves and thighs that needed the most improvement. It's then all about coming up with a game plan to get as balanced and symmetrical as possible, which is what separates the top pros from everyone else.

In the early 1980s, we didn't have the benefit of decades of research by high-end supplement companies or fancy gym equipment that isolated the muscles. We also didn't have the shared experiences of bodybuilders about contest preparation and working out that you can now find online with a few clicks. Instead, it was a lot of trial and error. A lot of one step forward, two steps back. A constant work in progress in which I would be learning as I went along in my bodybuilding journey.

Coming off the Mr. Summers win, my desire to get back onstage was off the charts. To be successful, I knew I had to take my training, nutrition, and supplement intake to an entirely new level. So I dove headfirst into my research, reading more books and asking as many people about their opinions and experiences as I could. If you don't ask, you don't learn, so I talked to contest judges like Bill D'Addio, bodybuilders like Mike Parsons, gym owners and coaches like Rafael Guerrero, and anyone who had a great physique and was willing to share their knowledge.

Mike Parsons

Bill had some great information for me and would end up helping me with my career even further. He had just bought the Delray Nautilus gym and took me and Bobby to see it. Bill offered us both jobs there—me as the trainer, Bobby as the manager. Bill eventually changed the name of the gym to Palm Beach Gym. It was a great gym with so many talented bodybuilders who would work out there, such as John DeFendis, Mike Quinn, and Tony Price.

I want to give Mike Parsons a big thanks. He was a few years older than me and more advanced in his bodybuilding career. He had an incredibly strong and shredded physique and was nice enough to share his techniques with me. He entered three shows and won every single one—Mr. Miami 1980, Mr. Gold Coast 1980, and Mr. Florida 1981—all in the heavyweight division. What a stud. Thanks, Mike!

With my all-in attitude, I signed up for three shows over the course of a year—the Mr. Golden Glades, the Mr. Gold Coast, and the Mr. Florida. I kept a meticulous daily journal of every meal and snack I ate, broken down into calories, carbohydrates, proteins, and fats, as well as when I ate it and how my body reacted to it. I used the *Nutrition Almanac* to accurately calculate and track my food intake.

By the way, the *Nutrition Almanac* has the most detailed and accurate information about every kind of food you can think of. Another great book to have handy for these purposes is *Prescription for Nutritional Healing*. I also wrote down all my workouts, including the body part, exercise, reps, weight, and how I felt before and after. I then took stock of and made detailed notes about my physique by looking in the mirror, using the tape measure, and weighing myself on the scale.

Me, Mom, Mike Parsons, and Aunt Millie

There are so many variables to bodybuilding. The crazy thing about it is that you can do everything perfect and still not get the muscle growth you hoped for. That's the challenge. Not everyone can be a great bodybuilder. It starts with good genetics—what your mom and dad gave you—and how your body responds to working out, supplements, nutrition, healing, rest, and recovery.

To most, bodybuilding takes on a negative image of guys doing steroids and developing huge muscles overnight, like Popeye with his spinach. If that were really the case, we'd have hundreds of Arnolds, Frank Zanes, Samir Bannouts, and Lee Haneys, and let me tell you, these guys are rare. Their bodies just fit together in a way that was pleasing to the eye. You can't get that from a drug.

To grow and achieve a professional bodybuilder's size, shape, and symmetry, I knew I had to bulk up above my target weight class. And then, at the ninety-day mark before the show, I'd dial it back in hopes of getting shredded. In other words, "peak."

MY WORKOUTS IN THE EARLY 1980s

I designed my workouts to hit each body part from at least three to four different angles twice per week. Each muscle is made up of thousands of fibers and has a left, right, top, and bottom to it. To fully develop a muscle, you have to hit it from all angles. I lifted heavy every day, every set. I now know it's smarter, more productive, and safer to mix it up with lighter weight and higher reps, but back then, my mindset was heavy, heavy, heavy. I'll get into this more later on.

I tried to train every body part to failure and could do so in a variety of ways. If I had a spotter, I would do forced reps and negatives at the end of each set.

Training partners are super important when you're training for a show. For starters, they hold you accountable to show up at the gym at a certain time to attack it. They also provide that necessary support and encouragement to get those extra reps in a safe way. Finally, good training partners bring out that competitive fire in you. Simply put, they make things more fun and productive.

If it weren't Bobby there to spot me, I would train a lot with Chris Duffy, one of the bouncers from Summers. He was a huge lineman who played for the University of Miami and trained like a beast. He pushed me hard in the gym, and I loved it. Chris had recently made the move to Venice with his wife, Marianne, to pursue a career in bodybuilding.

On the off chance I didn't have a spotter, I would do breakdowns, which is when, if you get to failure, you cut the weight in half and double the reps, over and over until you exhaust the muscle completely. The only way I felt like I had "reached" the muscle and had a good workout was if I was insanely sore to the touch the next day.

When you lift that hard, you get this intense "pump" where

you feel like you're twice the size and twice as hard as your normal self. Like you could conquer the world. All that adrenaline flying through your veins. Arnold wasn't lying when he compared getting a great pump to having an orgasm in his movie *Pumping Iron*. That's what makes it so damn fun and feel so damn good. It's what makes you come back for more, day in and day out.

For my workouts, I always liked the idea of keeping things simple. I loved the traditional, old-school, tried-and-true movements. But nothing is written in stone, so what worked for me might not work for you. I realize there are dozens and dozens of movements per body part, and you can ask ten bodybuilders the same question and get ten different answers.

Nowadays, I like to do three to four sets per movement, and the heavier I go, the fewer reps I do (in the ballpark of two to ten reps depending on the weight). The next time I work that body part, I go lighter and do fifty to a hundred reps. The point is, find out what works for you, and try to switch things up and keep your body guessing by varying the weight and the reps.

With that said, the following workouts are what worked best for me:

Workout Cycle

Monday: chest/back/abs
Tuesday: shoulders/triceps/biceps/forearms/abs
Wednesday: legs/abs
Thursday: chest/back/abs
Friday: shoulders/triceps/biceps/forearms/abs
Saturday: legs/abs
Sunday: day off

Movements per Body Part

Chest (Monday/Thursday)
Flat bench (overall chest)
Incline bench (upper chest)
Flies (center and depth)
Pullovers (rib cage, overall chest)

Back (Monday/Thursday)
Pull-ups (wide grip to create width)
Pull-downs (close grip to hit the center of the lower back)
Seated rowing motion (thickness and depth)
Bent-over rows (lower back)
Shoulders (Tuesday/Friday)
Behind-the-neck press (overall)
Side lateral raises (shoulder cap)
Front lateral (front deltoid)
Upright rows (traps, rear deltoid)
Triceps (Tuesday/Friday)
Pushdowns (overall)
Overhead extensions (shape)
Kickbacks (shape)
Biceps (Tuesday/Friday)
Standing curl with a bar (overall)
Seated dumbbell curl (length)
Concentration curls (the peak)
Forearms (Tuesday/Friday)
Fingertip curls (at the end of a bench)
Standing dumbbell curls across the body
Upper legs (Wednesday and Saturday)
Squats (overall, glutes, thighs)
Leg extension (front of thigh, above the knee)
Hack squat (front of thigh, shaping)
Leg curls (back of leg, hamstring, glutes)
Calves* (Wednesday and Saturday)
Seated raises (shape and roundness)
Standing raises (length)
Donkey raises (overall)

**Note: Do these exercises pigeon-toed to work the outer calf, duck-footed to work the inner calf.*

Abs
Rope crunches (upper abs)
Hanging leg raises (lower abs)

Hanging "around the worlds" (lower, overall, obliques)

Seated twists with a broomstick (obliques, intercostals)

Cardio

Offseason/non-peaking (gaining weight)—reduced cardio.

Peaking for a show—one-hour brisk walk after my last meal of the day.

Stretching

Between each set, stretch out the particular muscle group for sixty seconds.

Now, with competitive bodybuilding, whether amateur or pro, the name of the game is figuring out how to peak on a specific day and time so you look your best onstage. To peak properly is one of the most challenging things a bodybuilder strives to accomplish. Because bodybuilding is a subjective, judged event, if you don't hit your peak at the right time, you're usually not going to win.

What does it mean to peak? It means your muscles are full, round, hard, and separated. You have that paper-thin onion skin, so you can see every little striation. You look like an anatomy chart.

To peak for a contest takes months and months of discipline. As I said before, I went through a "gaining" or "bulking up" phase during which I tried to eat four thousand to six thousand calories a day. In those days, we drank Häagen-Dazs ice cream shakes supplemented with raw eggs and shitty protein powder between meals. I also took supplements like liver pills, amino acids, and multivitamins. Back then, they were huge pills that were hard to swallow and digest. Needless to say, all this wasn't for pleasure; it was for purpose.

As far as steroids are concerned, things back then were much more different from what they are now. About three months before a show, I would start taking 1cc of Deca once a week and 1cc of Primobolan every third day. Once the show was over, I would get off the steroids for three to four months, then start again once I began prepping for the next show.

I wanted to keep my eating simple, easy to follow, and therefore easy to stick to, like my workouts. During the ninety-day period when I was trying to peak for a show, the goal was to eat every three to four hours (about four to six meals per day) and have each meal consist of four hundred to five hundred calories. The focus was on a high-protein, low-fat, low-carb diet. This would maintain muscle size and burn fat.

A typical day looked like this:

Meal One: six egg whites (eat first); twenty minutes later, steel-cut oats (for a slow glycemic release) with one cup of blueberries and two cups of coffee.

Hit the gym.

Meal Two: grilled chicken breast, baked yam, and steamed broccoli.

Meal Three: grilled skirt steak and steamed brown rice.

Hit the gym.

Meal Four: grilled orange roughy fish, baked Idaho potato, and steamed spinach.

Meal Five: grilled turkey breast and vegetables.

One hour of rest, then a brisk walk for one hour.

Since this was a low-fat diet, I had to be careful how I prepared my meals. I would grill my proteins so any excess fat would drip off. For my yams or potatoes, I would bake them and eat them dry, meaning there weren't any of the traditional fatty condiments like butter or cheese on them. As for my rice, I would always boil it, never cooking it with butter or grease. To add a little flavor to my meals, I might add a little olive oil, Molly McButter, or seasonings like Mrs. Dash with some pepper, but no extra salt.

On paper, it sounded so simple, but it's one of the most challenging things I've ever had to do. To go from Mom's incredible Italian cooking to this type of bland diet wasn't easy. But that's how bad I wanted to change my physique and compete at the top level.

Without fail, though, I would go crazy every few weeks and

have super intense cravings for something crunchy, sweet, or cheesy. I would snap and stuff my face with so much junk food that I'd get sick. These days, it's common knowledge that one cheat day a week can actually be beneficial because it shocks your metabolism and keeps it from shutting down. But hey, stick close to this eating routine over a ninety-day period, and it will work wonders.

My first real show, the Mr. Golden Glades, was just around the corner, and I squeaked in just below 176 pounds to barely get inside the 154-to-176-pound middleweight division.

In the weeks leading up to the show, I practiced my mandatory poses and worked on a posing routine set to music, trying to time it so I hit my poses with the beats and breaks of the song. Doing that reminded me of doing my karate katas, where each strike, kick, or block ended by popping it into place, much like flexing a muscle.

Being graceful and flowing from one pose to another was a big part of it, which is why Arnold and Franco were filmed taking a ballet class in *Pumping Iron*. Ed Corney was one of the all-time great posers, which Arnold pointed out during the movie as he admired Ed onstage. Thank you, Ed, for your inspiration. RIP, brother!

Another very important thing I had to do was get as tan as possible. Here's why: Take the same two cars—one white, one black—and dent the doors exactly the same way. On the white car, you barely notice the dent; but on the black car, you see every little indentation, shadow, and crease. The point is, darker colors bring out more details. So, when it comes to the human body, a tanned physique shows off more muscularity and shape.

By the time the Mr. Golden Glades rolled around, I felt like I had hit my mark in terms of peaking. But, when I got to the locker room before the pre-judging, I saw that the other guys looked great. I couldn't help wondering if I had done everything I needed to do to compete with them up onstage. As we waited for our weight class to be called, I told myself to stay confident.

Any intimidation and nerves that I felt went away when they called my division to go onstage. I got a rush of adrenaline. Stepping out in front of the judges and the decent-sized crowd washed away a lot of my doubts. I struck my eight mandatory poses as best I could, and toward the end of pre-judging, the judges asked three guys to come forward. I was super excited to hear that I was one of them, which meant I made the top three for my division.

Once they called the three of us out, the judges lined us up and made us hit the mandatory poses next to one another. They then asked us to change places so they could compare us directly to one another.

It was pretty intense, but I loved it. And then, just like that, it was over in a blink of an eye. All I heard from the judges as they dismissed us was "Thank you."

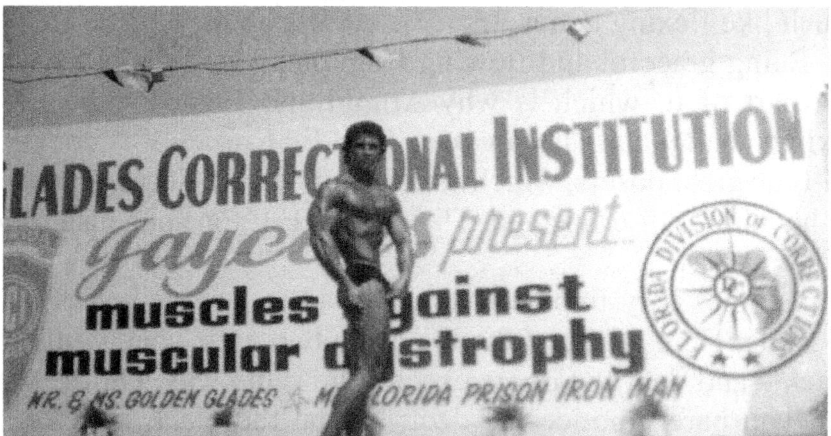

Me at Mr. Golden Glades

Pre-judging ended at about 2 p.m., and we were due back at 5:30 p.m. for the evening part of the show. During the break, I was excited and had some butterflies, but I managed to eat some carbs to keep my energy up and to prevent me from going flat. I then went back to my hotel room, got off my feet, and tried to rest for a few hours. Once back at the contest venue, I got oiled up and did a few towel pulls and push-ups to catch a pump.

The evening crowd was bigger and a lot more energetic than the pre-judging crowd. This is what people came to see—the posing routine that each of us competitors had choreographed to music. It was the performance part of the night that usually separated first from second when their physiques were super close on the scorecards.

When I got called up to do my routine, my rookie nerves came back, and to be honest, I was overthinking the whole thing. I tried to make sure every pose was perfect. It was hard to get out of my head.

For the 1981 Mr. Golden Glades, I placed second in the middleweight division. The result was bittersweet. I had placed well but thought I could have won it. In doing so, I learned a valuable lesson. Overthinking things did not serve my physique and performance well. Had I been living in the moment and just enjoying myself, I would have connected with the judges and crowd a lot better. I left the contest with a lot of optimism, then I did what all competitors always did after a contest—I went out to dinner with friends and ate, and ate, and ate.

Over the next four or five months, I did my eating and workout routine like I had done before, but this time I trained my mind as well. To do that, I made sure I knew my poses and routine like they were second nature, so much so that I could do them in my sleep. I focused on having fun and living in the moment onstage. It must have worked, because I won the middleweight division of the 1981 Mr. Gold Coast contest. My energy was much better, and I had a lot more fun. And that translated into a better performance that felt great and must have looked more graceful and aesthetically pleasing to the judges. Funny how your energy is so powerful.

The next show was going to be my biggest: the 1982 Mr. Florida. It was Florida's top show and pretty much the best show in the region. One of my goals heading into the Mr. Florida was to add size. I had to step up to the light heavyweight class because it was getting too hard to cut weight for the middleweight division. I had four months to prepare.

1981 Mr. Gold Coast Lightweight winner: Kevin Bruno

1981 Mr. Gold Coast Middleweight winner: Rick Valente

Gold Coast guest poser: Joachim Strzeletz

All Photos by Mike Hopkins

1981 Mr. Gold Coast Novice Gym Contest, L-R: Mike Nadeau, 2nd; Richard Terry, 4th; Jordan Zimmerman, 1st; Mike Rice, 3rd

1981 Mr. Gold Coast Over 35, L-R: Harold Collins, 2nd; Thomas Boles, 1st; Claus Hermanns, 5th

Mr. Gold Coast Over 35:
overall winner — Thomas Boles

Lightweight	Heavyweight
1. Thomas Boles	none
2. Harold Collins	
3. Rey Leone	
4. Arthur Gysin	
5. Claus Hermanns	

Judges: John Mese, Peter W. Potter, Marilyn Guzman, Wayne McCormack, Jim Cumby, Mike Pavlovich, Mike Bondurant

North County Bodybuilding Championships

Date: October 10, 1981
Place: Harding High School, St. Paul, Minnesota
Sponsor: Minnesota Bodybuilding Association
Contest Director: Cal Lueneburg
Reported by: Mike Sorrell
Guest Poser: Cal Lueneburg
contestants: Novice 17, Women 11, Open Men 21

Novice Division (closed):
overall winner — Richard Beckman

Lightweight*	Heavyweight*
1. Bob Peppe	1. Richard Beckman
2. Dennis Conway	2. Greg Van Ryswyk
3. Dan Smith	3. Nathan Wattenhofer

*175 lb. weight-break

Women's Division (open):
overall winner — JoAnne Johnson

Under 120 lbs.	Over 120 lbs.
1. JoAnne Johnson	1. Lisa Milbauer
2. Maxine Branson	2. Julie Stangl
3. Adele Jernberg	3. Annie Harrison

Men's Division (open):
overall winner — Al Palmer

Lightweight*	Middleweight*	Heavyweight*
1. Ron Regenwether	1. Dennis Stacy	1. Al Palmer
2. Michel Berube	2. Joe Pereira	2. Gary Hines
3. Mark Saranchuk	3. Laurence Henry	3. Cecil Squires

*Under 165, 165-187, 187 and over

Judges: Martha Blazek, Nancy Doring, Vicki Applin, Pete Moen, Mark McCue, Joe Lauenitis, Barry Darsow, Pat Spangler

34 PHYSIQUE ACTION LINE December, 1981

1981 Mr. Gold Coast winner

I want to give a quick shoutout to all the guys I was training with during this time at Gold Coast Gym. I had some great times and killer workouts with Jan Geerlings, Billy Comorford, Nick Stern, Mike Parsons, Tom Hannon, John DeFendis, and Big Mike. And over at the Pompano Gold's Gym, there was Steve Romanelli, Tony Little, John India, Chris Duffy, and Mike Quinn. Thank you all for your time, dedication, and inspiration!

John DeFendis, Mike Quinn, and me

The training went great. No injuries. No setbacks. I had gained enough size and weight to make the light heavyweight division. Coming into this show, I added a technique to my repertoire called "carb depletion."

Carb depletion is a process that starts a week before the show. The basic idea is that you cut out carbs for a few days, forcing your body to deplete most of its glycogen storage, thus making you very lean. About three days before the show, you add carbs back into your diet, and your muscles soak them up like a sponge. The result is a fuller, harder, and more shredded look.

Going into the Mr. Florida, I felt great and thought I looked like I was in peak form. The competition was pretty stiff in my new weight division. But I kept my head right, had fun, and put on a good performance for the judges and crowd. At the end of it, I got called out as a finalist and ended up placing third in the light heavyweight division. Given where I came from just a year ago, I was pretty excited with my progress and motivated to keep growing and learning.

My friend Nick Stern also competed in the show. He did really well, ranking high in the heavyweight division. I knew him from back at the hotel, where he used to lie on the beach. We're still friends to this day.

Nick Stern at Mr. Florida

That night, Bobby and I took out a couple of girls for a great Italian meal. We had steak, spaghetti and meatballs, ice cream, cannolis, and cheesecake. You name it, we ate it. I loved and savored every bite.

Over the next few months, I kept training as hard as I could while I tried to figure out my next show. The more I researched, though, the more obvious it became that I had to move to Los Angeles, where the top bodybuilders were. It's where the Joe Weiders were. All the magazines. The modeling and fitness agents, not to mention Gold's Gym Venice, "the Mecca of Bodybuilding." You have to keep in mind that this was way before the internet, so you had to physically be where the action was in order to build relationships, and to grow your name and brand. So I made my mind up.

"The Mecca" is where I needed to be.

I loved my time in Fort Lauderdale and loved all the jobs and great relationships I had built. I appreciated and was so grateful for everyone, especially Bobby, Suzanne, Alan, Bill, and my bouncer crew. I was also thankful for all the gyms and their owners, who let me work and work out without having to pay for a membership. I grew up a lot in Florida and attribute my personal growth to these people who showed me a different way to live.

I told my parents that I was off to Gold's Gym Venice to train with the big boys. Mom was a little concerned since I didn't know anyone in Los Angeles, but Dad once again was all for it. So was Bobby and the rest of my friends, who all told me to get out there and kick ass.

Bobby drove me back to the same airport where he had picked me up three years earlier in that same Corvette. The airport hadn't changed much, but I sure had. We hugged goodbye and vowed to see each other soon. And off I went to my gate, westward bound.

Bill D'Addio, me, and Bobby LeVine

I landed at LAX in the evening and took a cab to Venice Beach's Windward Circle, where I checked into the Marina Pacific Hotel. Once I got my stuff squared away in my room, I went to the front desk and got directions to Gold's Gym, which was several blocks away on the corner of Sunset Avenue and

Hampton. It was 9 p.m., but I didn't care. I just had to see it.

As I walked up Abbot Kinney, heading toward Gold's, my street sense kicked in. This was a tough neighborhood. There were gang signs and graffiti all over the place, not to mention gangbangers waiting on every corner. Every now and then, a high-end car would pull up, and there would be a quick conversation between the driver and the gangbanger. You didn't have to be a genius to figure out a drug deal was going down.

As I got closer to the gym, I saw that the front door was open, and I could hear loud rock 'n' roll music playing inside and that familiar sound of iron weights clanking together. As soon as I stepped inside, I was amazed—this place was as big as a warehouse, with a ceiling that must have been three stories high. On top of that, it was 9:30 p.m. and still packed. The energy was off the charts. People were pushing themselves to failure, and their training partners were egging them on to do more reps.

As I stood there and watched these top amateur and professional bodybuilders training like animals, I got goose bumps. Then it sunk in what I was really looking at—my vision board had come to life right before my very eyes. And I was about to step into it.

CHAPTER EIGHT

THE MECCA—GOLD'S GYM VENICE

"There are only two options regarding commitment. You're either in or you're out. There is no such thing as life in between."
—Pat Riley

DURING MY FIRST NIGHT IN VENICE, I lay in bed, staring up at the ceiling of my hotel room, with a shit-eating grin on my face. I was living out my childhood dream. I had gone from Ansonia, Connecticut, to Fort Lauderdale, Florida, to Venice, California, and was on the doorstep of the most famous gym in the world, "the Mecca of Bodybuilding," Gold's Gym Venice.

As I lay there, I thought about how my fearless pursuit of bodybuilding had saved me from the issues that plagued my brother and so many of my friends back home. I still couldn't believe Jimmy was fucking dead. Joey was in prison on a manslaughter charge. Gary had gotten shot five times walking out of a bar. And my brother Chas was constantly bouncing between prison, drugs, and rehab.

I felt grateful that I had found a passion that gave me the power and confidence to break away. Thinking about my friends and brother also inspired and motivated me to do more with my life. I thought if I could somehow make something of myself, then they would see that anything's possible. That you don't have to follow the herd; just follow your heart.

I didn't think I'd sleep a wink, but I'd obviously dozed off because before I knew it, the phone rang with my wake-up call from the front desk. I sprung out of bed, got dressed, and grabbed breakfast at a mom-and-pop restaurant next to the hotel. I remember it to this day—I had egg whites, oatmeal, and a large coffee.

After that, I grabbed my gym bag and made the half-mile walk to Gold's Gym. When I arrived, I stared at the famous Gold's Gym sign and logo on the front door. My adrenaline spiked as I stepped inside.

Tim Kimber, Ed Connors, and Pete Grymkowski

As with the night before, the gym was full of bodybuilders and the clanking of weights. I walked up to the front desk to pay for a membership, and Ed Connors happened to be standing right there. I didn't know it at that time, but Ed was one of the owners, along with Pete Grymkowski and Tim Kimber.

We got to talking, and Ed asked me where I was from, so I gave him my quick story of how I ended up at Gold's. I also told him that I had just arrived the previous day and was there to train for the Mr. Los Angeles contest.

"What did you say your name was?" Ed asked.

"Rick Valente."

"Oh, yeah, I've heard of you. Seen your name in the mags in

the Florida contest results section."

I was taken off guard. "What? Really?"

I pulled out some cash to pay for the day rate.

"Don't worry about it. Here's a pass for the week," Ed said.

Thank you, Ed!

I tried to play it cool as I walked around the gym, checking out the equipment, but it was hard not to be a little starstruck. I mean, there was Mike and Ray Mentzer, Robby Robinson, Mike Katz, Eddie Giuliani, Frank Zane, Ken Sprague, Tom Platz, Don Ross, Casey Viator, Mike Christian, Rachel McLish, Charles Glass, Samir Bannout, Kay Baxter, Pillow, Lynn Conkwright, the Barbarian Brothers, and Lisa Lyon, just to mention a few.

The Barbarian Brothers

It was one thing to see these people in the magazines or in *Pumping Iron*, but another thing to see them in person. They were huge and very impressive, putting up crazy amounts of weight. I'd go up to them, tell them I was a fan, and shake their hands. What really surprised me was how personable everyone was. They had done exactly what I was doing, moving to Venice to train at the Mecca. And they remembered what it was like to be a fan.

What made Gold's Gym so amazing was that it wasn't just

bodybuilders who trained there. It was the number of actors, wrestlers, comedians, rock stars, Playmates, boxers, football players, basketball players, and hockey players training there. It would blow your mind. The list was huge, but I'll get into more detail about that later.

What I noticed in the bodybuilders working out was that the intensity of their training was ten times more than anything I had ever seen before. These guys represented the best of the best from all over the world. They fed off one another's energy, driving their competitive juices through the roof, constantly trying to outdo one another.

As I warmed up, I watched Tom Platz squat 315 pounds for at least thirty-five reps. This guy was known for his massive legs and his intense training. His legs looked like tree trunks that could carry a car. When he finished his set, he racked the weights, lay on his back, put a wet towel over his head, and started hyperventilating like he was about to pass out.

I then saw Mike Mentzer do a high-rep set of leg extensions to failure. When it seemed like it was impossible for him to get another rep, he started grunting and got five more reps. That was also a set to failure!

The women held their own, too. I remember watching Kay Baxter supersetting biceps and triceps, going to failure and screaming as she did so.

When I finished stretching and sat down to do a warmup set on the bench press, I gripped the bar, and the 135 pounds felt like it was a broomstick. It's hard to put into words how light it felt. As I lifted,

Kay Baxter

I felt stronger than I had in my whole life. I put up more weight for more reps than I had ever done before. I wound up bench-pressing 315 pounds for eighteen reps that day, which was five reps beyond my personal best. Could the energy of a gym make that big of a difference? Absolutely!

Before I knew it, two hours had gone by, and my stomach started growling. After I cooled down, I told the guys I had met, "See you later" and "Nice to meet you." I couldn't wait to come back later that night for round two. Back then, two workouts a day was the norm.

Gold's Gym Venice is called "the Mecca" because it's the gym of all gyms, and it's where the top bodybuilders from all over the world went to train, take their physiques to the next level, get discovered by Joe Weider, and do photoshoots for the magazines. Again, there was no internet back then, so if you wanted to be in the muscle mags, you had to be where the photographers and magazines were located, which was Los Angeles.

Gold's Gym couldn't have picked a better location to set up shop. Venice, California, had it all. Its perfect weather and beaches attracted not only beautiful people but free spirits from all over the world. It was a melting pot of personalities and had an edge to it. People marched to the beat of their own drum in Venice.

For my new city and me, it was love at first sight. Aside from Gold's, my favorite part was the circus-like atmosphere on the stretch of Venice Beach Boardwalk that runs between Washington Boulevard and Rose Avenue. That stretch was like a zoo, with all sorts of people playing music, performing crazy acrobatic acts, or selling their art. On one side of the boardwalk was the beach, and the other side was lined with restaurants and shops selling everything you could imagine.

On one of my first walks on it, I stopped at one of the shops to buy postcards to send back home to my parents. When I went to the post office to mail them, I saw a bunch of old photos on the wall. The old-timer behind the counter must have seen this young, curious kid, and he launched into telling me all about the history of the area. He said way back in 1905, a millionaire by the name of Abbot Kinney founded Venice. He bought up a ton of land and turned Venice into a coastal attraction. He even dug canals (like Venice, Italy, and Fort Lauderdale, Florida) and built a massive pier that doubled as an amusement park. He also created the famous Venice Beach Boardwalk.

In the 1950s, Venice went through some tough economic times, which allowed a lot of artists and creative people to move there because the rents were so cheap. By the time I arrived in the early '80s, Venice was on a major upswing and had become a major tourist attraction. And it had also become a destination for celebrities and world-class athletes.

As for how Gold's Gym got started, the story goes something like this:

Joe Gold was a merchant marine who loved to work out. For years, he and his best friend, Irvin "Zabo" Koszewski, had been working out at the original Muscle Beach in Santa Monica, and later at Muscle Beach, Venice. Joe hated paying gym fees just to use someone else's equipment. A machinist by trade, Joe figured he could make better equipment and use it to open his own gym. With Zabo's help, Joe opened Gold's Gym in 1965 on Pacific Avenue in Venice.

Steve Merjanian, Zabo, and Joe Gold in the '60s

Gold's Gym was a place for real-deal bodybuilders. Joe kept the mood serious. No music. No bells. No whistles. If you were going to Gold's, you were going to work out. No fucking around.

Legend has it that if you didn't clean up your own weights, Joe would rip you a new ass.

It wasn't long after opening that Arnold, Franco Columbu, Bill Grant, Ken Waller, Manny Perry, Roger Callard, Robby Robinson, and lots of other top-level bodybuilders came to Gold's Gym and kickstarted what would become the Mecca.

In 1970, Joe sold the gym to Bud Danitz, but when Danitz got into some financial trouble, he sold it to Ken Sprague in 1972 for $15,000. That figure included the Gold's Gym business, brand, and equipment, along with the building and the house behind it. Talk about a steal!

Ken Sprague grew up in Ohio. After he won the Mr. Cincinnati at twenty-four years of age, he wanted to move to Venice, so he drove out to California and got an apartment near Gold's Gym. Sprague and his buddy would train at Gold's during the slow lunch-hour period, and he immediately fell in love with it. He was making good money producing commercials, so when Danitz put the gym up for sale, Sprague was at the right place at the right time to buy it. His main goal in purchasing Gold's was that he and the guys would continue to have a place to work out at.

Ken Sprague

Sprague was too busy to run the day-to-day operations of the gym, so he asked Ken Waller to be the general manager. Sprague's passion was more on the promotional side of the business, and he came up with the idea that Gold's Gym should sponsor contests. Not long after he bought the place, Gold's Gym sponsored the 1972 Mr. Western America. That contest was held in a little comedy club and had something like six competitors and fifty spectators. Sprague paid Arnold and Waller $50 each to do some guest posing.

From there, Sprague got an idea to utilize his connections in Hollywood by offering up Gold's as a free location for producers to film their movies, TV shows, or commercials. The only catch was, they had to put Gold's Gym T-shirts or other merchandise in the shoot. (For a bit of trivia, it was Ric Drasin who came up with the initial design for the Gold's logo—the bald bodybuilder with the bent bar.)

Similar to Summers in Florida and their T-shirt marketing concept, the entire world was soon seeing Gold's Gym T-shirts on their favorite actors onscreen.

It was in 1975 that Gold's Gym got its first real Hollywood break. Sprague heard about a soon-to-be-filmed documentary about bodybuilding that needed a gym to shoot in. He immediately reached out to the production company and bent over backward to make sure it would be filmed at Gold's Gym. His efforts to make Gold's the filming location included a promise to paint over the windows, thus creating the perfectly lit "studio" to film in, which he followed through on.

Ken Waller

Pumping Iron came out in 1977 and featured Arnold, Connecticut's Mike Katz, Lou Ferrigno, Franco Columbu, Ed Corney, Serge Nubret, Ken Waller, Eddie Giuliani, Tom Platz, and others training at Gold's to compete in the Mr. Universe and Mr. Olympia contests. It's a movie that inspired me and so many others. It took the still life photos of the magazines and made the bodybuilders come to life. It was huge for the sport of bodybuilding because it humanized bodybuilders in the eyes of the public. In doing so, it took what had been a little-known sport and introduced it to the mainstream public.

Another thing that took Gold's and bodybuilding into the

stratosphere was that Gold's sponsored the 1977 AAU Mr. America contest in Los Angeles. To promote the show, Sprague had an out-of-the-box idea to hold a parade featuring the competitors riding horses and elephants. The parade drew 250,000 spectators and was the second biggest in California that year behind the famous Rose Parade. According to Sprague, the contest got more press requests than the Academy Awards that year. A big reason for its popularity was that Sprague hired Mae West, the Hollywood icon, to host the show. Her presence brought out a different type of crowd, from old Hollywood to middle America.

After that, bodybuilding and Gold's Gym made it onto *60 Minutes*, the cover of *The Wall Street Journal*, and several other popular media outlets that were not geared toward sports or bodybuilding. To capitalize on the gym's growing popularity, Sprague moved it to a bigger space on Second Street in Santa Monica.

After 1977, Gold's Gym became the place to not only train at but to see and be seen for athletes, celebrities, and bigwigs from all over the world. Tourists would stop by to see the gym and the bodybuilders training there, take photos out front, and buy up Gold's Gym T-shirts and other merchandise.

By this time, Sprague had developed a friendship with Pete Grymkowski, who was a runner-up in the Mr. America three years in a row, from 1972 to 1974, and won the 1977 Mr. America. Pete was from Rochester, New York, where he worked the doors at various bars as a bouncer. He was a big dude, coming in at five feet, ten inches, and over 250 pounds.

One day while still living in New York, Pete was working at a bar when a guy named Tim asked him for some training advice. Tim had aspirations of being a competitive bodybuilder and got a tip to see Pete. They quickly developed a friendship, with bodybuilding being their common interest.

You can imagine that Pete saw a lot of things in his line of work. Eventually, the Feds wanted Pete to testify against the

Mob. Pete didn't want any part of that, so in the dead of night, Pete and Tim jumped into Pete's Corvette and hightailed it to Orlando, Florida. As for Tim, he moved back to Rochester.

In 1977, Pete took a one-way airplane ticket to California to train for the Mr. World contest. He trained at Gold's Gym during the day, and at night, he slept underneath the Santa Monica Pier. He did this for three months until he won the Mr. World title.

Pete Grymkowski

In December 1978, Sprague approached Pete to see if he would be interested in buying Gold's Gym for just $100,000. Sprague had made plenty of money and simply wanted to sell it to someone he knew would keep the Gold's brand and tradition going. Pete was game, but he needed some partners.

Now, as all of this was unfolding, Pete and Tim had kept up their friendship even though they lived on opposite coasts. Pete coached Tim, and in turn, Tim was the East Coast rep for Pete's Prima Pro line of protein powders.

Tim worked hard on his physique and ended up winning the 1978 Mr. Empire State. His goal was to make a run at the Mr. America title. This was around the time Pete got the opportunity to buy Gold's, so he called Tim to see if he wanted to buy in. Tim had just gotten married in October 1978 (a week after winning the Mr. Empire State contest) and had also bought a house, so he didn't have the cash. Pete ended up buying Gold's with Ed Connors and a third guy, Denny Doyle.

Tim didn't want to be left out, so he asked Pete if he could come out to Venice and work and train at Gold's. Pete was all for it, and so was Tim's wife. As luck would have it, within a few months, Denny Doyle bowed out of his ownership share, and because Tim had sold his house in Rochester for a profit, he had his own money to buy in.

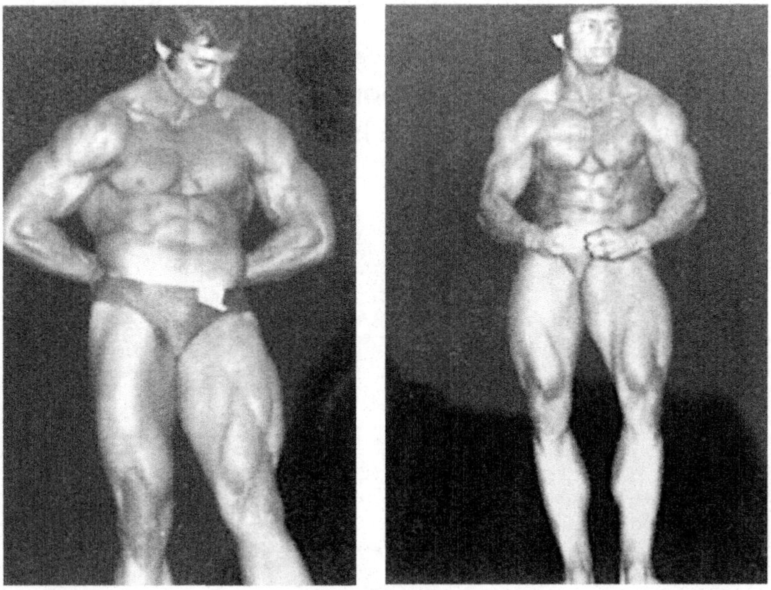

Tim Kimber

This all went down in early 1979. About a year later, Pete convinced his brother, Paul, to leave New York and move to Los Angeles, where he would become the president and international director of Gold's Gym Enterprises. From there, Paul created Gold's Gym Franchising, where Gold's would license its name to gyms all over the world.

The Gold's Gym name took off like wildfire. When Pete, Tim, and Ed sold Gold's Gym in 1999, it had something like 540 locations, including several that were owned and operated by celebrities and athletes like Pete Rose, Ric Flair, Barbara Mandrell, Reggie Jackson, Lyle Alzado, Ron Jaworski, Archie

Manning, Jermaine Jackson, Joe Klecko, Kevin Greene, B. Brian Blair, and Ken Norton.

In 1981, Gold's Gym moved from its location on Second Street in Santa Monica to its current home on the corner of Hampton Drive and Sunset Avenue in Venice. Soon after, a half-dozen or so restaurants, like the Firehouse and the Rose, sprung up nearby, with menus that catered to bodybuilders. In the beginning, the new location was five thousand square feet and consisted of one big warehouse room, where the front desk currently is. It expanded to the second room in 1986, the third room in 1988, and the fourth room in 1990, which is the layout you see today. It also includes a large open area in the front and back.

The original Gold's Gym warehouse room

When I arrived at Gold's in 1982, the Mecca was in full swing at its new location. I am so grateful for all the guys—Joe Gold, Ken Sprague, Tim Kimber, Pete Grymkowski, and Ed Connors—who had the passion for working out and growing Gold's Gym into the Mecca that it was when I got there. A perfect storm of characters, relationships, and passion.

New York City had its famous club, Studio 54, that attracted all the top celebrities and athletes, and Los Angeles had Gold's Gym. I know that sounds like apples to oranges, but on any given day at Gold's, you could work out next to one of the Lakers,

Dodgers, Kings, or Raiders. Guys like Lyle Alzado and Howie Long were always at Gold's Gym. And when opposing teams came to play in LA, their players would pop in to work out. And I'm talking players like Michael Jordan. It was truly the place to see and be seen.

Likewise, you could go in and pump iron next to a pop star, an Academy Award winner, or a world-famous artist. It also attracted commercial, TV, and film shoots, and on most days, there would be a shoot going on with an A-list actor, model, or athlete. The energy was unrivaled, just like at a nightclub, but instead of people dancing, people were lifting weights.

Rick Valente (in turquoise shirt) moves in some tough circles these days. We caught him just before he got down to work at Gold's the other day in the company of *General Hospital*'s Steve Bond and Lyle Alzado (in gray sweats).

Imagine how you feel when you see just one superstar, whether it be an actor, athlete, or musician, on the level of a Dennis Hopper, Larry Bird, or Janet Jackson. That's what it felt like to walk into Gold's Gym Venice in the '80s and '90s. Only there wouldn't be just one superstar; there would be several at any given time.

What follows are lists of most of the bodybuilders, actors, athletes, wrestlers, and A-list people from other professions who were members of Gold's Gym Venice during the '80s and '90s. I've tried to make these lists as comprehensive as possible to the best of my abilities. But memory being what it is, I'm sure some people were inadvertently left out. To those individuals, I want them to know they have my deepest respect and sincerest gratitude.

Bodybuilders

Martin Alamango
Ted Arcidi
Jack Armstrong
Jason Arntz
Aaron Baker
Samir Bannout
Kay Baxter
Laura Beaudry
Albert Beckles
Tim Belknap
Francis Benfatto
Reggie Bennett
Juliette Bergmann
Liona Bergmann
Sandra Blackie
D'marko Blewett
Monica Brant
John Brown
Sharon Bruneau
Carolyn Bryant
Brian Buchanan
Andreas Cahling
Dean Caputo
Mike Christian
Bob Cicherillo
Charles Clairmonte
Teagan Clive
Lynn Conkwright
Chris Cook
Chris Cormier
Joanne Lee Cornish
Porter Cottrell
Laura Creavalle
Jay Cutler
Steve Davis
David Dearth
John DeFendis
Paul Demayo
Jorgen de Meij
Berry de Mey
Diana Dennis
Chris Dickerson
Chris Duffy
Marianne Duffy
Carla Dunlap-Kaan
Matt DuVall
Kike Elomaa
Cory Everson
Jeff Everson
Lou Ferrigno
Lou Fortuna
Bertil Fox
Bev Francis
Jeramy Freeman
Johnny Fuller
Clare Furr
Rich Gaspari
Eddie Giuliani
Charles Glass
Sherry Goggin
Jeff Golini
Bill Grant
Lee Haney
Will Harris
Dave Hawk
Jeff Henry
Phil Hernon
Phil Hill
Raye Hollitt
Renel Janvier
David Johnson
Eduardo Kawak
Bill Kazmaier
Tonya Knight
Kent Kuehn
Lee Labrada
Anja Langer
Kevin Lawrence
Rory Leidelmeyer
Gary Leonard
Kevin Levrone
Fabian Lewkowicz
Dave Liberman
Jack London
Don Long
Perkins Lorenzo
Lisa Lorio
Ron Love
Lisa Lyon
Jim Manion
Arina Manta
Ludovic Marchand
Michael Matarazzo
Rico McClinton
Rachel McLish
Matt Mendenhall
Dimitrios Mentis
Mike Mentzer
Ray Mentzer
Erika Mes
Mae Mollica
Brian Moss

Lenda Murray
Jack Neville
Dennis Newman
Serge Nubret
Mike O'Hearn
Danny Padilla
Bob Paris
Mieczyslaw Parkita
David Paul
Peter Paul
Tony Pearson
Chuck Perez
Clyde Perry
Pillow (Theresa Jean Bell)
Jim Quinn
Mike Quinn
Janice Ragain
Shawn Ray
Victor Richards
John Richling
Sandy Riddell
Eddie Robinson
Robby Robinson
Ricci Rondinelli
Gunnar Rosbo
Don Ross
Denise Rutkowski
Ofer Samra
Gunter Schlierkamp

Actors

Rosanna Arquette
Ellen Barkin
Roseanne Barr
Angela Bassett
Steve Bond
Lisa Bonet
Barry Bostwick
Matthew Broderick
Charles Bronson
Pierce Brosnan
James Caan
Nicolas Cage
Dean Cain
Billy Campbell
Jennifer Connelly
Beverly D'Angelo
Ted Danson
Tony Danza
Robert Davi
Embeth Davidtz
Geena Davis
Dana Delany
Rebecca De Mornay
Laura Dern
Peter Dinklage
Kirk Douglas
Robert Downey Jr.
Richard Dreyfuss
Fred Dryer
Faye Dunaway
Sally Field
Ralph Fiennes
Laurence Fishburne
Carrie Fisher
Teri Garr
Mel Gibson
Whoopi Goldberg
Jeff Goldblum
Linda Gray
Jasmine Guy
Gene Hackman
Mark Harmon
Woody Harrelson
Lisa Hartman Black
David Hasselhoff
Rutger Hauer
Lawrence Hilton-Jacobs
Gregory Hines
Dennis Hopper
Matthias Hues
Kay Lenz
Ray Liotta
Tommy "Tiny" Lister Jr.
Dolph Lundgren
Kyle MacLachlan
Ron Maxwell
Mary McCormack
Penelope Ann Miller
Matthew Modine

Chuck Norris
Jason Patric
Nia Peeples
Michelle Pfeiffer
Bronson Pinchot
Jeremy Piven
Keanu Reeves
Ving Rhames
Victor Richards
Eric Roberts
Adam Rodriquez
Mickey Rourke
Kurt Russell
Stan Shaw
Martin Sheen
Charlie Sheen
Brooke Shields
Wesley Snipes
Kevin Sorbo
Sylvester Stallone
Mary Steenburgen
Peter Strauss
D.B. Sweeney
Heather Thomas
Sven-Ole Thorsen
Jean-Claude Van Damme
Ben Vereen
Lindsay Wagner
Mark Wahlberg
Fred Ward
Carl Weathers
Owen Wilson
Chuck Woolery
Bolo Yeung
Chuck Zito

Professional Athletes

Kareem Abdul-Jabbar
Muhammad Ali
Marcus Allen
Lyle Alzado
Tony Atlas
Brian Bosworth
Jennifer Capriati
Wilt Chamberlain
Chris Chelios
Nadia Comaneci
Bart Conner
Roberto Duran
George Foreman
Willie Gault
Julien Greaux
Laird Hamilton
Thomas Hearns
Evander Holyfield
Bo Jackson
Reggie Jackson
Caitlyn Jenner
Magic Johnson
Michael Jordan
Eric Karros
Vitali Klitschko
Wladimir Klitschko
Derrek Lee
Mario Lemieux
Kimo Leopoldo
Howie Long
Ronnie Lott
Greg Louganis
Ray Mancini
John McEnroe
Willie McGinest
Mark McGwire
Marty McSorley
Ken Norton
Hakeem Olajuwon
Mike Piazza
Gabrielle Reece
Mary Lou Retton
Dennis Rodman
Randy Stoklos
Danny Sullivan
Lynn Swann
Isiah Thomas
Rick Tocchet
Frank Trigg
Cathy Turner
Mike Tyson
Dave Winfield

Wrestlers

"Stone Cold" Steve Austin
Big John Studd
Big Show
British Bulldog
Brutus Beefcake
John Cena
Chyna
Ted DiBiase
Edge
Ric Flair
Mick Foley
Goldberg
The Hardy Boyz
Bret Hart
Jimmy Hart
Owen Hart
Mark Henry
Vince McMahon
Shawn Michaels
Kevin Nash
The Nasty Boys
Paul Orndorff
Diamond Dallas Page
The Patriot
"Rowdy" Roddy Piper
Razor Ramon
Jake "the Snake" Roberts
The Rock
Mike Rotunda
Tito Santana
Randy Savage
Sgt. Slaughter
Ron Simmons
Rick Steiner
Scott Steiner
Sting
Triple H
The Ultimate Warrior
The Undertaker
Rob Van Dam
X-Pac

Musicians

Kim Carnes
Billy Ray Cyrus
Sophie B. Hawkins
Janet Jackson
Jermaine Jackson
Lenny Kravitz
k.d. lang
Barbara Mandrell
Chynna Phillips
David Lee Roth
Frank Stallone
John Tesh
Adrian Zmed

Comedians

Carrot Top
Andrew Dice Clay
Billy Crystal
Joe Piscopo
Garry Shandling
Jimmie Walker
Damon Wayans

Directors

Peter Berg
Nick Cassavetes
Oliver Stone

Models

Linda Evangelista
Kate Moss
Sandy Taylor
Renee Tenison
Rosie Tenison

Photographers

Jim Amentler
Per Bernal
John Bialik
Jimmy Caruso
Paula Crane
Ralph DeHaan
Bill Dobbins
Chris Lund
Mike Neveux
Robert Reiff
Rick Sorenson
Russ Warner
Art Zeller

Writers

Jerry Brainum
David Horowitz
Shawn Perine
Donald Ross
Ruth Silverman

During that first week in California, I was doing everything I could to meet people, look for work, and find a place to live. This led me to a guy named Pat Hayes, who worked out at Gold's and needed some extra cash. We worked out a deal on rent so I could sleep on his couch while I looked for my own pad. Thank you, Pat!

One of the first guys I clicked with at Gold's was this dude named "Magic" Schwartz. He was a big biker guy, all tatted up, with long blonde hair. He lived in the back of Gold's Gym, in a converted school bus with his beautiful girlfriend, Reggie Bennett, who was a competitive bodybuilder. They had a beautiful brown-and-white pit bull named Blue, who had intense blue eyes. Magic had a Harley, and if there's ever a dude you'd want to ride across the country with, it would be Magic, because if you were to break down, he could fix anything.

I was lucky to have met Magic right away because he and Reggie had moved to Venice two years before me and already knew the lay of the land. They moved to Venice so Reggie could train at Gold's and get exposure in the fitness world, and so

Magic could pursue an acting career.

Reggie ended up becoming an A-list trainer, with clients such as Margaux Hemingway, Brigitte Nielsen, and many more. Magic went on to be in commercials and several movies, including *Over the Top* and *Lionheart*. He also became a successful trainer to celebrities like David Lee Roth, Jane Fonda, Michael Landon, Lance Henriksen, Mickey Rourke, Brian Bosworth, and David Hedison. He even did some pro wrestling. He did so many things, it blew my mind!

Reggie, Magic, and Blue in front of their bus

Right off the bat, Magic helped me get some work doing security. We ended up working lots of gigs together. One time, a rich guy in Beverly Hills had been getting death threats, so he bought some Uzis and paid us to stay at his house for a week. Another time, this guy's fifteen-year-old daughter ran away with a drug dealer, so he hired Magic and me to track her down and bring her home.

While I was still staying on Pat Hayes's couch, Magic told me about a buddy of his who had converted his garage into a single apartment. The beauty of this place was that it was close to Gold's, and his buddy didn't require a first and last month's rent, or a security deposit. I checked it out, and it had all I would need—a sink, a shower, a toilet, and a space to sleep—all in one room. I moved in with a thrift store cot, a sleeping bag, and a hot plate that I put on top of a milk crate. It wasn't much, but it worked perfectly.

Reggie

The more I hung out with Magic, the more I respected his creative energy and free spirit. He was one of those guys who thought outside of the box, and when he would have an idea, he would figure out how to make it a reality. He invented a total gym system before the real Total Gym was even invented. He also made a slider-type of machine that put you in a sprinter's stance and let you "run" in place in a nearly horizontal position. Lyle Alzado, the famous defensive end and tackle from the Los Angeles Raiders, and I did some photoshoots for Magic's slider-sled.

Having Magic and Reggie in my life was like having a second family. They took care of me and went out of their way to show that they cared. They really made me feel special when they threw me a surprise party for my twenty-fifth. Reggie had made a great birthday cake in the shape of a woman. It was delicious.

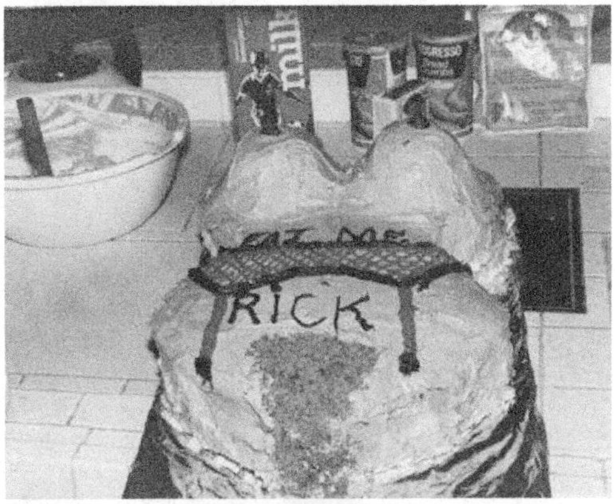

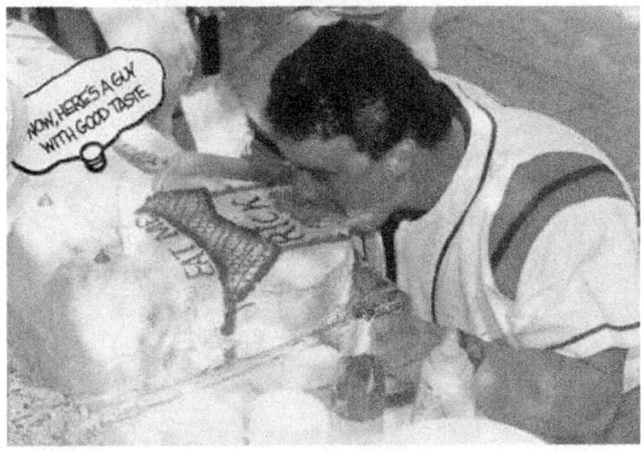

As I've said before, relationships are everything in your life's journey. Magic helped me out so much, and I can't thank him enough. We've kept in touch ever since we met. One of the best parts about reaching out to old friends is talking about the times we shared, going down memory lane, and hearing their take on our time together.

Thank you, Magic and Reggie!

With the security gigs keeping me afloat, I had some breathing room to look for a more consistent job. I'd spend mornings looking over the classifieds, and between workouts, I'd be pounding the pavement, going door to door on Main Street in Santa Monica to see who was hiring. The street back then was absolutely popping with clubs, restaurants, and bars. Everyone in LA knew it was the hot spot to grab a drink or a bite. On any given night on Main Street, you'd see your favorite movie star and all the paparazzi trying to get a photo. To see the glitz and glamour of it in person was a sight to behold.

Carré Otis and Magic

Sylvester Stallone and Magic

Luckily for me, my job search didn't last long, as I stumbled upon Charmer's Market. I applied and got a job on the spot as a security guard.

Charmer's Market was way ahead of its time. In addition to having all the regular sections of a grocery store, it had a butcher shop, a fish market, a bakery, a news and flower stand, a coffee shop, a bar, and a restaurant. It was located on Pier Street, at the corner of Neilson Way. Its owners, Doug and Jane, were both creative people who wanted it to be a place where you could take a break from grocery shopping, grab a bite to eat, and enjoy a glass of wine. The idea was a huge hit, and like Gold's, it attracted a Hollywood crowd. Actors like Ali MacGraw, Jane Fonda, Dustin Hoffman, Goldie Hawn, Warren Beatty, and others shopped and dined there.

It also attracted pro athletes. One day when I was making my security rounds, I saw the tallest dude I had ever seen. As I got closer, I immediately recognized the guy: Wilt Chamberlain, the NBA legend who scored a hundred points in one game and dominated the league in nearly every statistical category imaginable. I walked up to him, introduced myself, and told him that I was a huge fan. He was really humble, and we built a friendship from that initial conversation.

Me working at Charmer's Market

In fact, one time when I strained my groin trying to deadlift 550 pounds, Wilt noticed me limping around the parking lot. He asked me what happened, and after I told him, he suggested that I go see his sports doctor. The next day, I took the bus to see his doctor. After the doc evaluated me and gave me some treatment, I went to pay, and the receptionist told me Wilt had taken care of it. The next time I saw Wilt, I couldn't thank him enough.

A week later, I was working at the meat counter at Charmer's because the butcher didn't show up, and when Wilt came to get some cuts of meat, I gave him the best I could find and told him it was on me. It's the least I could have done, and I wish I could have done more. Rest in peace, Wilt.

Another famous athlete I saw at Charmer's was Lyle Alzado. Like with Wilt, any time I ran across an athlete that I recognized, I would approach them and tell them how much I respected them. It was always well received. I developed a friendship with Lyle, and we wound up training together at Gold's Gym (and doing the advertisement I mentioned above).

Another friendship that I was fortunate to have because of Charmer's was with a guy who had an antique car shop across the street called Ocean Park Motors. I had always kept my eye on it because it had so many beautiful classic cars parked in and around it. One day, I must have gotten too close to a car, and the owner, who was hosing down the driveway, tried to squirt me away.

Turns out he was just razzing me. We both laughed, and I introduced myself. We got to talking about cars and we just clicked. I don't know if it was because of our mutual interest, or the fact that we were both Italians, but the end result was a beautiful friendship that lasted thirty-eight years.

Bobby Scura was the guy's name. He was born in Rochester, New York, and moved to LA in 1952.

During high school, Bobby worked at Schaber's Cafeteria in North Hollywood and was fired when he tried to organize the kitchen staff into a union. From Schaber's, he moved on to work at Du-par's as a fry cook.

Me at Bobby Scura's car shop

After high school, Bobby went into the Air

Force in 1958, and after basic training in Texas, he was stationed in Hof, Germany, in the German state of Bavaria near East Germany. His job was to listen to code transmissions for intelligence gathering. Bobby told me all his stories about his very active social life with the ladies of the town. So we had a second interest in common after cars, and that was women.

When Bobby left the Air Force, he was hired by Playboy Clubs International and held jobs as a club manager in Chicago, Denver, and Los Angeles. Bobby saved up, and when he made enough money, he relocated to Santa Monica. Once there, he connected with Grand American Fare, a local real estate development group.

He was responsible for acquiring real estate and developing concept restaurants. At its peak, the group had twenty-two restaurants that catered primarily to college students with beer and tasty, reasonably priced food. In Santa Monica, the group owned and operated The Fish Company, Omelette Parlor, and The Oar House, to name a few. These were well-known, happening places on Main Street that helped create a jumping scene with great food.

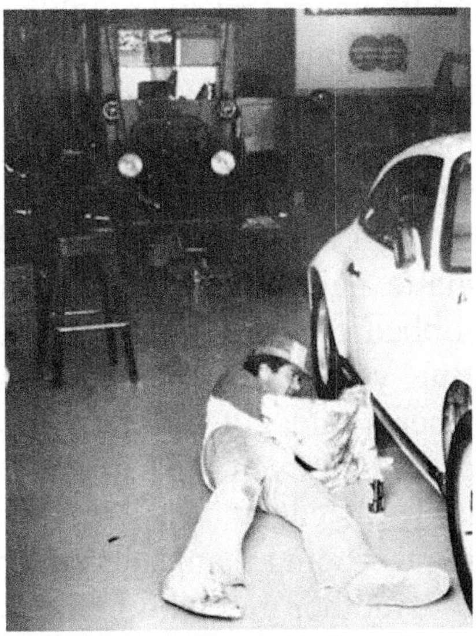

Bobby working on his Porsche

I found it amazing that Bobby was already "retired" at age forty, so he was able to indulge his passion, which was cars. He drove a white Porsche 911 SC, and he also had a fire-engine red convertible '57 T-Bird, the same car that Detective Dan Tanna drove on the TV show *Vegas*.

I'll never forget some of the beauties that came through his garage, and I'm not just talking about cars. Over the years, *Playboy* magazine held several photoshoots there. That was something to see. The wrap parties weren't half bad either.

Speaking of cars, it was about time for me to get my own. Up until then, I had used a bicycle or the bus to get around, but in Los Angeles, you really need a set of wheels. And so I did what I usually did—started asking around.

Bobby and me in his T-Bird

Some guy David from Gold's Gym told me about a used AMC Pacer that his neighbor was selling. Now, to be honest, it was a total piece of shit. Kind of like a Pinto, but way uglier and bubblier, if that was possible. This one came with a few issues, too. Its driver-side door was permanently locked, so I had to get in through the passenger door. The gray matte paint was so oxidized that it rubbed off on you if you touched it. But you know what, it had four wheels and got me from point A to point B. I even took girls on dates in it. It all came down to my state of mind—being thankful that I got a car.

Dennis Tinerino

Another guy who helped me out a lot was the famous bodybuilder Dennis Tinerino. Dennis won the Mr. Universe four times, from the late '60s to early '80s. One day, I was working at Charmer's when Dennis pulled up in the parking lot. I knew who he was and said hi to him. We got to talking, and after I told him my story, he said, "I know what it's like to just move here. If you need anything, let me know."

Bodybuilding back then was a small family of elite athletes, and Dennis was one of the really cool guys who treated me like a brother. People like Dennis made my transition so much easier. Thank you, Dennis. Rest in peace, bro!

One other thing I have to say about Charmer's was how great it was for meeting beautiful and cool women. One of them happened to be Hannele Sundberg, a powerlifter from Helsinki, Finland, who moved to Venice to work out at Gold's just like me. We of course hit it off immediately and worked out a lot together. We ended up dating, and one time she came home with me to Ansonia.

Hannele Sundberg and me

She fit in with my parents, who liked her right off the bat. And even though we didn't last, she became a great friend not only to me but to my parents. A huge thank-you to Charmer's Market for introducing me to so many great people.

With my jobs in place, I saved up some money and got a single apartment on Breeze Avenue in Venice, one block from the beach and walking distance to Gold's Gym. It was small, about ten by twelve feet, but it had all I needed.

With my essentials squared away, I then turned my sights onto what I came out here for—getting my pro card. The first step was to enter the 1983 Mr. Los Angeles, a contest that Gold's Gym was sponsoring. It was also a contest that would attract all the big-name magazines.

When I told Mom and Dad about it, they said they would love to come out with my cousin Mark to cheer me on. Knowing they'd be in the crowd pumped me up even more.

CHAPTER NINE

WINNING MR. LOS ANGELES

The key is not the will to win. Everybody has that. It is the will to prepare to win that is important.
—Bobby Knight

KNOWING MOM, DAD, AND MY COUSIN MARK would be flying across the country to watch me compete in the Mr. Los Angeles contest filled me with pure inspiration. I wanted to get into the best shape of my life. That meant tuning out the noise around me and staying laser focused. If it didn't have to do with making rent, training, eating, resting, posing, or tanning, then it wasn't part of my day.

The goal of each workout remained the same—to get that crazy pump and burn so the next day I would be sore to the touch. Now that I was training at Gold's Gym, the Mecca, I was exposed to a lot of new workout philosophies and techniques. Instead of having to run to the corner store and dig through the latest bodybuilding magazines, I got to watch the top bodybuilders in the world work out in front of me, and I got to ask them about their workouts and contest preparation.

Tom Platz training at Gold's Gym

Take for example Tom Platz. He had the biggest, most ripped legs in the world, and he trained them like no one else I had ever seen. The interesting thing about Tom was that he was always switching up his workouts, which sparked my curiosity big-time. I really lucked out one day when he had asked me for a spot. I couldn't say yes fast enough!

Tom did more intense forced reps and "negatives" than any other guy in the gym. If you don't know, a forced rep is when a spotter helps you get a few more reps after you've reached failure on your own. The idea behind negatives is that you start at the top of the movement and then resist the weight (and gravity) on the way down. You can do negatives with a weight that's beyond your max, or you can have a training partner push down on the weight.

As I spotted Tom, I got a front-row seat to these techniques. When he would do leg extensions, once he got to failure on his own, he would holler out, "FIVE MORE!" Then I would help him get five more forced reps. And just when I thought he was done, he would holler out, "Five more! Push down on the negative!" As before, I'd spot him to the top of his rep, then I'd start the negative by pushing down on the roller pad as he resisted on the way down. Tom was as strong as a bull, and sometimes I couldn't even force the roller pad all the way to the bottom! Crazy.

Likewise, if Tom were doing leg curls, once he got to failure, he would yell out for me to help him with forced reps, then he'd have me help him with negative reps. (For leg curls, the negative rep starts at the top, when the ankles are closest to the glutes.) By the time we'd be done, my arms were fried!

Tom was a super nice guy who was very generous with his time and advice. He gave me a lot of great tips on training, eating, and contest preparation. I will always be grateful for my friendship with Tom.

Back then, there was a camaraderie among all the bodybuilders (probably because there were no cellphones or social media to distract us). Most of the time, I didn't even have to ask for a spot because the guy training next to me would just offer when he saw that I needed it. Or I'd spot someone, and they'd spot me back. Sometimes I would have a training partner, like Chris Duffy, who left Florida to pursue a bodybuilding career in Venice. But most of the time, I wasn't tied to a single training partner and their schedule, which meant I could always do my two workouts a day, no matter what time I got in there. That was the beauty of Gold's back then.

Chris Duffy (right)

Another technique that I picked up from the guys at Gold's was called a "giant set," which targets one muscle group and consists of three to four different movements so you hit that body part from every single angle. Once you pick up the weights, you go through all the movements before you set them back down. Take shoulders, for example. I'd grab dumbbells and do ten to fifteen reps, starting with standing side raises, then go right into front raises, then upright rows, and finally finish with an overhead press. I'd do three to four sets of this "giant set," and trust me, by the time I got to the overhead press, my arms would be shaking, and my shoulders would be on fire.

While negatives and giant sets ended up working great for

me, you still need to figure out which of the many techniques and philosophies works best for you. The Mentzer brothers did one set per body part to failure, and that obviously worked great for them, as they both had beautiful physiques. The point I'm trying to make is that nothing is written in stone, and it takes some trial and error to find out what system your body responds to the best.

The most important thing, no matter what training technique you believe in, is mastering the mental part so you could bust through the pain barrier. I constantly challenged myself mentally to get those extra reps. To lift heavier weight. To get over the hurdle and keep pushing. Most of the time, I was surprised by how far my body would go when I mentally locked in and blocked out the pain.

The most strenuous training technique I ever did was doing fifty to one hundred rep sets. I had to check my ego at the door because I had to cut the weight down and then block out everything around me. When I would hit the fiftieth rep of a 100-rep set, I would gather myself and count the remaining fifty backward, which made it seem easier, as if I were going downhill. This and a lot of other mental tools helped me grow and shape the physique that I envisioned for myself.

Mike Christian and Charles Glass

Pushing through the pain is where a great spotter comes in handy. Someone who can either verbally root for you to do more reps or can offer a feathery, light touch to help you get past a sticking point, all the while making sure your form is correct. Having top pro bodybuilders like Charles Glass, Mike Christian, Casey Viator, Don Ross, Serge Nubret, and Lou Ferrigno, to name a few, cheering you on to do more reps got the adrenaline flowing like nothing else. Sometimes they'd yell, "Two more!" and I'd challenge myself to do four or six more, just to show them how competitive I was. And they'd do the same thing when I spotted them. I always loved competing against myself and other people.

Don Ross and Serge Nubret

Lou Ferrigno

Lyle Alzado became one of my best friends at Gold's over the years. To say Lyle was imposing was an understatement. In his prime, he stood at six feet, three inches, and 275 pounds. This guy would throw down with anyone, anytime. He even fought a match against Muhammad Ali; that's how much of a badass he was.

Lyle Alzado and me in a Gold's Gym ad

How I met him was kind of crazy. When I first arrived at Gold's, I'd be training in the morning and at night, and I started getting friendlier and friendlier with a young lady, Lee Winthers. One night, as I was leaving the gym, she asked where I was going. I told her I was going to walk home.

"I can give you a ride," she said.

"Thanks. That'd be great," I answered.

So she drove me home. We swapped phone numbers and started dating.

A couple of weeks later, Magic saw me with Lee at Gold's Gym. He grabbed me and pulled me aside.

"What the fuck you doing?" he asked.

"What?"

"Do you know who that girl is?"

I had no clue. To me, she was just Lee.

"That's Lyle Alzado's girlfriend," Magic said. "Brother, you better know what the fuck you're doing, because he'll beat the fuck out of you."

Me and Lee Winthers

Well, that was alarming, to say the least, but what the hell could I do? At the moment, I had a leg workout I needed to finish. So I went over to one of the squat racks and started training. After three or four sets, I was up to 405 pounds doing behind-the-neck squats when, in the mirror, I saw Lyle walking toward me.

"Oh, shit. He's gonna knock me the fuck out," I thought.

To my surprise, he just slapped me on the back and said, "Hello, Rick, I heard you're dating my ex-girlfriend. You make sure you take good care of her and treat her with respect."

"Absolutely, Lyle. Thank you, brother," I said.

I was incredibly relieved that Lyle responded to me like that. Thank you, Lyle!

Lee and I dated for about a year. She was great. I even took her back east to meet my parents, who, of course, loved her. Eventually, the relationship ran its course, but we remained friends. Lee, thank you.

It didn't take long for me to realize that when it came to my career, I had made the right choice by moving to Venice and training at Gold's Gym. Working out toe-to-toe with the pro bodybuilders there was something to behold. Their intensity was through the roof, and that pushed me to train harder than I ever had before.

Between sets, we'd stretch whatever body part we were working on, then we'd stand next to each other and hit the pose of that same body part in the mirror. Not only did this give me a greater pump, but it helped me work on my mandatory poses. This was a level of training that I only saw at Gold's.

Now, it's super important to remember that you can train until you're blue in the face, but if you don't eat the right foods for your body type, you will not get the results you are striving for. It's like putting regular fuel in a race car that needs premium. For muscle tissue to grow, you need to consume enough protein (like egg whites, skirt steak, fish, or chicken), slow-glycemic-burning carbs (like yams, vegetables, or rice), and high-quality fats (like avocado, olive oil, or nuts), then get adequate amounts of sleep so the muscle tissue can rebuild itself.

In Venice, I was essentially eating the same foods as I was in Florida, but I learned a really cool meal preparation technique from a bodybuilder at Gold's named Donny Gay. Donny was from Cincinnati, and we got to be really good friends working out together at Gold's. He was getting ready for the Mr. USA, and he had one of the most shredded physiques in the gym, with striations all over it.

We were working out together one day, and I just had to ask, "Dude, how do you get so shredded?"

Donny told me that he eats out of his stainless-steel steamer all year round, preparing every meal except breakfast in it. I thought, wow! I was interested in what exactly he ate and how he cooked it in the steamer. Donny told me he starts the morning with six egg whites and a cup of steel-cut oatmeal with a banana. Then he goes to the gym. After the workout, he puts water in the steamer and puts orange roughy fish, veggies, and a potato in it, and steams it. The fish is a natural diuretic and gets you ripped. And every four hours, he will have another meal in the steamer with a chicken breast, or some white fish with veggies and a potato or a yam. Eating that way is a game changer!

Donny Gay

Thank you, Donny, for your friendship, your workout, and all your knowledge about getting ripped! He and I are still friends, and we often talk about life and how we are blessed to be alive and still in shape.

It was ninety days before the Mr. Los Angeles show, and I was in a great rhythm with my workouts and eating. My days were dialed in and looked like this:

Me, Donny, and a lovely lady

6:00 a.m.: Wake up.

6:30 a.m.: Eat egg whites, steel-cut oats with a cup of blueberries, and coffee.

8:00 a.m.: Go to Gold's and work out for one hour.

10:00 a.m.: Eat steamed orange roughy fish, yam, and broccoli.

11:00 a.m.: Go to work at Charmer's Market.

4:00 p.m.: Get off work.

4:30 p.m.: Eat steamed chicken and a potato.

5:30 p.m.: Back to Gold's for round two.

7:00 p.m.: Eat steamed orange roughy fish, broccoli, and cauliflower.

8:00 p.m.: Walk for an hour.

9:00 p.m.: Work on my mandatory poses.

10:00 p.m.: Go to bed.

Whenever I had some downtime, I'd hit the beach to work on my tan, and in the evening, I really enjoyed my walk after I'd have my last meal. Back then, very few of us did cardio because we all thought we'd lose muscle mass, so a walk was what I did to keep my metabolism going. It helped burn that last little bit of stubborn fat around my waist and gave me some time to think about my day and my goals. By the time I woke up at 6 a.m. the next day, I'd be starving.

The thing is, though, when I got up in the morning, I was in this cramped studio apartment on Breeze Avenue. I had to cook my breakfast on a hot plate that was on top of my minifridge. As I did that, I would think how I'd really love to find an affordable one-bedroom apartment with a regular kitchen to cook in and a normal bedroom to sleep in. So I put that thought out into the universe.

A few weeks later, when I was making my rounds at Charmer's Market, my new friend Bobby Scura called me over to his antique car shop.

"Hey, a rent-controlled apartment in my building just opened up," he said. "You should go put in an application. The landlord, Florine, is expecting you!"

I was totally blown away! For those of you who don't know, getting a rent-controlled apartment near the beach in Venice or

Santa Monica was (and still is) like winning the lottery. It meant the landlord could only raise the rent a very small amount every few years, and they couldn't kick you out on a whim.

That very day when I got off work, I ran over to Bobby's apartment building on the corner of Fourth Street and Marine to fill out the paperwork and look at the apartment. It was a nice one-bedroom, one-bath unit. I liked how the building was well kept. I also loved that the complex had its own pool and an ocean view. Plus, it was about two blocks from Gold's, three blocks from Charmer's, and four blocks from the beach. And if that wasn't enough, Bobby lived in the unit right above the one I looked at. He had been there for so long that he fixed up his apartment with his own money and had put a ladder on his balcony going up to the rooftop, where he had his own little sundeck.

A few days later, I heard back from Florine that I was approved. I put in my deposit and the first month's rent, which was $400. (It currently goes for about $4,000.) Once I got the keys, I knew I was going to live there until the day I could buy my own place. Turns out, I'd be there for about fifteen years. Making the move from my little studio was easy enough because I didn't own much of anything. It was basically me, my steamer, a sleeping bag, and a few small items. I was so happy and felt so blessed to score this awesome new home. Thank you, Bobby!

Me and Bobby at the apartment

Now, the thing about Bobby was that he was a good-looking Italian guy, but he had never really worked out with weights.

I wanted to pay him back for helping me get the apartment, so I offered to train him for free, if he would be into it. He was game and started asking me all sorts of questions. Seeing and hearing his enthusiasm, I ran out and bought him a bench and starter weight set for his birthday. We set it up on the rooftop of our apartment building and worked out in the beautiful sunshine while we kept an eye out for girls down at the pool.

Bobby took to working out like wildfire. That's the thing about passionate people. If they're passionate about one thing, that same passion usually carries over to other pursuits. And that's exactly what happened to Bobby, who took his love for cars right to the weights.

I loved sharing my knowledge with him and was even more thrilled when his body started changing and responding to the workouts. His progress reminded me of when I trained my fellow classmates back in high school during Mr. Germe's gym class. It wasn't long before I got Bobby to train over at Gold's Gym. Helping other people get in shape is a really rewarding feeling.

Around this time, I got to thinking that it was time for me to get a new set of wheels. As it turned out, Bobby was getting ready to buy a new car. He said he'd give me a deal on this black Ford Ranger he had. So I bought it. I was so happy. It looked like new and had low mileage because Bobby had only lived a few blocks away from food stores and his car shop. It was a great truck.

It was forty-five days before the show, and I started to devote more time to working on my mandatory poses and my posing routine. Prejudging required each bodybuilder to hit eight mandatory poses, then strike our "most muscular" pose, which was usually the famous "crab" pose. The eight mandatory poses consisted of:

1) Quarter turns
2) Front double biceps
3) Front lat spread
4) Side chest

5) Side triceps
6) Rear lat spread
7) Rear double biceps
8) Abdominals and legs

Thankfully, Gold's Gym had a great posing room filled with mirrors at every angle so you could see every inch of your physique, just like the judges would. I learned from the pros that your stage presence while you hit your mandatory poses was crucial. You wanted to be the first person in the pose and the last one out of it, all while making eye contact with the judges and audience. You had to try to make it look effortless even though holding a pose while fully flexing was physically demanding. Those who didn't practice their mandatory poses would end up out of breath and have to cut the pose short because they'd start shaking, which looked terrible.

I worked on holding each pose for thirty to sixty seconds, which was a workout in and of itself. For me, the key was always making sure I controlled my breathing. In the posing room, I could also figure out exactly what angle made each pose look its best. A little twist here and shift of my weight there made a huge difference. Take my double biceps pose, for example: If I would give my hips a little twist, it would highlight my small waist while allowing me to flex my abs and obliques. All of that made my chest and arms look even bigger and more symmetrical. There were other ways to hit that pose, but for me, that was the most aesthetically pleasing for my body type.

Now, for the night show's posing routine, I knew I wanted to use a popular song that I could feel in my soul. Something that would get the audience all fired up and had a good, funky beat, like "War" by Edwin Starr, "In the Air Tonight" by Phil Collins, or "You Dropped a Bomb on Me" by The Gap Band.

I put in so much work making sure my timing and transitions between poses were on point so that I hit each pose on the right break of the song. I firmly believed that if two bodybuilders were super close in their symmetry and conditioning, the better posing routine would determine who took first.

Another thing I figured out from watching the best posers, such as Ed Corney, Mohamed Makkawy, Bob Paris, Lee Labrada, and Francis Benfatto, was that you got in and out of every pose starting and finishing with your hands and fingers. For example, the transition into a pose began by opening your hands, and the pose ended by popping into the pose and then clinching your fists shut. It gives the performance a nice flow and aesthetic, making it that much more graceful and entertaining to watch.

Back then, your posing routine was just as important as your conditioning. And so, as the contest neared, I practiced my mandatory poses and posing routine whenever and wherever I could, even in my head as I lay in bed at night. It took me back to being a kid, when I was learning karate katas and would repeat them over and over again to perfect them.

It was seven days before the contest, and I started my carb depletion. I gradually weened out the carbs from my diet, starting on Monday, until I ate zero carbs on the Wednesday before the show. Then on that Thursday, I ate about 300 grams of carbs, consisting of yams, potatoes, and pasta. And then I upped it to 600 grams or so on Friday. But again, be forewarned that, like workout techniques, peaking strategies are specific to the individual, and it takes some trial and error to dial them in.

Also, a few days before the show, I started the process of getting extra dark by using tanning dye, which was essentially like painting yourself a few shades darker. That began with a full-body shave, then using a sponge to spread out the dye. I hit the parts I could reach, then I had the girl I was dating at the time, Lisa Nunziela (she would go on to win *Star Search* a few years later), help me paint my back and the parts I couldn't reach. After we applied a thick coat of it, I then used a hair dryer to blow it all dry. I did this a few times before the show to make sure I had a nice, bronzed look that showed off my definition and muscularity.

On the Thursday before the show, I picked up Mom, Dad, and Mark from the airport. I was so excited to see them. Having them there and feeling their love and support meant the world to me. I put them up at a hotel on nearby Lincoln Boulevard. Since there were three of them, it'd be a tight fit in my one-bedroom apartment. If I couldn't hang out with them because of a workout or a shift at work, Lisa would fill in for me, showing them a really good time. My parents had a blast with her, and they especially loved that she was Italian.

Me and Lisa Nunziela

On the Friday before the show, I took Mark (who was fourteen at the time) to Gold's with me. When we went in, Mark's face lit up at the sight of all the bodybuilders, actors, and athletes he had seen in the magazines, movies, and TV. We then went into the posing room, and I went through my mandatory poses and posing routine one last time. After that, we grabbed a big bowl of pasta at the Firehouse. I then dropped him off at the hotel and went home to get off my feet.

My parents and Lisa

On the morning of the contest, I ate a light breakfast of oatmeal with peanut butter and honey. I then packed up for the show, grabbed my parents and Mark at their hotel, and made my way over to the Veterans Memorial Building in Culver City, about fifteen minutes away. Once inside, I walked through the large auditorium where the show would take place. It had a raised stage on one end, and seats for the judges and audience on the other. Behind the stage, there was a curtain that held a huge Gold's Gym banner on it. Seeing that banner and knowing that the most famous gym in the world was sponsoring the show reinforced how big of a deal this was going to be.

Even though it was still early in the day, a sizable crowd had already started to form. When I saw Bobby, Reggie, Magic, and some of my other friends from the gym who came to cheer me on, I smiled from ear to ear. I also recognized some older pros who came out to watch.

One guy in particular who caught my eye was Rick Wayne. He was a mega-stud bodybuilder who tallied up several Mr. Universe and Mr. World wins in the 1960s. I had a ton of respect for him and always admired his physique. When I was a kid, I put photos of him up on my vision board back in Ansonia. To have someone like Rick there, along with other top pros, made the energy in the room that much more exciting.

Rick Wayne

Once backstage, I ate a Snickers bar. I also had a little container with a half-glass of red wine in it, which I drank. The secret behind a small amount of red wine was to bring out the veins. And the idea behind eating the simple carbs was to top off my glycogen levels so that my muscles would look full and hard onstage.

Twenty minutes before my class was scheduled to hit the stage, I caught a pump doing push-ups, curls with a light set of dumbbells, and towel pulls with my training partner, Jeff Henry. I then had Kent Kuehn, who was backstage helping all the competitors, help me put on a thin layer of baby oil, just enough to create a little shine.

Kent was a super nice guy who worked the front desk at Gold's Gym after he retired from competing as a bodybuilder. He won the 1977 AAU Masters Mr. America and the overall at the North American Championships. Sadly, Kent passed away in June 2019. I'll always remember his positive energy and the inspiring words he shared with me as I was about to walk out onto the stage. Thanks for all your help, Kent. God bless you. Rest in peace, bro.

As we were called out onstage, I noticed that the place was packed, and there were a lot of reporters and photographers covering the show for the bodybuilding magazines. Even though it was a local show, it was an important one.

Mr. Los Angeles 1983 contest

The first part of prejudging consisted of quarter turns so the judges could get a good look at each of our physiques and see how symmetrical we were. From there, we each got to do the rest of the mandatory poses as the judges marked up their scorecards.

After that, the judges then called out the top three guys to do side-by-side comparisons. When I heard my name called by the lead judge as part of that first group, I knew that meant I had cracked the top three of my class. I was super pumped up about this, and so were my supporters, who all hooted and hollered when I stepped out.

I then hit each of the mandatory poses again for the judges alongside the two other guys who had incredible physiques, one of whom was Jeff Henry. Practicing so much in the posing room, I felt confident that I was hitting the right pose in the right position.

After we each finished our mandatories, the judges thanked us, and we returned to the lineup as the next group of three were called out. It went like that until everyone had a chance to pose, then the judges dismissed the entire class. Backstage, I gathered my stuff and kept thinking that prejudging went as good as I could have hoped for. I then found my parents and Mark, and we all went back to my apartment for the break between the prejudging and the night show.

At home, I ate a chicken breast, a yam, and a few cups of brown rice. I then got off my feet and rested my legs. As I did that, Dad drove down to Lincoln Boulevard to pick up some food, and when he was driving back, a woman flagged him down.

Dad pulled over to find out if she needed help, and then she said, "Hey, want a date?"

When he got to my place and told us the story, we all had a good laugh. Welcome to Venice, Dad!

When we got back to the contest, the crowd had swelled. The auditorium was packed with even more fans and press than before. Photographers with their big lenses were out in mass, and all the bright lights were on. It was time to put on the music and give a performance that would tear the house down.

Backstage, I caught a pump, got oiled up, and ran my posing routine through my head. When Kent gave me the heads-up that I was on deck, I stopped for a moment and just cleared my mind. I then reminded myself to go out there, live in the moment, and have fun with it.

"Go get it!" Kent said as I walked out.

Fortunately, I did just that. As I hit my poses in sync to the music, the crowd cheered. As the song went on and I kept nailing each pose, I struck what would become the signature pose of my life—the front double biceps with a slight twist at the waist, a giant photo of which would end up on the wall inside Gold's Gym and is still there four decades later.

For the few seconds I was in that pose, it felt like time stood still. I could see the faces in the crowd and the flashes of the cameras. Once the song came to an end, I gave a bow of gratitude to the crowd, then a big wave and smile to my family and friends.

After all the contestants in my class finished their routines, we waited for the announcer to read off the top five in the class,

My signature pose

and I was grateful to be one of them but of course was hoping for more. The five of us stood onstage as the announcer called the names for fifth, fourth, and third places, and none of them were me. I got a huge shot of adrenaline knowing it was just me and one other competitor.

When the announcer called out the runner-up's name and it wasn't me, I threw my arms straight over my head and let out a huge scream. I knew I had won.

When I finally heard, "First place goes to Rick Valente," it was the best thing I'd heard in my entire life. They handed me the trophy, and when I hoisted it up in the air, the crowd erupted with cheers, and the photographers snapped photos. I let out another huge scream, and the applause, whistles, and hoots drowned me out. It was a feeling you cannot buy. I felt so happy seeing everyone's faces light up, but it felt especially incredible when I saw Mom and Dad smiling and clapping, totally losing themselves in the moment. It was one of those times when I can honestly say I felt pure love and joy.

I gave one last wave and smile as I walked off the stage. "Congratulations, you look amazing!" Kent said once I got backstage, then he gave me a huge hug.

After I toweled off and changed, I headed out with my trophy in one hand and my bag in the other. I recognized Rick Wayne talking to some other people. And then, in a surreal moment, he pointed at me with a wide smile on his face.

"Congratulations. I'm Rick Wayne, the editor of *Flex* magazine," he said.

"I know who you are! I'm a big fan of yours. You were on

my vision board as a kid!"

He had a good laugh about that.

It was such an honor to meet him and shake his hand. I thought he just wanted to tell me, "Great job. Way to go." But what he said next is something I'll never forget: "Rick, I want to put you on the cover of *Flex* magazine."

This completely blew me away. I set my stuff down, gave him a big hug, and told him how thankful I was and that I'd be honored to be on the cover of *Flex*. I then ran out front, found my parents and Mark, and told them the great news. They were overjoyed and beyond happy for me.

"First place in the light heavyweight class goes to Rick Valente!"

Now it was time to celebrate. I took them all to Peppone Ristorante in Brentwood for a classic, old-school Italian dinner. We sat in a booth, and Dad had everyone laughing at his stories about me as a scrawny kid back home. We drank wine and ate fried calamari, spaghetti and meatballs, and steaks for dinner, and of course cannoli and sambuca to wrap it all up.

Over the next few days, I took my parents and Mark to see some of the landmarks around Los Angeles, like Universal Studios, the Chinese Theatre in Hollywood, and the Venice Beach Boardwalk. I had also booked a photoshoot that was going to be shot on the sidewalk in West Hollywood, which at the time I didn't know was nicknamed "Boystown." I thought it would be cool for them to see the shoot, so I brought them with me.

There I was, in my posing trunks, standing on a corner in West Hollywood, when I started noticing that guys kept tooting their horns and whistling at me as they drove by. It finally dawned on all of us what part of town we were in. We couldn't help but laugh.

After their weeklong vacation wrapped up, I dropped my parents and Mark off at LAX for their flight home. We hugged and kissed goodbye. I told them I loved them and that I'd be home for Christmas. I was sad to see them go.

It wasn't until I drove away from LAX and was alone in my car that my victory started to sink in. I replayed the contest in my head, reminding me of the feeling I got standing onstage holding the first-place trophy. I then busted out a huge smile, recalling how I met one of my idols, Rick Wayne. And that's when I screamed at the top of my lungs, "I'm going to be on the cover of *Flex* magazine!"

Ever since I was a little kid making my vision board, I always dreamed of being one of the guys on the cover of a bodybuilding magazine, and here it was becoming a reality. It just goes to show you, if you set a specific goal in mind, work your ass off, and stay focused, dreams do come true.

CHAPTER TEN

LIVING THE DREAM

"If you do the work, you get rewarded. There are no shortcuts in life."
—Michael Jordan

WINNING A CONTEST PROMOTED BY GOLD'S GYM, the Mecca of bodybuilding, with the title of Mr. Los Angeles, the center of the bodybuilding universe, was a huge stamp of approval. Bodybuilders and members at Gold's Gym suddenly started coming up to me, saying, "You looked fantastic!" or "Way to go!" We'd get to talking, and the next thing I'd know, they were asking me for training and eating advice.

When the top guys at Gold's Gym start treating you with more respect and asking you questions, it does wonders for your confidence. I always loved sharing my passion, and it was such a great feeling to be doing it at this level. Also, by giving advice here and there, I was lucky enough to land my first private clients—Chuck and Katie Arnoldi.

Me, Katie Arnoldi, and Chuck Arnoldi

Chuck is a famous artist who made a name for himself with oversized wall-mounted wood sculptures, as well as standalone sculptures and paintings. Katie is one of those people who always excels at anything she puts her mind to. She was a competitive surfer, a contest-winning bodybuilder, and an excellent writer with critically acclaimed novels.

Together, Chuck and Katie are a fun-loving, generous couple, and we clicked the moment we met. What started as a training gig soon turned into a friendship with both of them.

One time, they even took me to Hawaii on a vacation and gave me a room in a beautiful house they had rented right on the beach. It was my first time in Hawaii, and I loved feeling the warm ocean water on my skin. The beautiful sunsets, incredible views, colorful flowers, and fragrant smells were unlike anything I had ever experienced.

Chuck's artwork

From the moment I got off the plane and got "lei'd," I knew Hawaii was a special place, and it didn't disappoint. As a kid, I never imagined I'd go horseback riding to see a sunset in Hawaii. But I did on that trip.

Chuck, Katie, and me in Hawaii

Another time, Chuck was going to his doctor for a physical, and he asked me when I last had a physical. I told him I wasn't sure; it had been a while. So Chuck took me with him, and we both got complete physicals. And guess what? Chuck paid for the whole thing!

They would also often invite me to their home for dinner parties or to one of Chuck's art openings. I remember once wearing a custom suit and shirt that Chuck had his tailor make for me. He was so generous!

Their house was like an art studio compound, and I was always amazed at their guests, who included actors like Dennis Hopper, artists like Billy Al Bengston, and directors like Joe Pytka and Paul Abascal.

Me and Joe Pytka

Speaking of Joe, when I first met him at one of the Arnoldis' parties, I didn't know anything about him. I just remember seeing a very tall guy who looked like a wild man. We started talking about sports and got onto the subject of the Lakers, who were flying high at that time with their "Showtime" act led by Magic Johnson and Kareem Abdul-Jabbar, with coach Pat Riley at the helm.

Joe also happened to be from back east, having grown up in Pittsburgh, another working-class, factory-driven town, so we had that in common as well. At the time, I had no clue that I was talking to one of the most prominent, prolific, and well-respected commercial directors in the entire world. That's the crazy thing about Los Angeles, then and now—you never quite know who you're really talking to.

Okay, so if you don't know, Joe is a legend in his field. Over the course of his career (which is still ongoing at the young age of eighty-four), he directed more than 6,700 commercials. Of those, he directed more than eighty Super Bowl commercials for the biggest brands and featuring the biggest celebrity names in sports, music, and Hollywood. He also directed feature films like *Let It Ride* (1989), starring Richard Dreyfuss, and *Space Jam* (1996), starring Michael Jordan, and music videos for chart-topping megastars like The Beatles, Madonna, and Michael Jackson. He has won dozens of prestigious awards from organizations like the Cannes Lions International Festival of Creativity, the Emmys, and the Directors Guild of America, where he was recently awarded a Lifetime Achievement Award in Television. More on my friendship with Joe later.

Back in the gym, by training Chuck and Katie, I started to get more and more clients, so I was able to step away from doing the security gig at Charmer's Market. I charged people forty bucks an hour to train them, which was a lot back then. At that rate, I could train a few people a day, have plenty of time to work out, pay my bills, and have enough left over for some spending cash. I also started to pick up some local photoshoots and magazine work to supplement my income.

Me, Joe Pytka, and hairstylist Paul Abascal

As for my coaching style, I started out by asking my clients what their goals were, what their health and injury history was, and what they were currently doing for their workouts and meals. I also asked them about their lives to figure out what they were dealing with outside of the gym, how they were sleeping, and how much time per week they could commit to training. From there, I designed a specific workout and eating program that fit each client's body type and lifestyle, setting realistic goals for their needs.

During our actual training sessions, I focused on the mind-body-spirit connection, making sure my clients were aware that their success meant finding a balance between those three connections. In most cases, doing regular workouts automatically increased their spirit and worked as a great stress reliever to balance them out. If that wasn't enough, one of my favorite things to do was to give them a copy of *The Sky's the*

Limit by Wayne Dyer or *The Power of Positive Thinking* by Norman Vincent Peale. (Giving away books is one of my favorite things to do, by the way.)

It's important to remember that you need to feed and exercise your mind, body, and spirit. What you listen to, what you read, what you watch, who you hang out with—all these things are just as important to your happiness and overall health as your meals and your gym sessions. Surround yourself with positive, happy people, live in the moment, and life is that much sweeter.

Me and Katie Arnoldi

All in all, winning the 1983 Mr. Los Angeles turned out to be an amazing transformation for me, as I was able to combine my passion for bodybuilding with earning money. I felt so blessed to wake up near the beach, to spend my days at the Mecca training myself and others. Every day was different and always seemed to hold some sort of cool surprise. For example, I was at Gold's one day in the middle of a workout when Gregory Hines approached me.

"Hey, Rick Valente, I'm a big fan of yours!" he said.

"Thanks, but I'm a bigger fan of yours!" I said with a laugh.

Gregory then introduced himself as if I hadn't already known who he was. "Hey, I'd like you to train me. How much do you charge?" he asked.

"Forty bucks an hour," I replied.

Gregory started laughing.

"Oh, shit, is that too much?" I thought.

He then slapped me on my back. "No, I'll pay you seventy-five an hour," he said.

That's the kind of guy Gregory was. He knew I didn't have a lot of money and was very generous with me. It turned out to be the beginning of a beautiful, long friendship.

Gregory, for those who might not know, was a true triple threat with his amazing tap dancing, singing, and acting abilities. He got his start young, turning professional at the age of five, and went around touring with his older brother and dad as the Hines, Hines, and Dad show. Gregory moved to Venice in 1973 and got his big Hollywood break in 1981 when he scored a role in a wacky Mel Brooks comedy, *History of the World, Part I*. In the mid-'80s Gregory had great roles in *The Cotton Club* (a film about a nightclub in Harlem, directed by Francis Ford Coppola and starring Richard Gere and Diane Lane) and *White Nights* (about a Russian ballet star wanting to escape the Soviet Union, starring Helen Mirren and Mikhail Baryshnikov).

Me and Gregory Hines

Gregory Hines (right) in Hines, Hines, and Dad

While Gregory's movie career was taking off, he also had a music career with his silky smooth, jazzy voice. In 1986, he recorded a number one Billboard R&B single with the legendary Luther Vandross called "There's Nothing Better Than Love."

That title perfectly describes Gregory's approach to everything. When he performed that song once live in Los Angeles, he took me with him. Backstage, I got to meet Luther and other world-class performers like Anita Baker. Watching Gregory and Luther out there onstage doing their thing in front of thousands was incredibly awesome.

It wasn't long before we started hanging out and going to bodybuilding shows together or flying over to Vegas to watch a championship fight. Gregory's knowledge and passion for sports was insane. He'd love to pick my brain about all kinds of training and eating techniques, and I got to pick his brain about choreography for my posing routine. Ultimately, I would help Gregory put on fifteen pounds of muscle for his role in the amazing film *Tap*. He looked great for his part, and I was so honored and excited that I helped him achieve the body he wanted. (More on *Tap* later!)

Gregory was one of the most generous, caring, and humble guys I've ever known. He was nice enough to refer me as a trainer to his close circle of friends, including his manager and agent. He also hooked me up with Jeff Goldblum, who I ended up training as well.

Jeff Goldblum, me, and Gregory Hines

Jeff, who you know from so many movies, from *The Fly* to *Jurassic Park* and many more, was a great guy to train. He was super focused and had an all-in attitude every time he showed up. It's probably why he has been able to maintain such a long and successful career over all these years.

An awesome perk of training people was that, in so many cases, I developed friendships with them. One of my favorite memories about Jeff was going to dinner and a movie with him and legendary actress Geena Davis. That was pretty damn cool. Really nice people. Thank you, Jeff!

I wasn't the only bodybuilder working as a personal trainer. A lot of men and women were getting into it. There was Charles

Glass, a professional bodybuilder who ended up making a name for himself training other bodybuilders. Under his tutelage, his clients started winning contests, and that really established his reputation as a personal trainer.

Kay Baxter was another pro bodybuilder who worked as a personal trainer. In 1985, she started training former Van Halen lead singer David Lee Roth, as well as Cybill Shepherd. Kay was a lot of fun to be around. We used to train together, grab a lunch, then hit the beach to get some sun.

Kay Baxter and me

I was heartbroken when I heard that Kay had died in an automobile accident. Matters were made more tragic because she had recently become engaged. She was a true pioneer of the sport and is sorely missed.

Over the years, I had the privilege of getting to train all sorts of people from all walks of life, including Dennis Alexio (kickboxing world champion); Jermaine Jackson (entertainer); Beverly and Catya Sassoon (socialites); Tonya Knight (pro bodybuilder); Danny Sullivan (race car driver); Stan Shaw (actor); Chuck Woolery (television show host); Mike Quinn (pro bodybuilder); Janice Ragain (pro bodybuilder); Dave Snow (pro bodybuilder); Sally Field (actor); Sandra Taylor (actor and model); Tony Danza (actor), and several very successful businessmen and women, including doctors and dentists.

But before I get too far ahead of myself, I want to circle back to when I got the highly anticipated call from *Flex* magazine to shoot my first cover at Gold's Gym. The photoshoot took place in mid-1984, which was perfect timing because I was getting ready for my next contest and was in good shape. On the horizon was the 1984 Mr. California, then after that the 1984 NPC Nationals in New Orleans. Both would be important steps on my path to getting my pro card.

On the day of the shoot, famed photographer Michael Neveux showed up at Gold's Gym with his assistant to photograph my arm workout. Having them document my training session was an amazing experience. We attracted a small crowd of onlookers, and some of my bodybuilder friends stopped by to razz me. It was definitely one of those surreal moments in my life that stood out as a landmark achievement for me. Here I was, this kid from Ansonia, Connecticut, who was suddenly in front of the camera, doing biceps curls for *Flex* magazine. In my wildest dreams, even this felt too good to be true. Thank you, thank you, thank you, Rick Wayne!

It was an amazing day, to say the least, and I couldn't wait to see which photo they would use for the cover. But I also had a contest to get ready for, so I tried my best to stop thinking about the magazine coming out and put my focus on the upcoming Mr. California. I knew this show would be a big step up from the Mr. Los Angeles and that it attracted the biggest names from the amateur ranks.

For my preparation, my day-to-day routine of training, eating, and resting was pretty much the same as the Mr. Los Angeles, but having the support of so many people in and around the Gold's Gym family gave me an extra bit of confidence and inspiration. With each set I did and with each meal I ate, I was doing it not only for myself but for my clients, friends, family, and even Ansonia.

Flex photoshoot

The man with bodybuilding's most amazing triceps says:

"FOR TERRIFIC TRICEP[S] NOTHING BEATS THE

By Rick Wayne

Photography by Mike Neveux

A SURPRISING NUMBER OF competitive bodybuilders will tell you in earnest that they are the sum of parts that grow at the slightest stimulation and others that, no matter how much work is forced upon them, simply won't budge.

Nonsense, says Rick Valente. Muscles will react favorably every time to quality work. The problem resides in the fact that too many Johns do far too much of what's good for Harry and too little of what's best for John. Aspiring champions who plan their training programs by the goose-and-the-gander aphorism, says Valente, are destined to be turkeys, sitting ducks for the likes of Lee Haney, Bertil Fox, Tom Platz and Tony Pearson — all champions who swear by the principle of instinctive training, initially advocated in the early Fifties by Joe Weider.

"I learned the hard way," says Valente. "Like so many other beginners, I started out doing everything the magazines said my favorite champion did — whether or not I

Lat machine pressdowns are wonderful for the triceps, but just wait 'til you do them with a rope! Note how the latter method allows freer movement of the wrists for greater triceps contraction.

40 FLEX/JANUARY [illegible]

Another notable difference was that I had the king of rhythm and choreography, Gregory Hines, to dial in my posing routine. We had a blast in the posing room, and it was great getting help from such a talented man.

Everything was going great, but about a month before the show, I was riding my bike down the sidewalk when, suddenly, a lady pulled her car out of a grocery store parking lot right in front of me. I didn't see her, and she didn't see me because there was a big concrete wall dividing two properties. I slammed right into her front fender, which sent me flying across her hood. Talk about bad timing!

I landed on my right shoulder, slamming into the concrete sidewalk. Full of adrenaline, I jumped up and made sure nothing was broken, then I went over to the lady to make sure she was okay. Unfortunately, the front tire of my bike was totaled. I ended up having to call my friend Bobby Scura from a payphone and ask him to pick me and my bike up.

About an hour before my bike accident

The next day, my whole body was super sore, and my right shoulder started to turn black and blue. But it seemed like I lucked out and was blessed that I didn't suffer any significant injuries from the accident. Nothing was going to stop me. I just had to roll with the punches and take whatever obstacle came along, even a bike crash, in stride. So I made a few adjustments with my workouts and made sure to treat my shoulder with lots of ice and rest. It got better in about a week, and I was back on my game in no time.

The 1984 Mr. California was sponsored by Gold's Gym, and it was held at the Santa Monica Civic Auditorium, not even a mile from my apartment. As with the Mr. Los Angeles, I loved that I didn't have to travel for the show. Prejudging went really well, and I was called out with two other guys, Mel Hart and Armand Azurdia. Both guys had impressive physiques, and it was going to be a close call.

When it was time for our posing routines, I poured my heart and soul into my performance to win over the crowd and judges, but, of course, so did Mel and Armand. After the judges tallied their scorecards and called out the top five in my class, a funny thing happened as we made our way onto the stage. I was walking by Kent Kuehn, the backstage assistant, and he was holding the scorecard to take out to the emcee. I accidentally saw my name on it and that I had gotten second place.

Armand Azurdia, me, and Mel Hart at Mr. California 1984

Having to go onstage and pretend I hadn't lost was a tough thing to do, but hats off to Mel, who won. He looked great and definitely deserved the victory. And so did Armand, who took third.

I took the loss in stride. I didn't let it knock down my confidence. If anything, it just made me realize how much I loved the feeling of winning, and that I'd have to keep improving to get back in the winner's circle.

Now, between the Mr. California and the Nationals, the coolest thing happened—the October 1984 issue of *Flex* magazine hit the newsstands. And there I was, on the cover, doing a biceps curl in a yellow Gold's Gym tank top that matched the *Flex* magazine title. When I first saw it, my heart literally felt like it was beating out of my chest.

I was so humbled and honored that Rick Wayne followed through on his promise. Completing the full circle, from the time I was a kid and creating my vision board from bodybuilding magazines to being the guy on the cover of a magazine, made me feel a real sense of accomplishment and joy. To say I was happy would have been the understatement of the year.

Inside the magazine, there was a photo spread of my arm workout and a nice article written by Rick Wayne himself. Rick must have had a crystal ball because in his article, he said, "Valente's immediate future is, of course, synonymous with winning the upcoming American Bodybuilding Championships. Then it's on to the World Championships and the Big O [Mr. Olympia]...*That is, if Hollywood doesn't grab him first.*"

That very night after my cover shot hit the newsstands, my phone rang off the hook as my friends, such as Bobby LeVine, my parents, my cousin Mark, and even my brother Chas called to congratulate me.

It was the first time in a long time that I had a chance to talk to my brother at length. He told me he had cleaned himself up and was living in Florida with his wife, Sophia. Hearing he was sober and in a committed relationship might have been better news than my magazine cover. I told him I loved him and wished him the best, and then we both promised to keep in touch.

Soon after the cover came out, I also got a call from a reporter who worked for an Ansonia newspaper. He ended up interviewing me for a piece about the local boy who was making a name for himself in Los Angeles.

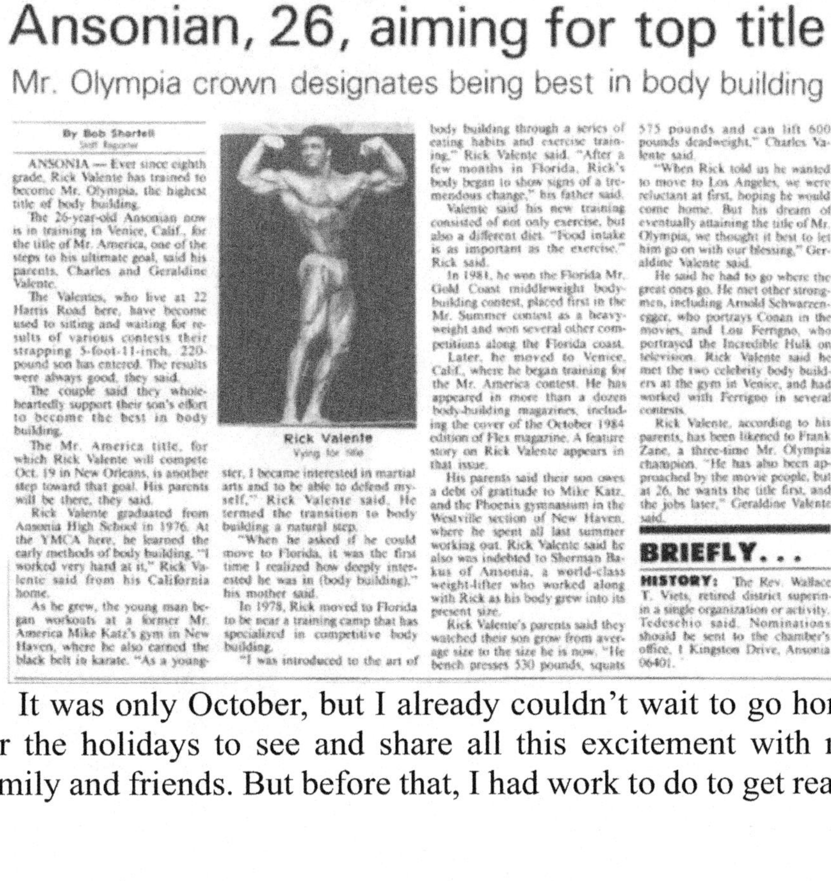

Ansonian, 26, aiming for top title

Mr. Olympia crown designates being best in body building

By Bob Shortell
Staff Reporter

ANSONIA — Ever since eighth grade, Rick Valente has trained to become Mr. Olympia, the highest title of body building.

The 26-year-old Ansonian now is in training in Venice, Calif., for the title of Mr. America, one of the steps to his ultimate goal, said his parents, Charles and Geraldine Valente.

The Valentes, who live at 22 Harris Road here, have become used to sitting and waiting for results of various contests their strapping 5-foot-11-inch, 220-pound son has entered. The results were always good, they said.

The couple said they wholeheartedly support their son's effort to become the best in body building.

The Mr. America title, for which Rick Valente will compete Oct. 19 in New Orleans, is another step toward that goal. His parents will be there, they said.

Rick Valente graduated from Ansonia High School in 1976. At the YMCA here, he learned the early methods of body building. "I worked very hard at it," Rick Valente said from his California home.

As he grew, the young man began workouts at a former Mr. America Mike Katz's gym in New Haven, where he also earned the black belt in karate. "As a youngster, I became interested in martial arts and to be able to defend myself," Rick Valente said. He termed the transition to body building a natural step.

"When he asked if he could move to Florida, it was the first time I realized how deeply interested he was in (body building)," his mother said.

In 1978, Rick moved to Florida to be near a training camp that has specialized in competitive body building.

"I was introduced to the art of body building through a series of eating habits and exercise training," Rick Valente said. "After a few months in Florida, Rick's body began to show signs of a tremendous change," his father said.

Valente said his new training consisted of not only exercise, but also a different diet. "Food intake is as important as the exercise," Rick said.

In 1981, he won the Florida Mr. Gold Coast middleweight bodybuilding contest, placed first in the Mr. Summer contest as a heavyweight and won several other competitions along the Florida coast.

Later, he moved to Venice, Calif., where he began training for the Mr. America contest. He has appeared in more than a dozen body-building magazines, including the cover of the October 1984 edition of Flex magazine. A feature story on Rick Valente appears in that issue.

His parents said their son owes a debt of gratitude to Mike Katz, and the Phoenix gymnasium in the Westville section of New Haven, where he spent all last summer working out. Rick Valente said he also was indebted to Sherman Bakus of Ansonia, a world-class weight-lifter who worked along with Rick as his body grew into its present size.

Rick Valente's parents said they watched their son grow from average size to the size he is now. "He bench presses 530 pounds, squats 575 pounds and can lift 600 pounds deadweight," Charles Valente said.

"When Rick told us he wanted to move to Los Angeles, we were reluctant at first, hoping he would come home. But his dream of eventually attaining the title of Mr. Olympia, we thought it best to let him go on with our blessing," Geraldine Valente said.

He said he had to go where the great ones go. He met other strongmen, including Arnold Schwarzenegger, who portrays Conan in the movies, and Lou Ferrigno, who portrayed the Incredible Hulk on television. Rick Valente said he met the two celebrity body builders at the gym in Venice, and had worked with Ferrigno in several contests.

Rick Valente, according to his parents, has been likened to Frank Zane, a three-time Mr. Olympia champion. "He has also been approached by the movie people, but at 26, he wants the title first, and the jobs later," Geraldine Valente said.

Rick Valente
Vying for title

BRIEFLY...

HISTORY: The Rev. Wallace T. Viets, retired district superin-
in a single organization or activity. Tedeschio said. Nominations should be sent to the chamber's office, 1 Kingston Drive, Ansonia 06401.

It was only October, but I already couldn't wait to go home for the holidays to see and share all this excitement with my family and friends. But before that, I had work to do to get ready for the 1984 NPC Nationals in New Orleans.

Speaking of the NPC, I have to mention a friendship with the president of the National Physique Committee, Jim Manion. He's an important figure in the history of bodybuilding. In the late '70s, he was president of the Physique Committee, which oversaw bodybuilding competitions for the Amateur Athletic Union. In 1981, Jim left the AAU, and with the support of Pete Grymkowski, he founded his own amateur bodybuilding organization, the National Physique Committee.

Over time, placing high in an NPC show became the requirement for obtaining a "pro card." Once an athlete gets a pro card, he or she can compete in pro bodybuilding shows. Jim went on to run the International Fitness and Bodybuilding Federation. Under his leadership, the IFBB went from only overseeing bodybuilding competitions to including Classic Physique, Women's Bikini Fitness, and Men's Physique.

Jim Manion

Debbie and Jim Manion

Whenever there would be an NPC show in California, he would come to California and train at Gold's Gym. I got to know him during this time. We even trained together a couple of times. After our workouts, we'd grab lunch at the Firehouse and talk about life. That was the beginning of our friendship. We remain friends to this day.

I'm blessed to have developed

this thirty-five-year friendship with Jim and his wife, Debbie. I'm also friends with his son, JM Manion, who runs his own multimedia company. And a quick shoutout to Jim's grandson, Tyler Manion, vice president of the NPC and the IFBB Pro League.

Tyler, Jim, and JM Manion

Now, let's get back to my preparation for the 1984 NPC Nationals in New Orleans. Training was going great, but a few weeks before the show, I got to talking to a doctor from UCLA who also worked out at Gold's Gym. This guy was a nutritional guru who helped Samir Bannout. I always admired Samir and the fact that he was able to create that hard-to-get-perfect "Christmas tree" shape on his lower back. The doctor told me a sodium-loading technique might help me get those results. I was easily convinced I had to do it to win.

And so, during my final week of preparation for the Nationals, I tried this new technique for the first time. Bad idea. Sodium loading is a complicated process, and in short, I didn't get it right. When the day of the show came along, my muscles looked flat, and I totally bombed. This was the first time I didn't place in the top five at a show. This experience taught me a valuable lesson, which was to never try a new technique one week before a show. I should have either stayed true to the same game plan that got me great results before or practiced the new technique well ahead of the contest.

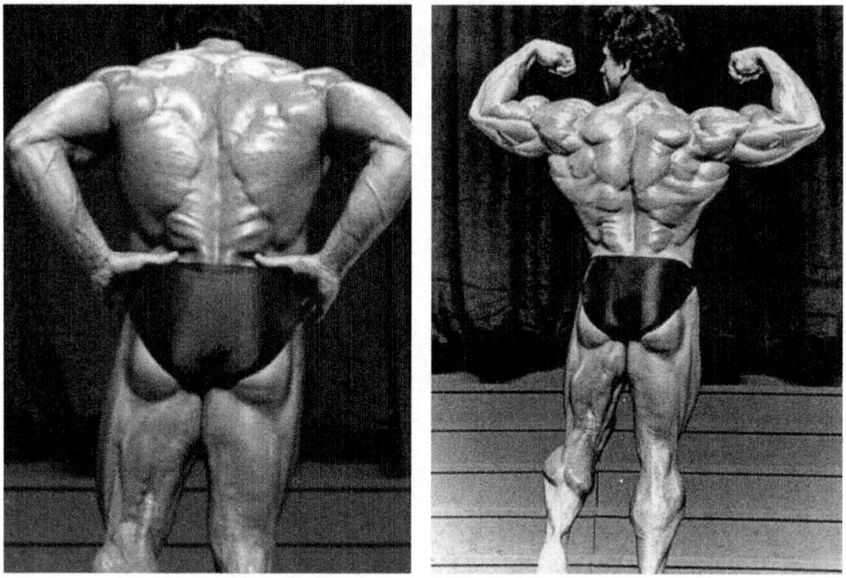

Samir Bannout's "Christmas tree" back

It turned out that a few days after the show, I looked totally shredded. My timing was off, but that's all it takes. That's the thing with life—you have to live it to learn it, and lessons come when you least expect or want them.

Getting second at the Mr. California and not placing in the top five at the Nationals was a tough one-two punch to take. It knocked me on my ass for a couple of weeks, putting me into a funk that I hadn't felt in many years.

As 1984 was winding down, I flew home for the holidays for a much-needed break. As bummed as I was about my contests, going home for the holidays was just what the doctor ordered. Feeling the love and respect from my family, friends, and the community meant the world to me. They didn't care that I had lost; they were just proud that I was on the cover of one of the biggest bodybuilding magazines.

One day, I was helping Mom in the kitchen when she told me that Dad wanted me to meet him at the St. Sebastian Italian Club. Dad and his brothers were still longstanding members of the club and had each done a bid on the club's board, so it felt like it was really their club.

Me at the 1985 NPC Nationals

That evening, I met up with Dad, a few of his brothers, and a bunch of his fishing and hunting buddies at the club. It had been years since I had gone there, and it brought back memories from when I was a kid, when Dad let me tag along.

I didn't think much of it other than that Dad and I were going to spend some quality time together. But once we were in the club, Dad started acting a little strange, as he kept looking at something behind the bar. Finally, I had to take a look myself. And what I saw brought a tear to my eye.

Dad had framed my *Flex* magazine cover, and it was now leaning up against the mirror behind the bar for all to see. I couldn't believe Dad had done that. I gave him a huge hug, and before I knew it, all his buddies started in with their compliments and congratulations:

"Way to go!"

"You son of a gun!"

"Proud of you!"

And, of course, a lot of their love came in the form of jabbing me:

"Nice hair!"

My biceps are twice that big!"

"Pretty boy!"

It was yet another surreal moment in my journey; I had gone from admiring Dad and his buddies to them admiring me and my story. Between Dad seeing me win the 1983 Mr. Los Angeles and framing my first-ever cover shot, I really felt like I had made it in his eyes. I think it's fair to say that all dads want to be proud of their sons, and all sons want to make their dads proud. I'll never forget that day or feeling. It was an incredible moment in my life.

After a few drinks, trading stories, and a lot of laughs, Dad and I headed home. It was bitter cold that day. I think my time in Los Angeles had thinned my blood. I wasn't used to the harsh East Coast wintertime.

When Dad and I got home, the warm aroma of Mom's cooking immediately wrapped its arms around me. She had sauce on the stove and was whipping up a cheesecake for dessert. We feasted that night on all the good stuff Mom loved to make—spaghetti and meatballs, shrimp cocktail, Italian salad, garlic bread, and some red wine. With no contests on the horizon, I had second and third servings.

Spending a week at home away from all the noise of Los Angeles was good for my mind, body, and spirit. Mom and Dad's love and laughter provided a nice reset. When they took me to JFK to fly back to Los Angeles, I felt energized and ready to get back at it. The crazy thing was that at that time, I didn't know the universe was working its magic in ways I would never expect.

For starters, when I got back to Los Angeles and went to Gold's Gym, one of the first things I noticed was that Gold's had hung up a large photo of my double biceps pose from the 1983 Mr. Los Angeles contest. For a bodybuilder, to have your picture up inside of Gold's Gym Venice is a dream come true. It blew my mind to see myself up there, and it immediately started my year off on the right foot.

My poster at Gold's Gym

I walked over to Pete and Tim to thank them for putting my picture up, but they had another surprise for me. They handed me a Gold's Gym membership card. I already had a membership card, so it seemed weird that I was getting a second one. It wasn't until I looked closely at the card that I realized this one was very different. In the "Membership Number" space, there was no number. Instead, it read "comp life." Pete and Tim had given me a complimentary lifetime membership to Gold's Gym. That really blew my mind.

Gold's Gym for life!

"If there's anything I can do to help Gold's Gym, you let me know," I told Pete and Tim.

"Go upstairs and see my brother, Paul," Pete answered. "He has a lot of Gold's Gym grand openings coming up and he wants you to be there, pose for pictures, and do a seminar."

"Absolutely. My pleasure," I said.

I have so much gratitude for everything Pete and Tim did for me. What's been extra special is developing lifelong friendships with them. They always were, and continue to be, a lot of fun to be around. Back in the day, Pete would show up at the gym so cordial to everyone and always smiling. He's got this presence that is infectious. And he likes to enjoy life. Whenever I'd see him, he'd have a new muscle car, like a Porsche with a giant 351 motor, or a Ferrari. He knew I loved cars, so he'd take me for rides.

Paul Grymkowski

Tim was always fun to see in the gym because he was really into working out. I always had fun talking to him because he loved women and loved talking about them. I still talk to them to this day. Whenever they're in town, we get together for lunch or dinner. We always talk about how amazing Gold's Gym was throughout the '80s and '90s. In Gold's Gym, Pete and Tim created a place that felt like a home away from home. Everybody was like family.

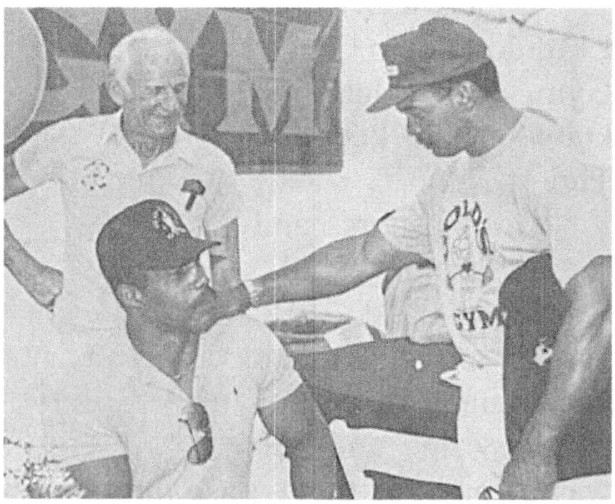

Pete Sr., Ken Norton, and Reggie Jackson

Someone else I really like was Pete's dad, Pete Sr. He'd always be in the gym, cleaning the windows, the mirrors, the equipment, etc. We'd always go to lunch, telling each other stories and having a good laugh.

Another amazing guy I was inspired by was Derek Barton.

CHAPTER ELEVEN

SMACKED DOWN

"If you let your head get too big, it'll break your neck."
—Elvis Presley

THE GOLD'S GYM MOTION PICTURE AND TELEVISION DIVISION opened in early 1985 with Derek Barton at the helm. The division was run directly out of Gold's Gym Venice in an office on the second floor. The way it came about was the way most things do, through relationships.

As 1984 was winding down, Derek, who was an actor, stuntman, and writer, played softball on Sundays at Fairfax High School with a group of celebrities, athletes, and other notable people. One of those people happened to be Tim Kimber.

Derek Barton

During that year, Tim had been getting calls from casting companies looking for bodybuilders to cast in commercials, TV shows, and movies, so Tim wanted to figure out how Gold's Gym could potentially run a talent agency of athletes. Once Derek and Tim got to be friends, Tim learned that Derek had some marketing and branding chops, and so he invited Derek to meet at the gym to brainstorm ideas about how to start up a talent agency and how to maximize it to grow the Gold's Gym brand.

Derek was game and took the meeting with Tim and Pete Grymkowski. The three bounced ideas back and forth until they zeroed in on an idea to create a casting agency at Gold's Gym. They hashed out how the concept would work and all the logistics involved.

Having thought his consulting work was done, Derek thanked Tim and Pete and told them to call him if they needed anything else. When Derek got up and started to walk out, Pete and Tim gave each other a confused look, and that's when Pete yelled, "Hey, Derek! Don't you want the job? We need someone to run it!"

"I didn't think this was a job interview," Derek stopped at the door and said, "I have a job acting and doing stunt work."

"You can still do those jobs and do this one, too!" Pete smiled. "It will be bea*uuuu*tiful!"

Tim and Derek

Pete and Tim made Derek an offer he couldn't refuse. So, at the beginning of 1985, Derek became the director of the Gold's Gym Motion Picture and Television Division, as well as the director of Advertising and Public Relations. As time went on, Derek would prove to be indispensable in growing the Gold's Gym brand. His contributions resulted in Gold's Gym being listed in the *America's Greatest Brands* book.

Anyway, getting back to when Derek set up shop at Gold's, the first thing he did was assess the pool of talent at Gold's Gym, and then he started to sign people up. And it just so happened that one day while I was working out, Derek approached me to see if I would be interested in being his very first client.

I was so honored, and, of course, I didn't hesitate to say, "Hell, yeah!"

According to Pete Grymkowski, signing me was part of a plan he had. Pete wanted to broaden the appeal of Gold's Gym, to get it into the mainstream. His strategy was to find a bodybuilder who wasn't too huge and would appeal to mainstream America. I was very lucky to be at the right place at the right time. Pete picked me because he thought I had crossover appeal.

Here's a list of some of the other Gold's Gym members Derek signed up for the Gold's Gym Motion Picture and Television Division:

Lyle Alzado
Mike Aparo
Reggie Bennett
Sandra Blackie
Steve Bond
James Caan
John Cena
Mike Christian
Diana Dennis
Andrew Dice Clay
Cory Everson
Lou Ferrigno
Willie Gault
Sherry Goggin
Jeff Golini
Jennifer Goodwin
Bill Grant
Olivier Gruner
Steve Henneberry
Jeff Henry
Gregory Hines
Raye Hollitt-Olson
Matthias Hues
Carlo Imperato
Tonya Knight
Pete Koch
Marianne Kopie Liggett
Kim LeBlanc
Christian Lettier
Tom Magee
Mike Matarazzo
Rico McClinton
Mae Mollica
Ken Norton
Tony Pearson
Shawn Ray
John Richling
Annie Roe
Ofer Samra
Magic Schwarz
Stan Shaw
Crista Videriksen Worthy

Leslie & Jack Wadsworth	Carol Ann Weber	Troy Zuccolotto
Carl Weathers	Janet Wilson	

Derek would look over the Hollywood trades for casting calls for men and women who were good-looking and in great shape. Then he would contact the casting directors and offer the use of Gold's Gym as a site to hold their auditions. This was a way for Derek to get his clients into the auditions. Soon, word got out, and production companies had started to call Derek with specific requests.

If the shoot or production wasn't located at the gym, Derek would send me, or whoever landed the gig, with a bag full of Gold's Gym apparel to hand out to the director, producer, and crew. If the shoot was inside Gold's Gym, then the production company could use the location for free, so long as the models and actors wore Gold's Gym merchandise. It was a brilliant idea.

Me and Derek

Visibility was the name of the game, and Derek was a natural at figuring out - how to get the Gold's Gym brand into the public eye. Now remember, there was no internet back then, so getting your brand out there was a totally different ball game. Derek was one of the first pioneers of "product placement," and as they say, the rest was history!

Once Derek had started sending me out on auditions, it was like "lights, camera, action!" in the blink of an eye. Everything happened so fast, and before I knew it, I was booking dozens and dozens of gigs. I was heading in the Hollywood direction just like Rick Wayne foreshadowed in his *Flex* profile of me.

Now, this didn't mean I stopped bodybuilding. In fact, I still worked out just as much because at most auditions, the first thing they would ask you to do was take your shirt off. And they expected you to be in great shape. For this, I tried to stay within ten pounds of my contest weight year-round, as opposed to the cycle of gaining twenty-five pounds in the off season and trying to lose any excess weight for a contest.

Each audition or shoot turned out to be its own little show. There wouldn't be a formal winner, but by showing up in shape and taking the work seriously, I started to build a good reputation, as well as strong relationships. This new venture was something that I dove into headfirst. And what that meant was learning and studying the craft. This included reading a book about acting, asking a lot of questions, and taking a commercial acting class. Getting coached on how to relax and to be yourself really helped me in front of the cameras. It all came back to having fun and not putting too much pressure on myself. It reminded me of doing bodybuilding shows, where I had my best performances by being focused and relaxed.

Going to two or three auditions a week became the norm. The only challenge was the notoriously bad Los Angeles traffic. One time, I was driving to an audition, cruising up the 405 freeway, heading into the Valley in my black Fleetwood Cadillac. I was heading up the hill just past the Getty Center when all of a sudden, a puff of smoke came off a big rig's rear tire. And then the next thing I knew, a five-foot-long piece of tire tread was flying straight at my windshield! I had no time to react and SMACK! Just like that, my windshield cracked so bad that it sent tiny shards of glass into my face and all over the inside of my car. Luckily, I was able to pull off to the side of the highway to regroup.

After an accident like this, I could have gone home, canceled the audition, and I'm sure the casting director would have understood. But I thought, fuck it, I want to get this gig. And so, I drove the rest of the way to the audition with my head hanging out of the side window because I couldn't see through my windshield.

When I finally arrived at the audition, the casting people were about to shut down for the day. They weren't happy and understandably annoyed at how late I was, but once they saw my nicked-up face and the glass in my hair, along with hearing my story, their attitudes did a 180-degree turn.

They ended up admiring my perseverance and passion for the project, and I ultimately landed the gig. It was a television commercial for a very popular radio station in Los Angeles called Z100. In the TV spot, I had the pleasure of dressing up like Rambo and firing off a machine gun. It was a blast, and I'm grateful the casting director let me audition!

Now, the crazy thing about auditioning was that you're expected to show up early and sit around for what seemed like forever, before getting called into the room to audition. Once it was your turn, you were expected to dive right into the role, whether it was screaming like Tarzan or putting on camouflage and firing a machine gun. It wasn't always easy, but I'd do my best to step right into whatever character I was supposed to be. I'd also try to spark up a conversation with the casting team, to build a personal connection with them, which seemed to work well for me.

Something I'd learned from my actor friends was to have professional headshots and some creative "leave behind" photos. For my leave behinds, I chose my front double biceps pose from the Mr. Los Angeles contest and a photo of me shirtless, riding a horse.

The horse photo came from a shoot that I had booked in Malibu. They dressed me in a leopard print loincloth with my ass hanging out, along with a matching leopard print headband and wristbands. And then they put me on a horse, bareback. I spent all day long on that horse, and we got to be pretty good friends. I love animals, and getting to hang out with one while getting paid was awesome. Oh, and by the way, they got hundreds of shots, and I got a sunburn! Ha!

When the shoot was over, the photographer told me she would mail me a check for my fee once she got back to New York. A few weeks later, a check for $500 arrived, along with one negative of me on the horse. But when I went to cash the check, it bounced! Son of a bitch!

That really pissed me off, but the silver lining was getting that one photo. It turned out to be an awesome picture that got me tons of gigs, and I also sold signed copies of it at gym openings and guest appearances. I probably made a few thousand dollars off that photo, so the fact the check bounced didn't even bother me.

My professional headshots

I've said it before, but I really do think my seven-eleven birthdate gave me a ton of amazing luck. Here's another example of what I'm talking about.

One day, I was laying out in the sun on Venice Beach, when all of a sudden, a production assistant approached me and asked if I wanted to be in a commercial they were shooting for Pepsi. I said, "Of course!"

When I walked over to where they were shooting, guess who was directing it? Joe Pytka! I thought, "Damn, how lucky am I?!"

Because of this commercial, I got my SAG-AFTRA card on April 30, 1985, and have been a member ever since. Thank you, Joe!

Joe is a great guy, and I'm fortunate that I got to develop an incredible friendship with him over the years. We initially bonded over sports, and later I learned he was a huge car guy, so we connected over that as well. Joe was also nice enough to let me watch him and his team edit and cut raw footage in his studio, which was a block away from Gold's. Everything they did fascinated me, and I got to see their behind-the-scenes work. Joe's attention to detail was amazing, and his directing was insanely creative. I've always had a curious mind and love to watch talented people like Joe work on their craft. This was a real gift for me and something that would pay dividends down the road.

Thanks to Derek and Joe, I found myself in all sorts of commercials and photoshoots over the years for companies such as Pepsi, Coke, Apple, Nike, McDonald's, Del Taco, and tons of others. I got to be the face of several national campaigns, including the Gulf Oil Company, L.A. Gear, Caesar's Palace, Nike, NFL, Outdoor Products Monthly, Atlas Computer, Moda Italia, Body Alive, Vidal Sassoon, Zero Boogie, NPC Active Wear, Weider Sportswear, Better Bodies, American Pit Bull Body Armor, Ruthless Sports Wear, and many others.

I was also doing a lot of magazine work, both nationally and internationally, for publications such as *MuscleMag*, *Muscle & Fitness*, *Powerhouse*, *Flex*, *Reps*, *Muscle Magazine*, *Iron Man*, *Natural Body and Fitness*, *Max Muscle*, *Muscle Training*, *Bodybuilding & Kraftsport*, *Popular Mechanics*, *Midland Reporter*, *Gold's Gym Monthly*, *TV Times*, *Body and Fitness*, *GQ*, and many more. Over the years, I wound up doing more than fifty magazine covers and forty-two commercials, and I was also featured in hundreds of articles.

In addition, I got to do ads for Gold's Gym Marketing, which was promoting the gym's clothing line. These were fun to do because some of the shoots consisted of not just me but other Gold's Gym alumni such as Lyle Alzado, Mike Christian, Mae Mollica, Steve Bond, Mike Torchia, Sherry Goggin, Gary Strydom, and Pete Grymkowski. These ads were featured in all the bodybuilding magazines.

WEIDER Sportswear
Für Bodybuilder und fitness- und sportbegeisterte Damen und Herren vom Meister persönlich für Sie entworfen.
Joe Weider
© Trainer of Champions since 1936
WEIDER
Vertrauen ist etwas Besonderes. Das Gefühl des Vertrauens kann man nicht dem Zufall überlassen. Es muss ehrlich erarbeitet und über viele Jahre hinweg bewiesen werden. Seit einem halben Jahrhundert haben wir die Qualität aller unserer Produkte über alles andere gestellt. Unser familieneigener Betrieb basiert auf dem Versprechen, für alle unsere Produkte nur bestes Material zu verwenden. Wir folgen nicht dem höchsten Standard – wir haben ihn!
Die WEIDER-Produkte sind erhältlich bei der
Shark Vertriebs AG
Altstetterstr. 187
8048 Zürich
Tel. 01 432 58 58
BODY IN SHAPE 9

Look what Gold's Gym can do for your body.
How to get your body into Gold's Gym.
GOLD'S GYM

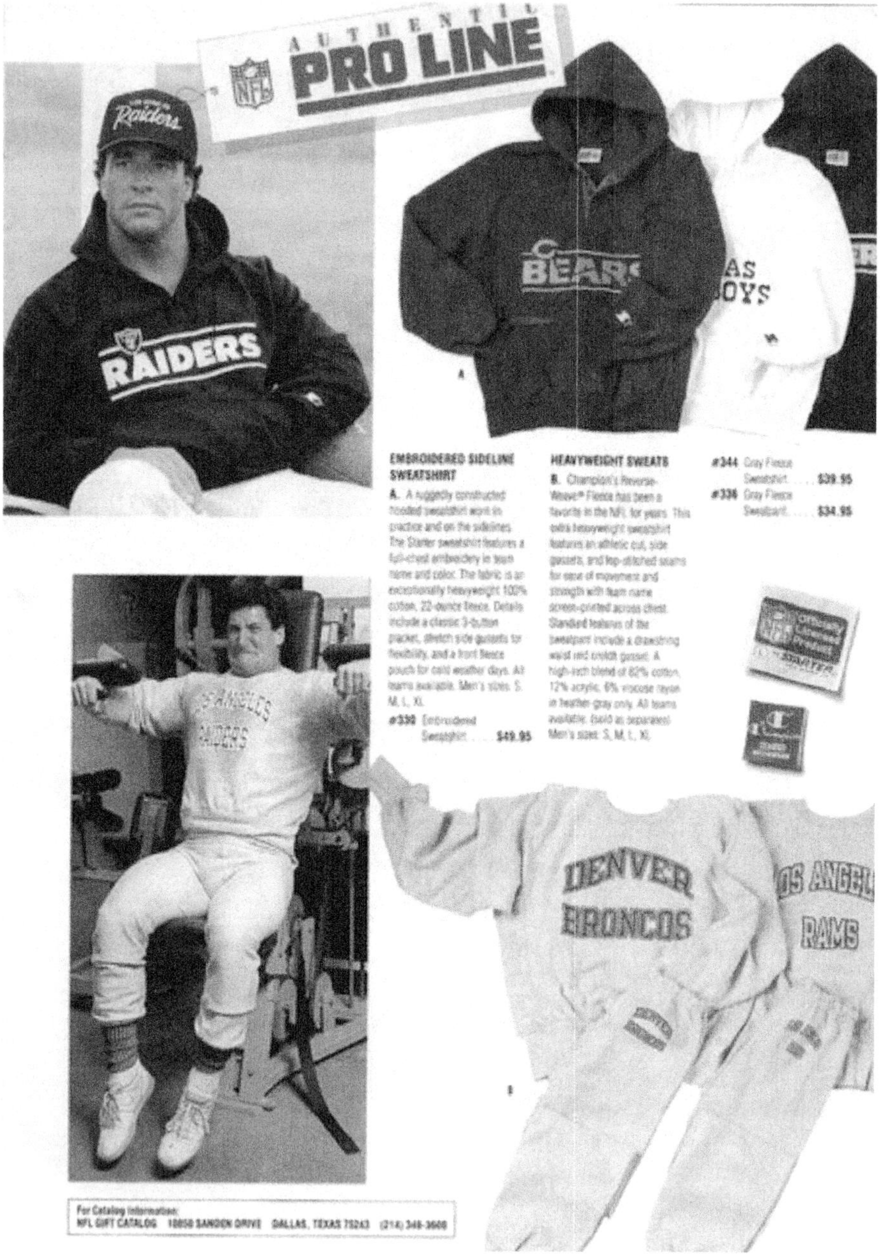
AUTHENTIC
PRO LINE
NFL
Raiders
RAIDERS
BEARS
DENVER
BRONCOS
RAMS
EMBROIDERED SIDELINE SWEATSHIRT
A. A ruggedly constructed hooded sweatshirt worn in practice and on the sidelines. The Starter sweatshirt features a full-chest embroidery in team name and color. The fabric is an exceptionally heavyweight 100% cotton, 22-ounce fleece. Details include a classic 3-button placket, stretch side gussets for flexibility, and a front fleece pouch for cold weather days. All teams available. Men's sizes: S, M, L, XL.
#330 Embroidered Sweatshirt $49.95
HEAVYWEIGHT SWEATS
B. Champion's Reverse-Weave® Fleece has been a favorite in the NFL for years. This extra heavyweight sweatshirt features an athletic cut, side gussets, and lap-stitched seams for ease of movement and strength with team name screen-printed across chest. Standard features of the sweatpant include a drawstring waist and crotch gusset. A high-tech blend of 82% cotton, 12% acrylic, 6% viscose rayon in heather-gray only. All teams available. (Sold as separates) Men's sizes: S, M, L, XL.
#344 Gray Fleece Sweatshirt $39.95
#336 Gray Fleece Sweatpant $34.95
For Catalog Information:
NFL GIFT CATALOG

"I'm in the money! I'm in the money!" That's the song Rick Valente's singing these days, what with five commercials currently on TV. Wonderful to report, even though Rick has a hard time finding shirts that fit, success hasn't swelled his head one bit.

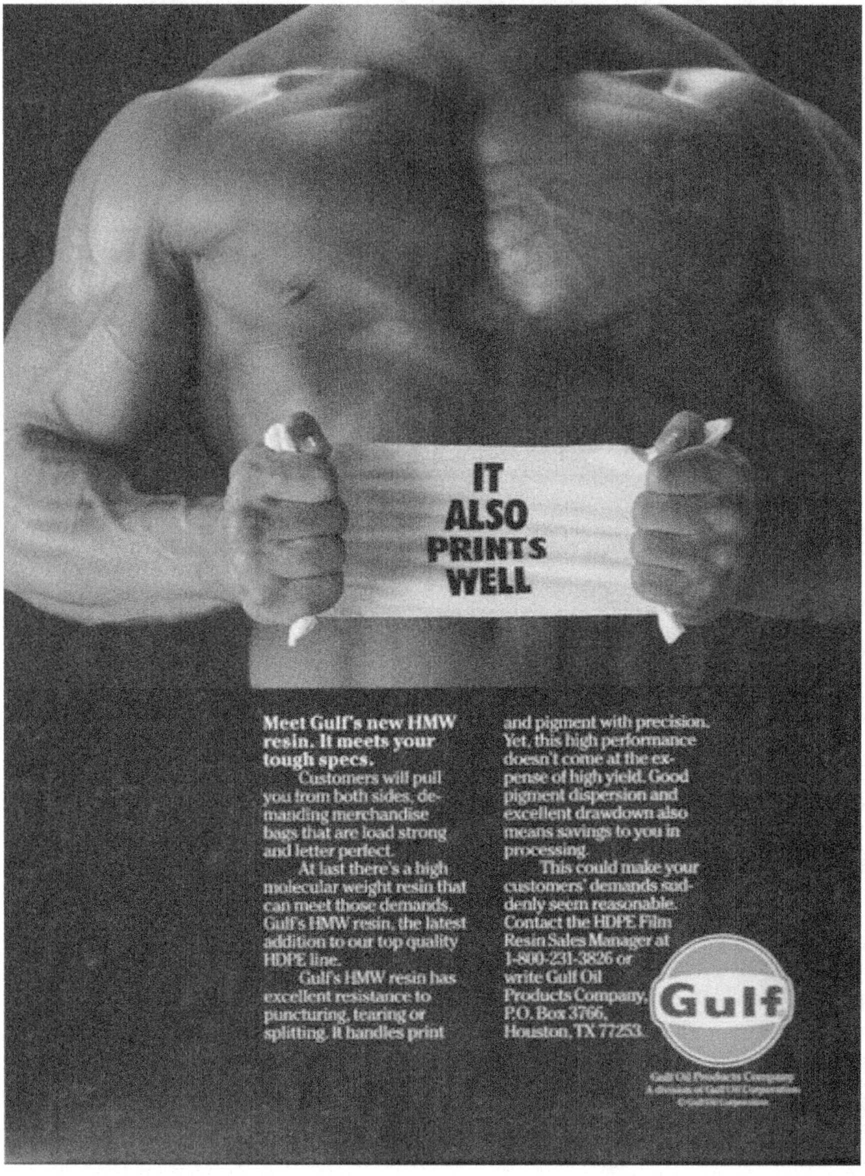
IT ALSO PRINTS WELL
Meet Gulf's new HMW resin. It meets your tough specs.
Customers will pull you from both sides, demanding merchandise bags that are load strong and letter perfect.
At last there's a high molecular weight resin that can meet those demands. Gulf's HMW resin, the latest addition to our top quality HDPE line.
Gulf's HMW resin has excellent resistance to puncturing, tearing or splitting. It handles print and pigment with precision. Yet, this high performance doesn't come at the expense of high yield. Good pigment dispersion and excellent drawdown also means savings to you in processing.
This could make your customers' demands suddenly seem reasonable. Contact the HDPE Film Resin Sales Manager at 1-800-231-3826 or write Gulf Oil Products Company, P.O. Box 3766, Houston, TX 77253.
Gulf
Gulf Oil Products Company

WHAT THE HECK IS THE
PEPSI SUMMER CHILL OUT
HAND GESTURE?

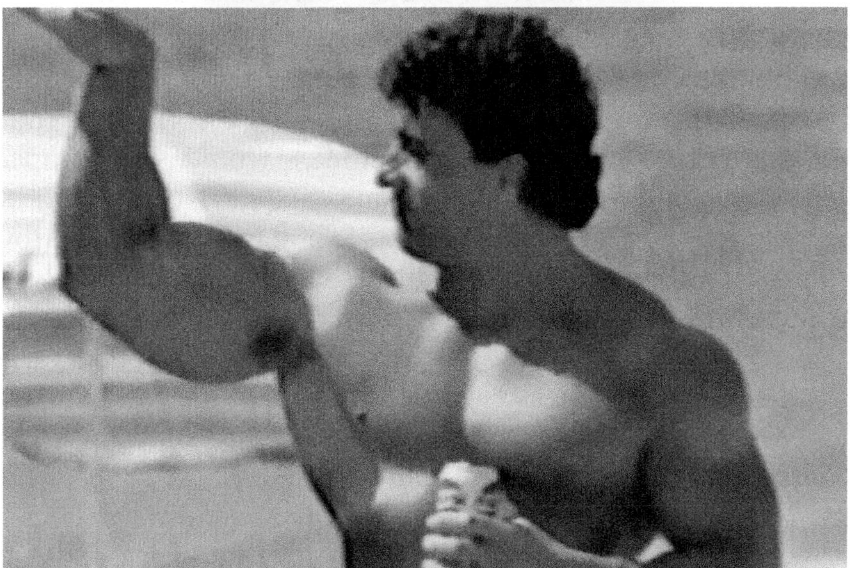

In 1988, Paul Grymkowski hired Rich Minzer to be Gold's Gym's assistant director of Franchising and Gym Operations. Rich was a businessman with a great sense of how to grow a company. He was also in charge of installing and maintaining all the equipment in Gold's Gym each year. He had over 100 vendors to deal with, and he was able to get them to donate a million dollars' worth of equipment every year to the gym.

This was a win-win for everybody. The gym got equipment for free, and the vendor got free marketing whenever photoshoots were taken in the gym. During that time, you could open any bodybuilding magazine and see a pro bodybuilder at Gold's working out with their equipment.

L to R Pete Grymkowski, Paul Grymkowski & Rich Minzer

Rich gave a lot of attention to where the equipment was placed in the gym. He made sure that all the equipment for each body part was grouped together. So, if you were going to train arms, the biceps and triceps machines would be grouped together. The same thing went for legs—squat racks would be lined up along the wall, with leg presses and hack squats nearby.

Gold's had its own nutrition department, known as Nutritionalysis. It was run by a bodybuilder by the name of Neal Spruce.

Neal had won the heavyweight division in the Mr. Western America competition. Ed Connors was at that show and had spoken to Neal about an opportunity to work at a soon-to-be-opening Gold's Gym in San Francisco, where Neal was living at the time. Neal took the job.

At the gym, Neal would write up a nutrition plan for every member. This plan was based on the member's fitness goals. It contained not just information on what foods to eat and their quantity but also specified the best supplements for that member, including which ones were the best brands.

Rich's Gold's Gym equipment

Eventually, word reached the Gold's Gym corporate office about the work Neal was doing. It was decided that he would be a great asset to Gold's Gym Venice. So, Neal moved to LA and started writing nutrition programs for members at the Venice location, including the bodybuilders and celebrities who trained there. As the Gold's Gym brand grew, Neal would be sent to all the other locations to set up their nutrition programs.

Neal Spruce

Like me, Neal grew up loving motorcycles and got into his fair share of trouble as a kid. Needless to say, when I first met him, we really hit it off. Today, Neal runs his own company, dotFIT, which is a nutrition provider for more than forty thousand sport and fitness professionals.

Teagan Clive

During this time, female bodybuilding was on the rise, and there were a lot of talented female athletes in the gym, including Lisa Lyons, Kay Baxter, Pillow, Reggie Bennett, Lynn Conkwright, Rachel McLish, Carla Dunlap, Val Streit, Juliette Bergmann, Liona Bergmann, Cory Everson, Cameo Kneuer, Janice Ragain, Marjo Selin, Sharon Bruneau, Debbie Dobbins, Mia Finnegan, Laura

Creavalle, Mary Roberts, Shelley Beattie, Lenda Murray, Anja Langer, Bev Francis, Carol Semple, Lisa Lorio, Monica Brant, Erika Mes, Diana Dennis, Maria Gonzalez, Amy Fadhli, Lena Johannesen, Yolanda Hughes, Alphie Newman, Anja Schreiner, Kiana Tom, Marla Duncan, Raye Hollitt, Carolyn Bryant, Sha-ri Pendleton, Tonya Knight, Teagan Clive, Cathy LeFrancois, Jodi Friedman, and Katie Arnoldi.

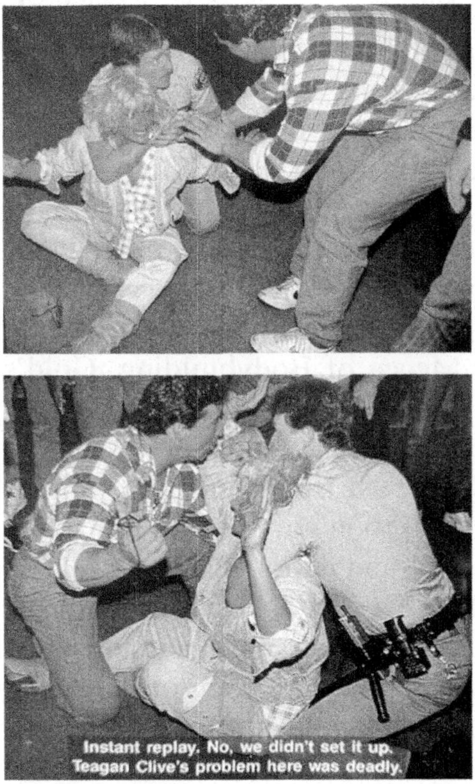
Instant replay. No, we didn't set it up. Teagan Clive's problem here was deadly.

You might remember Teagan Clive from David Lee Roth's *California Girls* music video. At five feet, nine inches, and one hundred and sixty pounds, with bleach-blonde hair, she was impossible to forget.

We once went together to a bodybuilding show in Anaheim. We had just arrived and were talking in the lobby. Teagan then went into the ladies' room, and I waited for her outside. A few minutes later, a woman ran out of the bathroom and over to a policeman, telling him there was a man in the women's bathroom. So, when Teagan walked out, the cop tackled her, getting her in a headlock. She couldn't breathe, her face was turning red, and she started crying. It freaked me the fuck out. I ran up and pushed the cop in the back of the head.

"What the fuck are you doing? She's a woman!" I yelled.

"I can arrest you for assaulting me!" the cop said.

"Let her go, and we'll talk about it," I shot back, pleading with him.

Finally, I got him to let Teagan go. After I calmed her down, I explained to the cop that Teagan was a very strong female bodybuilder; that's why she was so big. The cop apologized. I walked out with Teagan, and we went home.

This incident had reminded me that as popular as female bodybuilding was, it still had a long way to go before it would be accepted by mainstream society.

The Gold's Gym franchise operation really took off in the mid-'80s. I found myself being flown out to Gold's Gym openings all over the country. Pete once told me, "You were the patriot of Gold's Gym." He and Derek were making me the face of the brand. I felt so blessed by this opportunity. It was such an honor to be of service to people I respected, as well as being associated with the legendary Mecca of Bodybuilding, Gold's Gym.

There were so many gym openings that Paul would send out other top guys like Jim Quinn, Mike Christian, and many others. We'd fly out on a Friday, go to a ribbon cutting ceremony, and then do seminars, training sessions, and radio talk shows to help drive memberships throughout the weekend. The owners of the specific franchise would always take us out afterward and show us a good time. It was a great way to see a bunch of cities and states I hadn't seen before, not to mention meet a lot of good people.

During this growth spurt, Gold's grew from one gym to opening five to ten new gyms per month. Eventually, they had over five hundred locations by the '90s. The gym management was able to use its connections to World Wrestling Entertainment (WWE) to land famous wrestlers such as Hulk Hogan to help promote the Gold's brand.

I think everyone knows who Hulk Hogan is. The guy is a giant and has his trademark handlebar mustache, along with his yellow-blonde locks. And of course, he had one of the biggest personalities wrestling and the world had ever seen. It was a blast working alongside him, helping Gold's expand.

I'd met tons of other pro wrestlers while doing grand openings, including "Macho Man" Randy Savage, Big John Studd, Dwayne "the Rock" Johnson, "Stone Cold" Steve Austin, the Ultimate Warrior, the Undertaker, Diamond Dallas Page, Sgt. Slaughter, Brutus Beefcake, John Cena, and so many others.

One of my favorite openings, though, was with Ric Flair, who bought a few Gold's Gym franchises in North Carolina. Ric was a huge superstar in the wresting world and had an incredible personality, so you can only imagine how entertaining his gym openings were. I always liked and admired Ric. He was great to work with and even more fun to go out with. I'll just leave it at that.

Derek and I had a great relationship, and without his creative marketing skills, who knows how my story would have turned out. To show him how much he meant to me and how grateful I was, I bought Derek a nice Movado watch for Christmas in 1985, which he still has to this very day! The Movado was all the rage back then, having a unique clean face with no numbers.

While writing this book, Derek and I had some great conversations that brought back so many incredible memories. During one of our talks, I was taken aback by Derek's kind words when he told me: "You and I helped change the course of Gold's Gym. You were the first member of the Motion Picture Division and the most successful one. You seemed to get everything I sent you out on, and the casting people loved you. You were to Gold's Gym what Michael Jordan was to Nike. You really helped popularize the brand."

Derek's Motion Picture Division brought the Gold's Gym brand to mainstream America, making it feel more accessible to people from all walks of life and fitness levels, as opposed to just hardcore bodybuilders. Before we knew it, franchises were popping up in almost every major city in the U.S., and plenty of locations abroad. According to the Gold's Gym website, it ended up having 540 franchise locations, all growing out of that one location in Venice.

Welcome to the Gold's Gym Family!

I have so much respect and gratitude for Derek, what he accomplished, and that I got to go along for the ride. Because of him, I landed one of the coolest gigs of all time—a photoshoot for the cover of Van Halen's *5150* album.

It was in early 1986 when Derek had put out the casting call for the cover of Van Halen's newest album, *5150*. Back then, all of us treated rock 'n' roll bands like they were gods. To score an album cover would mean that you'd be connected to a badass rock 'n' roll band forever. And even though booking huge commercials for companies like Coke, Nike, Pepsi, and Apple was super cool, this seemed a whole lot cooler.

Van Halen was riding high after a successful run of albums in the late '70s and early '80s. They had just put out their first number one single, "Jump," in 1984, and were one of the biggest rock bands of the '80s. The album that I was auditioning for marked a transition for them, as the former lead singer, David Lee Roth, and the band had a falling out, so Sammy Hagar had joined the original members, Eddie Van Halen (guitar), Alex Van Halen (drums), and Michael Anthony (bass guitar).

These guys were some of the most talented musicians in the world, and in late 1985, they were recording *5150*, which would be finished and released in the early part of 1986. The album title, *5150*, came from the California Welfare and Institutions Code Section 5150, which allows authorities to lock up psychotic individuals in a psychiatric facility. On the street, "5150" was a slang term that people used to describe someone who was losing their shit or acting insane.

For the audition at Gold's Gym, the line stretched out the door and around the block. When it was my turn to go into the posing room in front of the casting director, I introduced myself, took off my shirt, and did a few mandatory poses. I then left my two favorite "leave behind" photos, and that was that. It was a few weeks later that I got the call from Derek. Van Halen had chosen me. When I hung up, I celebrated like I had just won the Mr. Olympia.

The photoshoot took place at a studio in LA. The concept for the cover was for me to be the Greek god Atlas, holding a globe on my shoulders to signify bearing the weight of the world. The back of the album was me being crushed by the globe, which was cracked open, revealing the band inside of it. The globe had a big "VH" on it, and I wore a chain around my neck with a pendant that said "5150."

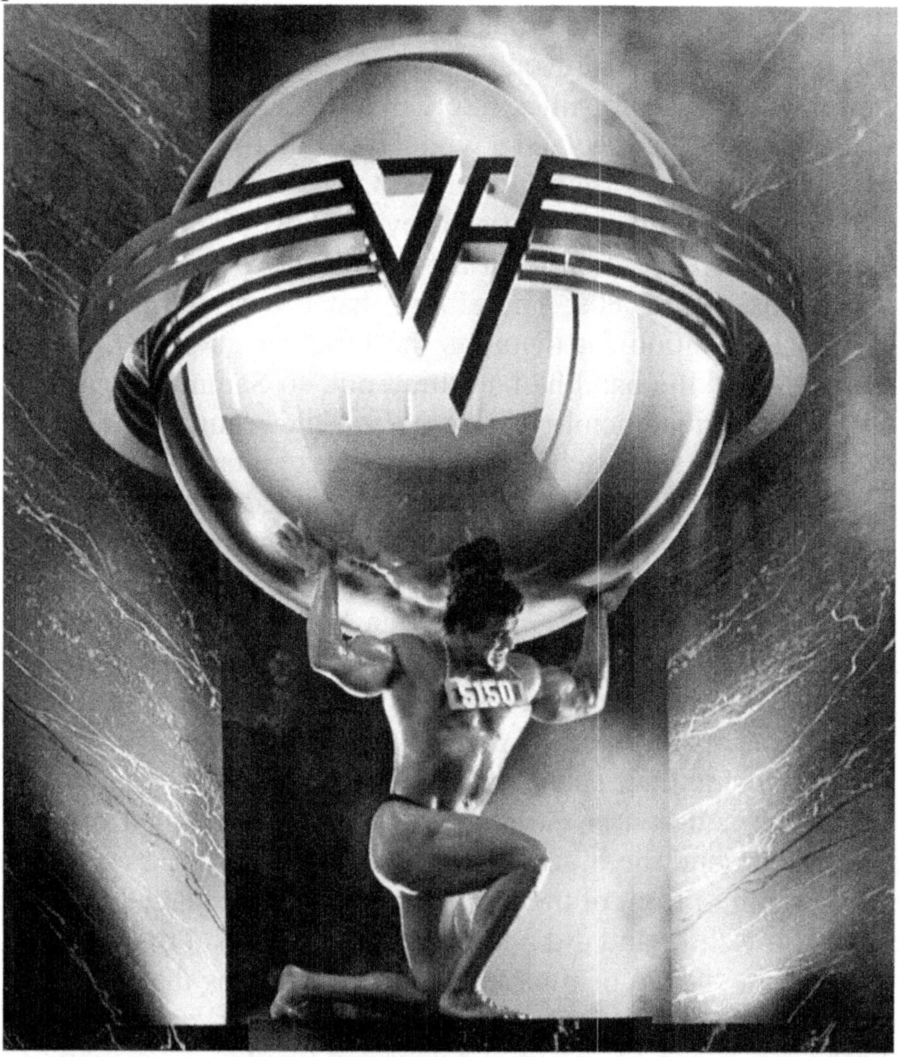

The shoot lasted a couple of days, and it was an absolute blast getting to hang out with rock 'n' roll royalty. All the guys were so cool and fun to work with. We had a lot of laughs and even partied some. Getting to know them is another moment I'll never forget, and it was by far one of the most incredible gigs I ever had the honor of doing.

Another amazing thing about the Van Halen shoot was that Rick Wayne's son, Kevin Wayne, and his girlfriend at the time, Karen, came to capture some of the behind-the-scenes photos for the bodybuilding magazines. Kevin was an excellent up-and-coming photographer and writer, and we had such a blast on the set, cutting jokes and pinching ourselves to make sure we weren't dreaming.

Yes, it's that Valente chap yet again, this time with Van Halen and Teen Scene reporter Karen Friedman. The occasion? Rick modeled for the rock group's latest album. You gotta admit our Rick's got it over the other bare-chested machoman!

After that photoshoot, Kevin and I had developed a great friendship. Over the years, we did a few photoshoots together at Gold's, and he wrote some great articles about me. We also did a lot of social activities together, like going to Westwood on double dates back when Westwood was one of the hottest spots to hang out at. I'll never forget the time we were driving down Sunset Boulevard and saw a huge billboard advertising Van Halen's *5150* album, with me holding the globe on it. I can't even explain it, just that it was an amazing feeling.

When *5150* hit the shelves, it sold like crazy, going six times platinum in the United States and selling a ton overseas as well. It hit the number one spot on the Billboard chart in 1986 and had several hit singles, including "Why Can't This Be Love," "Love Walks In," and "Dreams." Knowing that the album sold so well and that I was on its cover is insane. I'm forever grateful to Van Halen for giving me the opportunity to be on the cover. What can I say but thank you, thank you, thank you!

Me and Ray "Boom Boom" Mancini

With all the exposure I was getting, I started to get attention from bigger names in Hollywood and pro sports, and I developed some great friendships. Incredible actors like James Caan and Ray Liotta, and amazing athletes like Lyle Alzado and Ray "Boom Boom" Mancini, to name a few. Hanging out at restaurants, bars, and clubs with these types of people has a way of making you feel pretty cool.

It was a crazy, fast lifestyle that I hadn't really been a part of before. It was nothing to hop on a private jet and pop over to Las Vegas for a night or two, or to score ringside seats at the best fights. And as my luck would have it, it was around this time that I struck up a friendship at Gold's Gym with one of the baddest dudes in the whole world, Dennis Alexio, who was the full-contact karate champion of the world.

Dennis was a beast in the gym and became one of my favorite training partners. When we would work out at Gold's Gym, he would step into my world. And of course, when we would go to the dojo together, I would step into his world. I loved being part of his team, and it was an honor (and challenge) to get to spar with him. Even though I was padded up, I was amazed at how powerful his punches and kicks were. It was crazy how the karate I had studied as a kid was paying off once again.

Me and Dennis Alexio

Art Zeller

Partner with punch: Rick Valente's new training buddy is none other than Heavyweight kickboxing champ Dennis Alexio.

Brawn

by STUART McROBERT

Deceit-Free Bodybuilding

This is the second part of a three-part overview of how hard-gainers should approach their training. Last time, I covered focus, goal, progressive poundages, safety, and individualization.

Dennis Alexio and training partner, Rick Valente

PERSPECTIVE

Some people argue that to categorize yourself as a hard-gainer sets up a negative "I can't do much" attitude that can even start a self-fulfilling prophecy in motion. How little they know. Understanding that you are a hard-gainer *liberates* you from screwed up aspirations, stupid training routines, and a messed up life while sparing you from being ripped off by the charlatans who promise you the earth and then rob you of your money.

It's only when you recognize you are a hard-gainer that you can set the scene for adopting realistic role models, sensible and practical training methods, a sane long-term strategy, bags of patience, and loads of persistence. Then while keeping training in its place and not having it consume your life, you put into practice time-proven and result-producing routines for hard-gainers and thus actually start getting the results you have been craving and lacking while using inappropriate but conventional training methods. As long as you consider yourself anything other than a hard-gainer, you are almost certainly not going to train according to your ability to respond to exercise. You will be consumed by despair and frustration as you invest so much for so little return. You will become easier prey for being ripped off by charlatans, and you will become another bodybuilding failure and possibly take the drug route because conventional training methods don't work for drug-free typical people. The well intentioned or, in many cases, the overtly dishonest "you can do it too" and "forget all about genetics" mentality fuels bodybuilding failure, supports the ripping off of the masses, and encourages drug abuse. Watch out!

While realism is the hard-gainer's watchword, you don't know how far you can go unless you actually take yourself there. Even average genetics can go a very *long* way. As mentioned in the previous issue, set initial key goals for yourself (set long term ones if you are inexperienced in weight training) of 5 or more reps with 275 pounds in the bench press, 350 in the squat, and 400-440 in the deadlift. (As well as these three lifts being among the very best exercises you can do, what you can lift in them is a barometer of what you can do in all exercises and thus these three movements reflect your overall muscular development.) Relative to the masses that lift weights, very few drug-free bodybuilders can lift the aforementioned poundages. You simply should *not* look to higher achievements until you have these first. When you've gotten there, look to the next 10%, and then focus on achieving it; then look to the next 10%, and focus on achieving it, etc. Bite off a bit at a time and focus on the *now*, getting each day right, again and again and again...

EFFORT AND DEDICATION

While intensity cycling means you don't train full-bore at every workout, there's no getting away from the fundamental need for hard work. Getting big and strong demands, at least for some of the time, *very* hard work. It takes years to become outstanding, so dedication over the long haul is a necessity. Effort and dedication rrectly applied) rule the day.

Very few people train hard. Many people train with exaggerated grunts groans, but few really push themselves hard. There's nothing you can and nothing you can take to the gym with you that can make you drive rself to the limit enough times to make gains unless you *really* want to it yourself. The buck stops with you. In the final stage of a training cycle en you are training full-bore at every workout, only you can push yourself ough the pain and discomfort, again and again.

Of the average bodybuilders that do train hard, few take enough rest between rkouts to permit themselves to grow. So effort *and* recovery time is the mbination to get right--the effort must be correctly applied. The opportunity d ability to train hard, to be really able to pour in the effort work your body to its limit, is a joy, a blessing, d a privilege. Make the most of it!

INTENSITY CYCLING

The proper application of effort is the substance of intensity cycling--the variation of training intensity. Intensity cycling is at the root of long-term and successful training.

Very hard training is an irreplaceable component for building greater strength and muscular size, but not if it's done every workout of every week of every month of every year. It must be interspersed between periods of less stressful workouts.

We can't progress in absolute size and strength in a long-term linear fashion. We need to plan to take two steps back in order to take three steps forward. Even the genetically-gifted and drug-assisted athletes use intensity cycling to some degree. The difference between them and us is that we need to take longer steps backward and, when we do take our forward steps, they are smaller than the easy gainers'.

The neophyte needs not be concerned much, if at all, with intensity cycling. The novice can productively stick to a simple, basic, and not-too-frequent routine, training hard under his or her own steam--no forced reps, drop sets, negatives, pre-exhaustion, etc. The novice can productively maintain this for a year or more. All that's needed is a week off followed by a break-in week or two every three months or so, and perhaps a few exercise changes for variety.

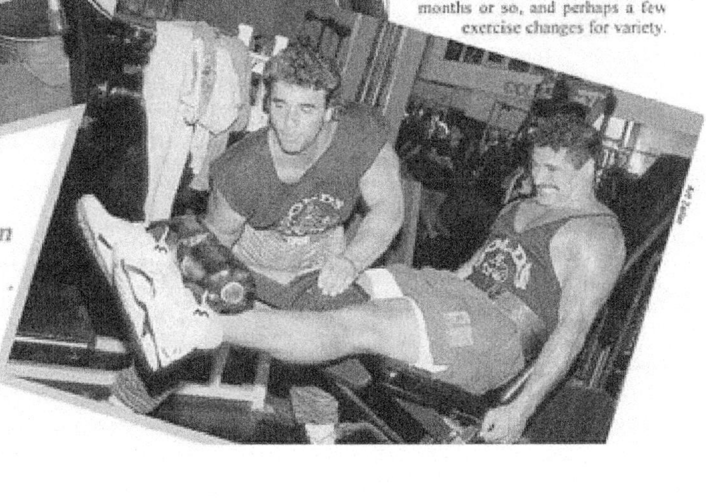

ennis Alexio, orld Champion ck Boxer, kes his eight training ry seriously.

Once gains dry up, it's time to start taking advantage of cycling.

Beyond the very impressive gains of the properly trained beginner, the near-linear progress ceases. From this point, progress is irregular--full of plateaus, valleys, and peaks. Cycling is an organized and planned effort to arrange the irregular progress into a regular progression of ups and downs, with each new up or down being a little higher than the previous one. Cycling is about taking steps backward to prepare for enough forward steps to go beyond previous best achievements.

"Cycling is about taking steps backward to prepare for enough forward steps to go beyond previous best achievements."

Not only does the body rebel against consistent full-bore effort, so does the mind. To strive to do more reps and/or more poundage than you have ever done before, every workout, every week, every month, becomes a colossal burden. Always having more to do when you are already at the limit of your current capacity is too much. There must be slack periods. There must be workouts in which you purposely avoid pushing yourself to the limit. This is very difficult to accept if you have been locked into the "hard all of the time" philosophy.

There are many ways of cycling training intensity. One basic formula is to spend half a training cycle, slowly returning to your previous best poundages, and then spend the second half of the cycle moving in new poundage territory, using small discs and notching up steady, weekly poundage gains. Don't keep piling on 5-10 pounds each week on each exercise, or you'll grind to a halt almost as soon as you hit your previous best lifts. Add less, but do it every week. When the cycle is scheduled to end, try to keep it going a few extra unplanned weeks by using very small plates--half to one pound discs. So a cycle has several components: an easy start in which you only handle about 80% of your previous best working poundages for your *usual* reps, a gradual increase in poundages as the intensity picks up, then hard work starts as you get close to your previous best poundages, then very hard work as you move into best-ever poundages again and again and again...and for as long as you can keep the gaining momentum going. (Younger people who don't have heavy demands of careers and families and who can rest and sleep enough can train full-bore for longer stretches than people who are far more stretched throughout their lives and are thus much more easily overtrained.) The shorter the cycle, the less you are likely to gain from it. When poundage gains finally dry up, end the cycle, layoff for about ten days, and then start a new cycle with poundages a little higher than you started the previous cycle with, and so on.

Cycling is not a perfect system. It depends on many variables and fine tuning according to current and changing circumstances. Here are three important misuses of cycling: first, don't overdo the easy workouts or neglect to push yourself in the second half of each cycle. Second, don't reduce the number of easy and not-quite-difficult workouts in your haste to get into the very hard sessions as soon as possible--it's *crucial* to set up a gaining momentum. Third, don't rep out to the limit with the reduced poundages during the early part of the cycle--be patient, the intensity will pick up soon enough without forcing it on prematurely.

Part three of this summary of how hard-gainers should approach their training will appear in the next issue of *Muscle Media 2000*. ▲

EDITOR'S NOTE: *Stuart McRobert publishes and edits* Hardgainer, *a magazine for genetically-typical and drug-free bodybuilders. For a 12 month subscription, send a check or money order for US $25.00 payable to* Hardgainer, *to the magazine's new address:* Hardgainer, *P.O. Box 6365, Dept. M2, Louisville, KY 40207.*

McRobert is also the author of Brawn, *a must-read 230-page book for all drug-free and genetically-typical bodybuilders. It's available from* Muscle Media 2000. *Please see the ad on page 101 of this issue.*

I went with Dennis to his fights, whether it was in Vegas, Inglewood, or wherever. Being backstage as Dennis hit the pads to get warmed up was intense. His focus and energy were second to none, and it was a real blessing to see someone in their prime, doing what they were born to do. It was a huge adrenaline rush to walk out to the ring with him as the crowd went wild—a high that I can't put into words, and I wasn't even the one fighting!

Me and Dennis (center) shaking hands in the ring

Over the years, Dennis racked up several championship belts, and I was lucky that he had let me carry one of them into the ring while the rest of his entourage carried the others. As a kid, I always wanted to be a fighter, and this was the second-best thing. Dennis hit so hard that he knocked out sixty-five of his seventy opponents. Think about that for a second. He only lost twice (and one of those was because he broke his ankle). He had one tie and two no contests.

Me carrying one of Dennis's belts

Apart from the training, sparring, and going to the fights, Dennis and I had really clicked and became incredibly close friends.

Between all the stuff we were doing to stay in shape, we ended up eating a lot of meals together and hanging out often. We would get into some heavy-duty conversations, and he ended up being like a brother to me. I was so lucky that I got to be close friends with a world champion, and thankful that he let me be part of his wild journey.

Now, the only problem with all of this, if you can even call it a problem, was that I was having so much fun that I didn't realize I was getting sucked back into my party days. We got VIP treatment wherever we went, skipped long lines at the latest and greatest clubs, sat at the best tables, and met the most beautiful women. And so, of course, living that lifestyle, I started drinking, doing recreational drugs, and staying up all night.

It was that same restless, unstoppable energy I had experienced as a teenager back in Ansonia. Only this time around, I was running around with fellow bodybuilders like Mike Christian, Michael Torchia, and Mike Quinn (the three Mikes) all over Hollywood and the Sunset Strip.

Mike Christian

Mike Christian was a rising star, having won the Mr. California in '83 and the Nationals in '84. In 1985, he launched a highly successful line of gym clothes, and things really took off for him. In addition, he became a pro bodybuilder and bought a house and a custom Mercedes convertible. But most importantly, Mike was a lot of fun to be around. He had an infectious laugh, and we got along great.

Mike and I would do a lot of Gold's Gym photoshoots, sometimes to advertise the gym's clothing line or to sell the brand. These were big ads that were in all the muscle magazines, so we got a lot of exposure. A few times, Mike, Gary Strydom, Shawn Ray, Chris Cormier, Flex Wheeler, and I would be flown out to Germany as special guests at the FIBO fitness convention. We would do some fun guest posing onstage, give seminars, and take photos with the fans.

Me and Mike Torchia

Michael Torchia is an Italian guy, so we clicked right away. He is a bodybuilder who held the titles of Teenage Mr. America, Mr. New York, and Mr. California. Whether it was training, going to clubs, partying, or eating, we did it all together and had a great time. We also did photoshoots for Gold's Gym marketing and clothing. Mike liked women as much as I did, and these shoots were fun because there was always a beautiful fitness woman with us. To this day, I still keep in touch with Mike.

Me and Mike Quinn

Mike Quinn was an East Coast guy with an edge, but once you got to know him, he'd do anything for you. He was another guy I liked to train with. He had won Teenage Mr. America at his bodybuilding debut in 1981. I remember in 1987, as he was prepping for the Mr. USA, I helped him with his mandatory poses, his posing routine, and finding the right music for it. He ended up winning the title.

Mike sadly passed during the writing of this book. His sister had called me to give me the news. He was sixty-one, far too young.

Back in the day, we were four young, single, good-looking guys doing what most guys in their twenties do. We knew all the bouncers at the hottest clubs because they either trained at Gold's Gym or had seen us in the bodybuilding magazines. We were treated like celebrities everywhere we went. That kind of energy feeds on itself, and it's easy to fall into the trap of wanting to do more and more.

There's no doubt that going out was a blast, but in reality, it was just a big distraction that took me away from my passion. Looking back on it, I realized that the further I got away from bodybuilding, and the more I had gotten into modeling and acting, the partying and goofing off took over. Like in high school, I knew that I couldn't stay up all night and then be productive in the gym. The two simply didn't mix.

It was early 1987 when it all hit home one day. I woke up in the late afternoon after a night of partying and the sun was already setting. It shook me up that I had missed an entire day, and so I asked myself for the second time in my life, "What the fuck are you doing, Ricky?"

I knew the answer to that question and immediately picked a bodybuilding show to enter. It was time to get focused and back to my original passion. It had been two years since I had last competed onstage, and so my first contest back was going to be the Mae Mollica "Grand Prix" at the Wadsworth Theatre in Brentwood, just a few miles from where I lived.

Getting back into the contest scene felt incredible. I loved having that singular focus and not having to run around town to do auditions and gigs. In my three-month peaking phase, I got back to my training and dieting roots, having learned my lesson from the sodium loading experiment. I thrived on the laser focus it took to properly peak and to create a really entertaining posing routine. The feeling I got from that was something you just can't buy with money.

I was back in the zone, feeling amazing, when one day after a great workout, I was at home preparing my lunch when my mom called and told me that my good childhood friend and neighbor, Stevie Picard, had crashed his welding truck and died. That was May 25, 1987. It was sobering news to hear.

Stevie Picard

I felt so awful for Stevie and horrible for his mom and family, who had lost a husband and father in a work accident, and now a son and brother in a car accident. Shit like that reminded me of how lucky I was to be alive. I'll never forget when his prayer card arrived in the mail from Mom. I still have it to this day and think about him often. Love you, Stevie. Rest in peace!

I dedicated my contest preparation to Stevie and had a great summer working out and preparing for the show. I thought my physique was as good as it had ever looked, and I went into the show expecting to win it.

During the show, I hit my mandatory poses and knocked my posing routine out of the park. At the end, I got called out in the top five, and then it came down to me and one other guy who I thought I had beat. And so when the announcer called out my name in the second-place position, I put my index finger to my temple and pulled the trigger.

After the show, I grabbed my gym bag and stormed out of there, pissed off that I had fallen short of winning. I ignored photographers who wanted to take some pics of me, even though it would have likely led to positive things and even some paid gigs. My mind was fucked up and totally in the wrong space, so instead of being grateful that I took second, I was pissed off that I had lost first. I knew better, too.

My reaction when I lost

You have to accept losses in stride, but this time, I couldn't let it go. I let my ego take over my head.

Posing in the Mae Mollica Grand Prix

During the weeks after the show, I did my best to put it behind me, but it was difficult. Every day I walked into the gym, someone would say, "Hey, you should have won that show."

I know they meant well, but the constant reminders made it impossible for me to get past the loss.

Luckily, I had booked a Nike commercial, and that put me in a better mood. The commercial was part of the "Bo Knows" campaign. My good friend, the one and only Joe Pytka, was directing it. It featured a song by the legendary rock 'n' roll guitarist Bo Diddley.

This commercial had the most insane cast. It was a who's who of athletes from the '80s, including Kirk Gibson from the Los Angeles Dodgers, Jim Everett from the Los Angeles Rams, Michael Jordan from the Chicago Bulls, tennis player Pat McEnroe, Wayne Gretzky from the Los Angeles Kings, and myself along with four other amazing bodybuilders, including John Richling and Armand Azurdia. And it of course featured Bo Jackson, the multisport superstar whom Nike used to boost its cross-training shoes and apparel. The commercial ran through all the sports Bo "knows" about and got a lot of laughs when Gretzky was about to say, "Bo knows hockey" but instead he skated up to the camera, shook his head, and said, "No."

The shoot was a blast, and Bo Jackson was so down to earth and easy to speak with. During one of our conversations, we got to talking about his sneakers, and out of the blue, he asked me, "What size do you wear?"

Soon after that, he had Nike send me a half-dozen sneakers. What an amazing guy. I was so blessed to be in the presence of greatness and saw up close how a true legend should carry himself.

A few years later, I ran into Bo at a custom motorcycle shop in Marina del Rey, where we were both buying new bikes. I couldn't thank him enough for the sneakers. Thanks again, Bo!

As for the actual commercial shoot, my scene was to be shot at the Venice Beach weight pen.

There was a lot of down time between takes. While we were waiting around, Joe asked me how many reps I could get benching 405 pounds. Some of the other athletes heard this and they gathered around to watch. After warming up with 225, I did fifteen reps with 315 pounds like it was nothing. And then, I bench pressed 405 pounds for ten reps. A big dude jumped on the bench after me and tried to bench the weight but couldn't do it. I felt good showing them how it's done. I guess after my disappointing second-place finish, my ego needed a little stroking, and this was probably my way of doing it.

A couple of days later, I was back at Gold's Gym for my chest workout. I warmed up fast, doing a few quick sets of lighter weight before going up to 315 pounds for ten reps, then 405 for eight reps, and then 450 for three reps. After that, I jumped up another fifty pounds to 500 for a single rep. With that much weight, I needed a spotter, so I grabbed this girl next to me to help out.

Now, when you go to bench press 500 pounds, it grabs people's attention. It wasn't that rare to see someone benching that much weight at Gold's Gym back then, but it always looked impressive.

After giving my spotter the game plan, I laid down on the bench and gripped the bar like I had done thousands of times before. As I got my hands and breath ready, I counted down, "Three, two, one," and then my spotter helped me lift the bar off the rack. But, as I started to lower the weight, my right pec locked up, and the next thing I heard was a sound like someone was ripping a piece of plywood in half. Then, the bar crashed down on my chest.

I was in total shock. "Fuck!" I screamed.

A bunch of guys ran over, including Lyle Alzado, to help get the barbell off my chest. After that, I sat up in a daze. My right pec and arm felt like nothing I had ever felt before. I was in pain, but more than anything, my pec felt numb and detached. I touched my pec with my left hand, and it was all rolled up into a ball. I knew it was bad, and the look on everyone's faces confirmed my worst nightmare, that my pec was torn in half.

Lyle, having been through plenty of his own injuries, got me up, walked me to his car, and took me to the emergency room in Marina del Rey. But because I didn't have any insurance, no one would touch me. That's when Lyle put me back in his car and took me to see the Los Angeles Raiders' team surgeon, Dr. Robert Rosenfeld, at Cedars-Sinai Hospital in Los Angeles.

Because of Lyle, I got right in to see the doctor, but unfortunately, the diagnosis wasn't good. The doctor had asked me if I was in a lot of pain. When I told him that I wasn't, he was pretty sure that I had suffered a third-degree pec tear. With a tear like that, there was only one way to fix it: surgery.

As I signed out of the doctor's office with a prescription for two different types of painkillers in my pocket, I scheduled my surgery for a week later since I had to let the swelling and bleeding subside. On the way home, we stopped at a pharmacy and filled my prescriptions. Lyle then dropped me off at my apartment and handed me over to my friend Bobby Scura. It was really a blessing that Bobby lived in the unit above me because he ended up helping me until my surgery.

Outside my apartment after my pec tear

Once I was alone in my apartment, the reality of what happened had sunk in. I was overcome with shock and depression. Bodybuilding had been my passion for the last seventeen years. I had accomplished a lot, but there was so much more I wanted to do competitively. I felt like I had only scratched the surface of my potential. The sport of bodybuilding and all the gigs I was booking were all based on my looks. I was judged on how symmetrical and muscular my body was. This was my first serious injury, and it totally destroyed my feeling of invincibility.

The injury fucked with my head. I kept on wondering why this happened to me. I wanted to lash out at somebody. None of it made any sense. What had I done to deserve this? I finally figured out that I only had myself to blame. Showing off at the commercial shoot so soon after the Grand Prix, then heavily working out right away, made me susceptible to tearing a muscle.

I became reckless, and the result was catastrophic. Had I taken the loss in stride and had the necessary patience to ease back into my workouts, I don't think I'd be writing this story. But what happened, happened, and by sharing this story, I can hopefully help someone else avoid an injury like this. And for me, that would be an incredible victory.

Up until this moment in my life, I had taken so much pride in being able to stand on my own two feet. I hadn't ever felt this helpless before, with my entire world flipped upside down and facing a whole bunch of uncertainties. I resorted to taking as many painkillers as I could to numb myself. I would doze off on a cot that was rigged to keep my torso upright and end up having all sorts of nightmares. I'd wake up in a cold sweat, hoping that it was all a bad dream. But the sling, the bruising, and the inability to use my arm reminded me that it wasn't. I'd then take more pills to knock myself out, and the cycle would repeat. I saw why these high-powered drugs were so addictive and why people, like my brother and so many others, could easily fall prey to them (and this was decades before the opioid crisis would sweep across America).

Sadly, self-medicating and checking out from reality seemed like the right thing to do that week. Third-degree muscle tears are no joke. I knew that even if the surgery were successful, my body would be like a sports car after an accident that bent its frame. Like the car, my body would never be in true alignment again, and other body parts would have to compensate for the tension coming from the torn pec.

After that week, one of the worst in my life, Bobby took me back to the hospital for my surgery. In the operating room, the anesthesiologist gave me his spiel about going under. I had never had surgery before and didn't know what to expect. As he hooked me up to the IV drips, the anesthesiologist assured me everything would be okay.

Just before he put me under, he asked me, "Where is your happy place?"

My mind flashed to my trip with the Arnoldis. "A beach in Hawaii," I replied.

And so, he started the drip. "Aloha," he said, with a little smile on his face.

And that's when everything faded to black.

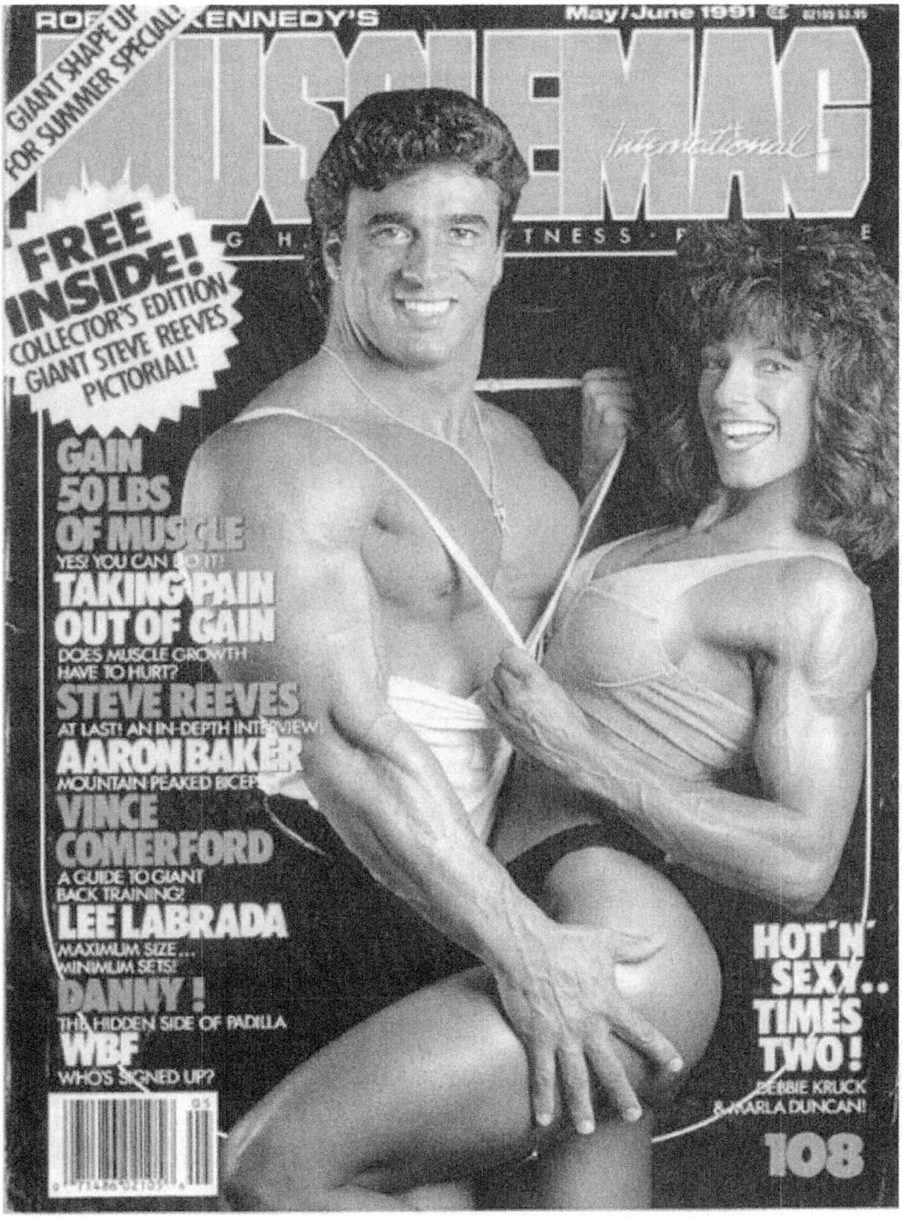
May/June 1991
International
GIANT SHAPE UP FOR SUMMER SPECIAL!
FREE INSIDE!
COLLECTOR'S EDITION
GIANT STEVE REEVES
PICTORIAL!
GAIN
50 LBS
OF MUSCLE
TAKING PAIN
OUT OF GAIN
DOES MUSCLE GROWTH
HAVE TO HURT?
STEVE REEVES
AT LAST! AN IN-DEPTH INTERVIEW
AARON BAKER
MOUNTAIN-PEAKED BICEPS
VINCE
COMERFORD
A GUIDE TO GIANT
BACK TRAINING!
LEE LABRADA
MAXIMUM SIZE...
MINIMUM SETS!
DANNY!
THE HIDDEN SIDE OF PADILLA
WBF
WHO'S SIGNED UP?
HOT 'N' SEXY.. TIMES TWO!
DEBBIE KRUCK
& MARLA DUNCAN!
108

THE NEW
BODYBUILDING
FOR EVERYONE!
Built!
REVISED
AND
EXPANDED
EDITION!
Beginners:
The Step-by-Step
Natural Bodybuilding
System to Improve
Energy, Strength
and Physique
Hardcore
Bodybuilders:
Hot Routines and
Explosive Muscle-
Building Strategies for
Advanced Trainers
Robert Kennedy and Maggie Greenwood-Robinson

THE POWER OF
NPC
NATIONAL PHYSIQUE COMMITTEE
ACTIVE WEAR
Spring 1991 Catalog $3.00
PHOTOGRAPHED BY J.M. MANION

CLOTHING FOR THE WELL BUILT
BODY ALIVE

Precio: 325 Ptas. • Año III • N.º 14
Precio Canarias: 317 Ptas.
NUEVO
CULTURISMO
Así entrena la campeona del mundo
LOS AMINOACIDOS
DONATO atleta ejemplar: 25 años compitiendo
Consiga un físico perfecto
MUSCLE & FITNESS
CAMPEONATO MUNDIAL POR PAREJAS EN MADRID

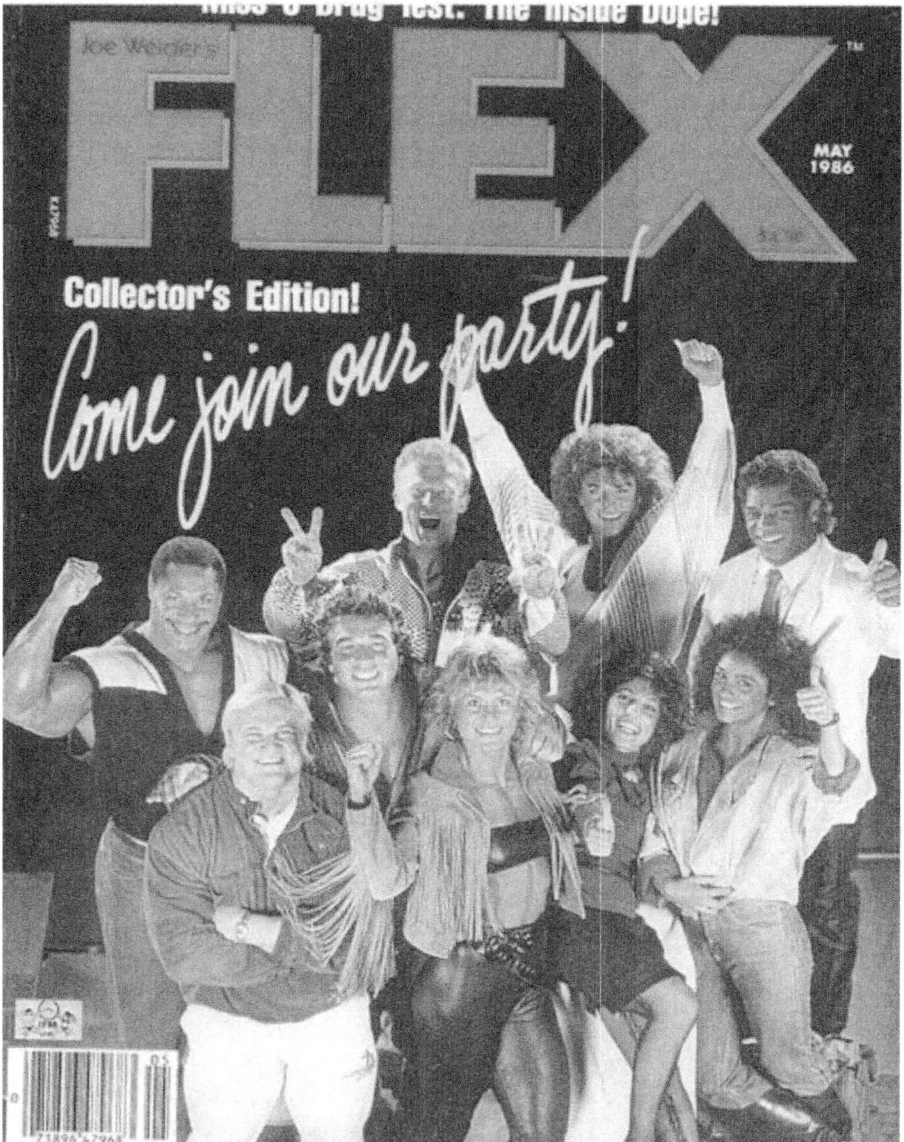
Joe Weider's
FLEX
MAY
1986
Collector's Edition!
Come join our party!

MTI
MUSCLE
TRAINING
Illustrated
$4.00 CAN.
SEPT. 1987
LOVE
AND
AEROBICS
POTENT MUSCLE ADVENTURE!

winter · spring
AMERICAN
PITBULL
BODY ARMOR
1994 · 1995

BODYBUILDING
SURGE
By John Everett
Photos by Paula Crane

muscle
MAGAZINE
N° 1
TRIMESTRIEL
FRANCE : 35 F
AVRIL - MAI - JUIN
LE BODYBUILDING : POURQUOI et POUR QUI ?
ENTRAINEMENT - MATÉRIEL - DIÉTÉTIQUE
SUPER DOSSIER : DÉBUTER et PROGRESSER

Le monde du
MUSCLE
MENSUEL
DOSSIER :
LES PSEUDO-VITAMINES
DANS CE NUMÉRO
DES CARTES POSTALES MUSCLÉES
FRENCH NEWS
BRAS D'ACIER
avec
RICK VALENTE
CYBORG avec
J.-C. VANDAMME
Hervé LEWIS L'ENTRAINEUR DES STARS
Brian BUCHANAN
Stoney Lee GRIMES
En direct de
MIAMI BEACH
2 POSTERS
M 2025 - 76 - 25,00 F
N° 76 MARS 1989
FRANCE : 25 F

BestFitness

AMERICAN
PITBULL
BODY ARMOR
PITBULL
Fall • Winter 1997 / 1998

THE NEW LEADER IN FITNESS
POWERHOUSE
FALL 1993
$2.95 U.S.
$3.95 CAN.
POWER INTERVIEW:
DOLPH LUNDGREN
KIANA
POWERHOUSE GYM
KIANA TOM & RICK VALENTE GALAXY Competition Hosts
SIMPLY THE BEST.

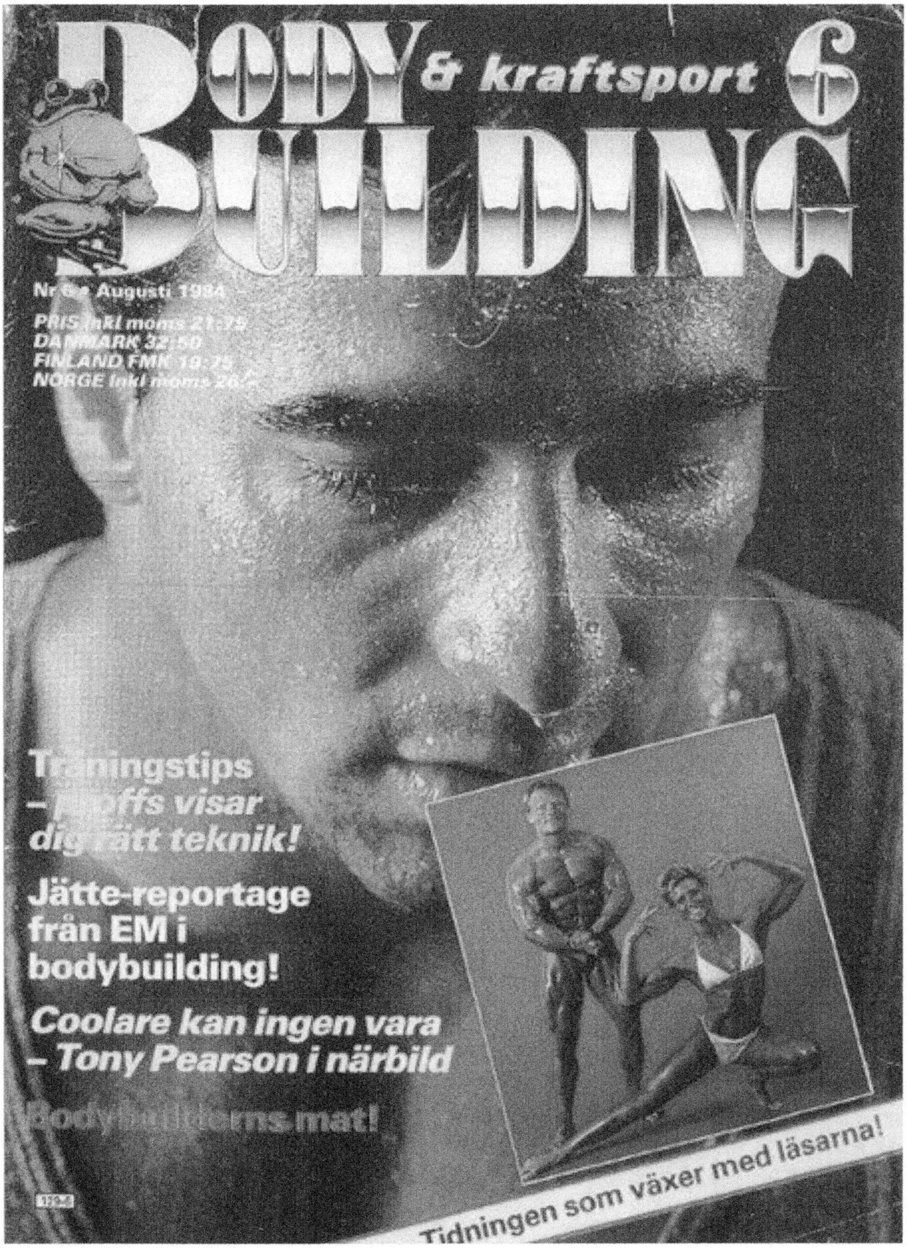
BODY BUILDING
& kraftsport
6
Jätte-reportage från EM i bodybuilding!
Coolare kan ingen vara – Tony Pearson i närbild
Tidningen som växer med läsarna!

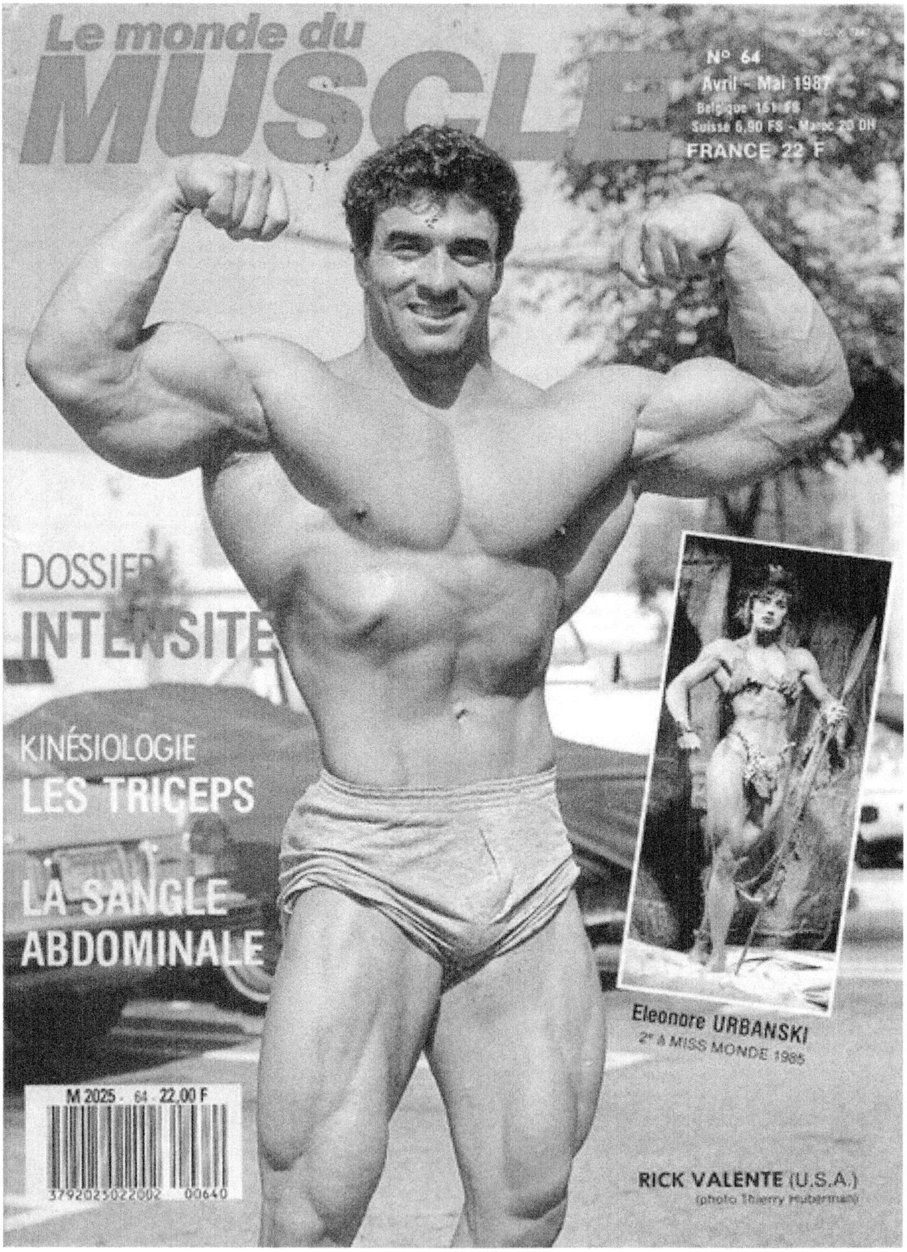
Le monde du
MUSCLE
N° 64
Avril - Mai 1987
FRANCE 22 F
KINÉSIOLOGIE
LES TRICEPS
LA SANGLE
ABDOMINALE
Eleonore URBANSKI
M 2025 - 64 - 22,00 F
RICK VALENTE (U.S.A.)

CHAPTER TWELVE

GETTING OFF THE MAT

"It's not whether you get knocked down; it's whether you get back up."
—Vince Lombardi

THE CONCEPT OF SURGERY IS PRETTY WILD. You go to the hospital, put complete trust in the doctors and staff, and then submit yourself to them. It's a big leap of faith when you stop and really think about it. I mean, the last thing I remembered was the anesthesiologist saying, "Aloha," and then the next thing I knew, I was waking up in a quiet room, with my right arm in a sling wrapped tightly to my body. The time in between was a dreamless sleep, during which Dr. Rosenfeld and his team sliced me open, repaired my pec, and stitched me back up.

When I woke up, I was in a groggy, dreamlike state, and so I wasn't sure if there was a tall dude with long hair sitting in the room. Was I imagining him, or was he real?

He must have noticed that I was having trouble making him out because I heard a laugh and then a voice say, "Hey, Rick, it's me, Joe…Joe Pytka."

The news of my pec tear had made its way around my circle of friends, so when Joe had heard about it, he made sure he was there when I woke up. Now that's what I call a friend.

Since meeting Joe, I had appeared in many of his commercials, and he had also given me an open-door invitation to his office so I could watch him edit raw footage. His office was close to Gold's Gym, and I'd often stop by after a workout to see what was going on. Most days, there were a lot of talented people there doing a lot of amazing stuff within their craft.

My relationship with Joe really took off when I started to train him in a gym he'd built at his office. Like I said earlier, when you train people, you get to know them really well because they open up and tell you just about everything going on, not only with their fitness but with their lives.

Joe was about twenty years older than I was, so he kind of became like an older brother to me, someone I could go to for advice or to bounce some thoughts off. We had formed a tight bond.

Actions speak loudly, so the fact that Joe had showed up at the hospital meant the world to me. He hung out for a while and we talked about sports, life, cars, and all kinds of other interests that we had in common. He did his best to cheer me up and to let me know that life goes on, that what doesn't kill you only makes you stronger. Unfortunately, at that moment, I wasn't exactly believing any of it.

When the young intern came into the room to do a post-surgery check, Joe gave me a hug, a final word of encouragement, and took off. The intern checked my vitals as he went into detail about my surgery, what they did, and that they felt it went well considering the severity of the injury. Then, he said something I've never forgotten. This was partly for the actual words and partly for how he delivered them.

"That was the worst third-degree pec tear we have ever seen," the intern said in an excited, giddy voice. "Your muscle looked like raw hamburger meat ripped completely in half!"

Hearing that from this intern who was part of Rosenfeld's team was powerful, and not in a good way. I knew Dr. Rosenfeld was the LA Raiders team doctor, and that his sports medicine group treated their fair share of muscle and pec tears. And so here I was, a guy in his late twenties, whose entire world revolved around bodybuilding, and there's this kid talking like he's celebrating my injury. You've got to be kidding me.

These were the last words I needed to hear. Talk about being demoralized. His words made my stomach knot up and made me feel shitty on so many levels. What the intern failed to realize was that my whole persona and purpose was tied to my physique. That my livelihood depended on my body being muscular and symmetrical. That these were the things I was judged on to either place well in a contest or get booked for a gig.

He also failed to realize that I *loved* to lift weights, that training was the most fun thing to do. It truly does feel good to do forced reps, negatives, and push around tons of weight. Now, all that pleasure was gone.

I dwelled on his description for what felt like hours but got a boost when Dr. Rosenfeld stopped by to check on me. He was an older guy who had been around the block.

"You're a young, healthy guy, and you're going to be just fine," he said.

I took that to heart. Hearing that from the main man gave me some hope. His choice of words let my brain imagine a future where I actually would be fine and be back doing what I love.

Dr. Rosenfeld told me to rest up and that he'd be back soon with his discharge instructions. He then gave me an assuring pat on my good shoulder before walking out the door.

It was after he left that I had noticed an envelope with "Rick" handwritten on it, sitting on the bedside table. I opened it up and my jaw dropped. Inside was a stack of cash amounting to a few thousand bucks. You son of a bitch, Joe!

What an amazing guy to not only leave the cash but to do so on the down-low, not wanting to take any credit for it. From our conversations, I guess he had put two and two together that I wasn't sitting on a pile of cash and that being out of work for at least a few months would put me in a financial crisis. I was truly blessed he had helped me out like that.

That cash turned out to be my lifeline until I could work again. There are people in our lives who might not be there during the little stuff, but they will sure as hell step up when the big shit goes down. Joe, thank you. You are the man!

It was only a few hours after my surgery, but I was already experiencing the roller-coaster ride that recovery would be—the high of Pytka, the low of "intern burger meat," and the inspiring words from the seasoned surgeon. The night-and-day difference between the doctors was a defining moment in my life. The two opposite approaches really showed me how much words matter. How the saying, "Choose your words wisely," was not just a cliché but something that was 100 percent true.

When someone is dealing with life altering adversity, you have to put yourself in their shoes and be compassionate. Think before you talk because what you say to them is very powerful. The young intern must not have realized this and let his enthusiasm for surgery and medicine take over.

It came time for my discharge, and the doctor's orders were to keep my arm and shoulder completely still and immobile for six to eight weeks. I also had to keep my arm as close to my body as possible, to make sure the stitches wouldn't stretch or break. This included sleeping upright to make sure I didn't roll onto it during the night. As the doctors explained to me, doing all of this would give the muscle fibers the best chance to regenerate and grow back together.

As the doc spoke, I tried to focus on the discharge instructions, but my mind drifted to the thought of being laid up for six to eight weeks and not able to work out. I was about to leave the hospital and enter a huge void, not having any clue what it would be like. That thought scared the shit out of me and made me sick with anxiety.

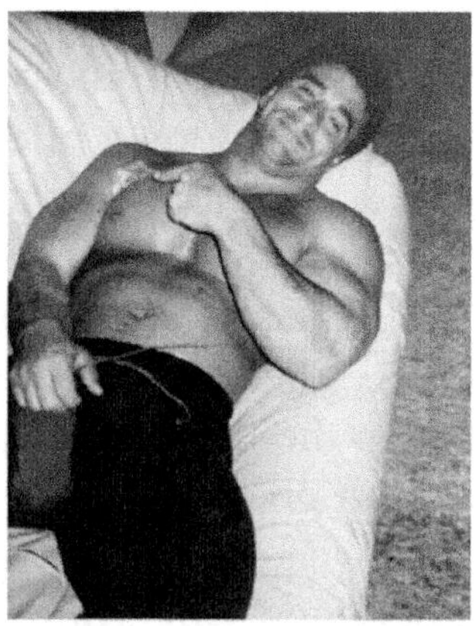

I was accustomed to training every day, which provided a huge release. What was life going to be like without that release? Without seeing my friends and competitors at the gym? Without getting to train like an animal at Gold's Gym? Without going to auditions and booking gigs? Without training my clients? My mind went on and on and on. I couldn't make it go quiet. I know athletes can relate to this, but it also applies to anyone facing an uncertain future, whether because of an illness, injury, career change, loss of a loved one, or anything like that.

The desolation of my apartment was a lot to deal with. Much like the week between my injury and my surgery, I escaped reality with Vicodin, Percocet, and smoking joints. Looking back on it, I was probably going through the five stages of grief—denial, anger, bargaining, depression, and acceptance. And right after surgery, I was firmly stuck in the denial and anger phases. I didn't want to see anyone and didn't want to do anything. But I had to eat, and hunger will make you do things you don't feel like doing, like leaving your apartment. And so, when I was out of food one day, I walked the few blocks over to the Firehouse to grab a bite to eat. As luck would have it, I was walking into the Firehouse just as Joe Gold was walking out. There I was, my arm in a sling, and Joe using a walker.

It goes without saying that Joe Gold is a legend, and when I had moved to Venice, I was dying to meet him. But Joe had already sold Gold's Gym before I arrived, so I had to venture over to World Gym to find him. Joe opened World Gym in 1977 in Santa Monica, and it ultimately moved to a space over in Marina del Rey. He ran that gym until the day he died on July 11, 2004, the same date as my birthday. Kind of crazy, huh?

One cool thing about World Gym was that it had some of Joe's original equipment that he had designed and built when he first opened Gold's Gym. But by far the coolest thing about World Gym was that most of the old-school legends had trained there. Guys like Eddie Giuliani, Zabo Koszewski, Roy Goldman, and Manny Perry, as well as the generation of guys just before me like Arnold Schwarzenegger, Lou Ferrigno, Tom Platz, and lots of others.

The old-school guys were super loyal, so when Joe had opened his new gym, they all flocked to it together. This gave World Gym a family feel. And as the old guys got older, they all took care of one another—a clan that would never break up. It was a cool thing to see and something that probably doesn't happen that often anymore, if at all. Those guys represented the best of the best from their respective generations and laid the pavement for guys like me. I admired them for that and thought to myself that if these guys need anything down the road, I'd do my best to help out.

Now, from the time I met him, Joe had been nothing but nice to me. I had a ton of respect for him, and he seemed to respect me as well, even going so far as to let me train at his gym for free. I never became super close to Joe, but what I knew about him reminded me of my dad and my grandpa. He was a surly, no-nonsense kind of guy. When he spoke, he spoke his mind. He ran his gym like that as well. No music, no goofing off, and if you didn't rack your weights after you used them, you'd get an earful.

I hadn't seen Joe for a while, so when I saw him walking out of the Firehouse restaurant, I was a little surprised. I think his hip situation made him a little more ill-tempered than usual because when he saw me, instead of saying hello or, "How's it going?" he said, "What the fuck happened to you?"

I laughed him off. "Ah, damn, Joe, I tore my pec in half," I said. "A third-degree tear."

"You stupid fuck," Joe said matter-of-factly, shaking his head. "You'll never be the same."

His words stung. I did my best to let it slide, knowing that Joe didn't have a filter and was dealing with his own shit. Maybe it was his tough-love way of saying, "That's too bad, man."

Instead of grabbing food, I headed toward the beach. I knew in my gut that he was 100 percent right. I would never be the same. At a minimum, I would have a five-inch scar on my right pec that goes from under my armpit across the top of my chest and angles up toward my throat. I would always have a little dimple-like depression on the outer head of my pec close to my armpit, where the internal stitches were placed. And who knows if I'd ever get full range of motion back, let alone be able to bench press anything close to what I could bench before.

Joe's words put me in an awful mood, and then seeing people playing on the beach with the full use of their arms sent me spiraling. I returned to my apartment, took more drugs, and vegged out. I had at least five to seven more weeks of being in a sling, and I knew that was going to be tough to get through.

I think a lot has changed since then in terms of post-surgery rehabilitation. I'm pretty sure nowadays the surgery would be less invasive, and you'd be doing physical therapy soon after the operation, making sure the muscles didn't atrophy too much and the joints didn't lock up. Unfortunately, that wasn't the case for me.

My daily routine was essentially taking drugs, getting food, and watching a lot of television. I didn't want to talk or hang out with anyone and certainly didn't want to go to Gold's Gym, where I'd see a bunch of bodybuilders doing what I couldn't. My attitude was shitty as I was dwelling on the past and not seeing much of a future. But that all changed just a few weeks into my post-surgery blues.

On that fateful day, I had left the confines of my apartment to get some food. The plan was to walk down to the Firehouse, eat, get some more food to go, and then head home. That was it. But as I was crossing the street, something caught my attention. That something was a young man in a motorized wheelchair that he controlled with his mouth. I was amazed to see that he didn't have fully formed arms or legs. One of his arms, that wasn't even elbow length, had three fingers on it. His other arm had two. His legs were about a foot long and he didn't have any feet.

As he passed by me, he saw my sling and he gave me a huge smile.

"Sir, what happened to you?" he asked.

"I tore my pec," I said. "What happened to you?"

He told me that he was born like that, so it was all he had ever known. He pulled out a little harmonica and played a few notes for me. He played beautifully. Every day, he earned money by playing music on the Venice Boardwalk.

I couldn't believe that as he spoke, his eyes glowed full of energy and life. His smile went from ear to ear. I was floored that he was truly happy, that he had chosen to look at life from a glass-half-full perspective. He wasn't focused on what he didn't have or couldn't do. Instead, he spent his energy on what he *did* have and what he *could* do.

The more we talked and the more I learned about him, I could feel a shift inside of me. That shift started with recognizing how pathetic I had been acting. How could I complain about anything when this kid was out there taking on the world in spite of his obvious challenges?

I walked with him for about half an hour. At the end of our conversation, I handed him a hundred bucks.

"Wow! Thank you, sir!" he said.

"No. Thank *you,*" I answered.

Life's journey is so much about how you respond to adversity. And I realized I was responding badly. I was being controlled by depression. Rather than wallowing in self-pity, I needed to focus on a solution to my situation. I had to remember the words I would tell my clients—that the power of positive thinking and taking action is the best cure for anything that you're going through. This was a huge chapter in my life and made me really understand the connection between mind, body, and spirit.

After we said our goodbyes, I walked off and couldn't help but think that somehow, God and the universe had put him in front of me. My chance meeting with this young man had completely turned my attitude around, and I made a pact with myself right then and there that I would get off my ass and get back to doing what made me happy—lifting weights.

The rest of that day, I didn't take any more drugs and let the ones I had taken wear off. I went to the grocery store and bought my usual types of food to prepare my bodybuilding meals.

When I woke up the next day, I felt better than I had in weeks. My head was clearer than it had been, and the knot in my stomach wasn't there anymore. I got out of bed and made six egg whites, followed by a bowl of oatmeal with blueberries.

Eating my bodybuilding breakfast lifted my spirits but was nothing like I felt when I had returned to the gym. Entering Gold's after being away for a month gave me a huge spike of adrenaline. Seeing, hearing, and smelling the gym was a much-needed antidote to my depression. Tim, Ed, and Pete welcomed me, along with the rest of my friends at the gym, who patted me on the back and gave me words of encouragement. That day, I did a light leg workout, and it was truly the beginning of my road to recovery.

After eight weeks, Dr. Rosenfeld finally gave me the green light to take that damn sling off. I asked him how much I owed him because I had never got a bill in the mail.

"Nothing. Joe took care of it," he answered.

That blew my mind. Not only had Joe Pytka paid for my surgery but he paid for my entire hospital stay and subsequent checkups.

The next time I saw Joe, I told him I would pay him back.

"Don't insult me," he replied.

From that moment onward, I knew I was going to do whatever I could for Joe. Having a friend like him is a true blessing. Thank you, Joe. Love you, and God bless you.

With the sling gone, I could now move into my rehabilitation phase, which would include going to a physical therapist as well as doing my own workouts. To begin with, therapy was super simple. I was basically just working on straightening out my arm and unlocking the joints. One of the "exercises" was crawling my fingers up a wall to awaken my shoulder joint and get that range of motion back. This movement, which I never had to think about before, was now almost impossible to do because my right shoulder, pec, and arm had atrophied, and it was painful, too. But slowly and surely, session after session, I kept working my way up that wall until I could get my hand above my head. I also worked hard to lift my arm laterally, just to get my elbow up to the height of my shoulder.

All in all, my physical therapist was amazing and really

drilled into my head the need to be patient and to approach all movements with humility.

Once I got a decent range of motion back, I was able to start working on getting some size back. To do this, I'd be working with five- and ten-pound dumbbells. That's 480 pounds less than what I was able to bench press prior to tearing my pec.

It was imperative that I remained patient during this recovery period. I had to fight the urge to lift heavier before I was ready. I really had to keep my ego in check and do everything correctly, or else I would risk injuring myself again. And I know there are many people reading this who have had major surgeries and know exactly what I'm talking about.

When I finished that first upper-body workout at Gold's, I weighed myself and took a good look in the mirror at my physique. I was astonished that I had lost at least twenty pounds of muscle, and at how scrawny I had looked weighing in at under two hundred pounds. In addition to losing weight, I had also lost a lot of definition and tone. It was a punch to the gut for sure, but I thought at least there's room for improvement.

As I gradually increased the weight (and I mean very gradually), the reality of the injury itself set in. For starters, I loved to bench press. It was my favorite movement, and now I couldn't bench heavy anymore. Then there was the lost range of motion. The pain of having to rip through scar tissue. The visible scar and depression in my pec. And of course, there was the imbalance that the weakened pec placed on the rest of my body.

But the truth is you can work around any injury. You can alter your movements and your workouts to accommodate whatever the body is going through. This takes a good trainer or physical therapist, and in my case, I could also rely on the knowledge of my body and muscles that I had built up over the years.

To deal with my pec surgery and the fact that the muscle was out of alignment, I had to pretend to be a master mechanic who had to fix a sports car after its chassis was bent in an accident. The game became, how could I get my body as close to perfect alignment in spite of the injury so that it could perform optimally? This was my new challenge, and one that I took head on.

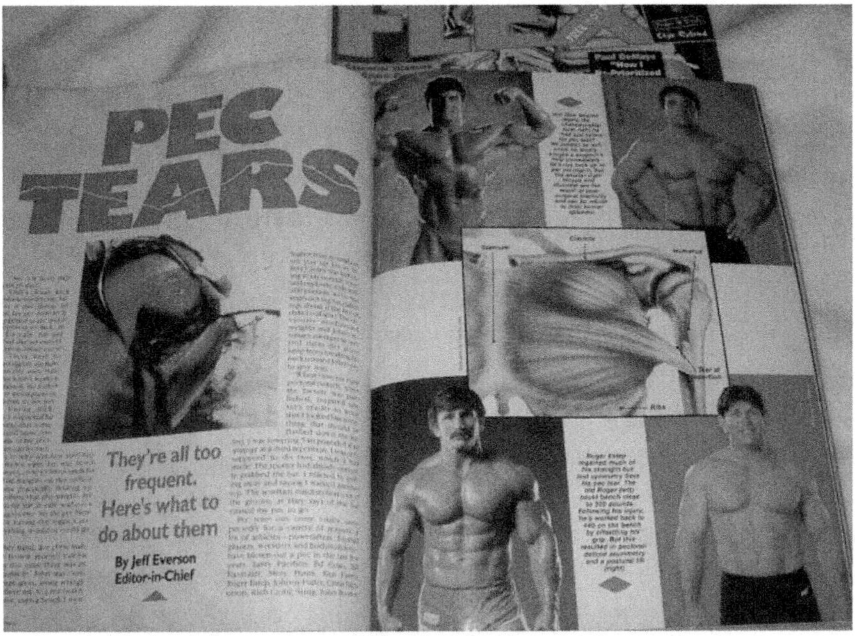

Me (top) featured in a "Flex" magazine article on pec tears

In writing about this, I hope to help others avoid an injury. To say, listen to your body and let it rest. Be patient and make sure you cycle your workouts and training to give your body a much-deserved break. Nowadays, you can't always train heavy, and you have to put the phone down between sets and stretch your muscles and joints. Also, don't forget to exercise your mind because, as you might remember, it was my ego and anger that got me into this predicament to begin with.

More than that, though, if you end up having an injury, whether in the gym, on your bike, in a car crash, or whatever, just know that it's not the end of the world. The temporary defeat will be replaced with hope, new discoveries, and great opportunities. I know it sounds cliché, but it's true. Just weather the storm and keep a positive attitude and good things will come of it.

On the flip side, if you are dealing with an injured person or someone going through a major life event, be kind and compassionate. We are all susceptible to injuring ourselves or being injured by others. No one is above that, so think before you speak, and try to be like Dr. Rosenfeld. If you see someone training and their form doesn't seem perfect, don't judge them because they may be working with an injury or recovering from a surgery. Do whatever you can do to support them, even if it's just a word of encouragement to let them know you see them.

I was lucky to have a lot of support from my friends in the gym and from my family as well. Those close to me knew how hard I worked on my physique over the years, and they knew how devastating my pec tear was to me. So, they all rallied behind my rehab as I was working my way back to my regular self. Everyone roots for a good comeback story, right?

Even so, I wasn't sure what my comeback would look like. I knew in my heart of hearts that I wouldn't be able to compete onstage anymore at the highest level. This wasn't me being negative or anything like that; I was just being realistic. I knew how symmetrical and perfect your body had to be just to crack the top three, let alone to get second or first place. The competition was fierce, and the difference between the guys at the top level was measured in fractions of an inch. I also knew how intense the training was to peak properly, and I wasn't sure I could train that hard safely. I knew guys that got back to competing after significant muscle tears, but not third-degree pec tears that required surgery.

Beyond competing, I had to question whether I would be able to continue to book gigs at a steady rate like I had done before. Luckily, I had Derek in my corner, as well as Andy Woolf and Don Franklin, two agents from World Class Sports Agency, and Jim Crabbe, an agent from William Morris. They had promised that they would loop me back into auditions once I was ready to do them. But would I be able to compete against a bigger and stronger dude that was trying out for the same gig? Only time would tell.

Until that part of my career regained some steam, I started training clients again, as well as helping top amateurs and pros get ready for contests. Derek was awesome as he kept sending people my way, including high-profile actors who needed to get in shape for upcoming roles. I would talk to them about my injury, stressing the importance of cycling your training and not maxing out every time you go to the gym. They also took in my words that you have to train your mind and spirit just as much as your body. Inevitably, pretty much everyone I had talked to about my injury was dealing with, or had dealt with, a major injury, illness, or life setback, whether it was themselves, a loved one, or a close friend. Sharing my nightmare injury with others helped me heal.

I have so much gratitude for Gold's Gym, Derek, and my other agents, who all helped me get back in the game so I could earn money to pay my bills and rent. That's the cool thing about being part of an incredible family like the one at Gold's Gym back then—they always had your back. One hand washes the other. I would do whatever I could do for them, and they'd do whatever they could do for me.

When my body finally got back to having enough muscle so that I could take my shirt off, I jumped back into doing gym openings for Gold's. And boy, did that feel great.

During one of my workouts, a well-known and respected fitness photographer named Paula Crane had approached me and asked if I wanted to be in a shoot with a young, upcoming female pro bodybuilder. I didn't hesitate to say yes. I quickly followed Paula upstairs, and that's when I met Tonya Knight.

Before I continue with Tonya's story, I have to give you some background about the writing of this book. Whenever I would think of someone I wanted to write about, I would call them and get their permission. It had been years since I last spoke to Tonya. I had no idea what to expect when I called her.

Over the years, I've cherished the time I spent with her. She made a big impact on my life. So, imagine my surprise when I called her and the first thing she said was, "I'll marry you now, Rick."

Me and Tonya Knight

This was so out of the blue that I started laughing.

"No. No. It's not a joke," she said.

"Oh, I love you, too," I replied.

Then I told her I was writing my autobiography and I wanted to cover the time we spent together. She said she'd love to be in the book and promised to send me a couple of pages about our time together and what it meant to her. A week later, she sent me a three-page letter. It was very sweet and brought back a lot of memories, but there was one thing she wrote that just floored me.

"I've always believed you made a bigger impact on my life than I did yours because I was at the age where I was discovering myself and I fell into the arms of the perfect person," she wrote.

Wow! I had no idea she felt that way.

About nine or ten months later, I received word that Tonya had passed away. This broke my heart. She died too young.

Hi Rick,

This is how I remember us, correct me if I'm wrong.

I was living in Kansas City and had been training and competiting for several years and had just turned Pro. I believe I had competed in my first pro show (The World Pro). After that I somehow had a few photo shoots in LA. then I received a call from the Producer of "American Muscle" magazine to cast as the spokesperson for this new ESPN show. I got the job and had to go to California to do some filming near Venice Beach Gym (?) and Golds Gym. I was interviewing a few people at Golds Gym and I met Paula Crane and she ask if I would do a photo shoot with her. At this time they had a room upstairs in the gym and that is where she shot her photos. While doing the photo shoot she said let me go see who's here today and maybe get shots w/ a male. She came back w/ you. WOW! BTW, I was with my boyfriend at the time. A month or so passes and our picture is in a magazine and my boyfriend at the time said "you and Rick should compete in couples. From there, somehow, he got your phone number. Somehow, we started talking and you explained to me you had just torn your pec so competing would be out of the question. We continued to talk on the phone, sent photos to each other. I couldn't wait for you to call but I was still quite nervous. I remember when I called, sometimes, your answering machine would go off and your message said 'I'm unable to get to the phone, leave a message and I will get back to you, Ciao... I thought that was so Kool.

OK, moving on... I landed a job w/ the Sharper Image Catalog in San Fransisco and for some reason I had to be back in LA. Photo shoot or just to see you, I'm not sure

you said that I could stay at your place (How sweet, lol)
for the 10 days I was there. So, from San Fransisco I
flew to LAX and you picked me up at the airport
and for me it was love at first site. I believe it
was for you also, because you had an engagement ring
with you. We headed back to your place
and within an hour you pulled us into
the bedroom and (I was inexperienced) started
tugging at my pants and I said no, lets
wait a little bit (I was nervous). This little
tug of war went on until I felt you on
my thigh and I changed my mind. Wow is
good. You rocked my world that day and it
was a great 1st experiance in Calif Ricks world.
Of course, I had the Ms Olympia
coming up soon and we were excited about
having the same love & knowledge of bodybuilding.
I was your student and absorbed everything
you said... You were very protective of
me and gave me advice on a few Bodybuilding
Gurus (lol) that were in the business of experimenting
on female body builders and almost turning
them in to men in a matter of months. You
were st. (Dan Duchaine). You taught me to
keep it classy in photoshoots. Which, I am
grateful for to this day. You went on photo
shoots w/me and had you not been there
on one occasion I'm not sure I would be here.
I had my first cup of coffee with you. You
introduced me to Sweet Potatoes. I vow they
are the best complex carb you can eat while
in prep for a show! I also remember you
introducing me to great music. We fell in love

with Tracy Chapman together. I remember you
playing "Its a wonderful world" but
mostly you played a song by your dear
friend, Gregory Hines (R.I.P.) and Luther Vandross.
You danced with me in the living room to
that song many times.

Anyhow, back to my contest prep. I thought
was training hard & doing cardio hard back
home but. You put me on a stricter diet. We
really weighed things out. My cardio was
increased to 2 hrs a day. Plus, lifting and
posing practice. I was incredibly tired and
starving. (Remember, when you taped the fridge
door shut, lol) Anyhow, my personality was
becoming dull and I was only focused on one
thing the Ms. O. I wasnt the best girlfriend-
No one is in contest prep! *I dont know
if you want to talk about the drug test scandal
or not (its probaly more my story)

Ive always believed you made a
bigger impact on my life than I did yours
because I was at the age where I was discovering
myself and I fell into the arms of the perfect
person. I had so many "firsts" with you. Like, the
love of sushi, coffee, the workout close of the 80's +
early 90's, the Love Eric scrunch sox, etc, etc, etc.
You were so cool and the Epitome of the laid
back California HOT guy!

*Im not sure if you want to talk
about why I moved out or how it ended. Well,
you probably have to. We can discuss that over the phone
♥ T

It turned out that Tonya had just gotten her pro card and was in Los Angeles at Gold's Gym filming a TV show and doing a photoshoot with Paula. They needed a male in the shoot, and that's where I came in. Right off the bat, I could tell Tonya was a sweet, adorable young woman who had a small-town vibe to her. She also happened to have an amazing physique and was very beautiful.

During the shoot, Tonya and I hit it off, joking and teasing each other as Paula snapped photos of us. When I had learned Tonya lived in Kansas City, I razzed her, telling her that she needed to be where the pros trained, at Gold's Gym Venice. More than that, though, she needed to be in Los Angeles, where Joe Weider and all the fitness magazines were.

After our shoot, Tonya went back to Kansas City, and over the next few weeks, we talked on the phone about bodybuilding and how Tonya could market herself. Sometimes, our conversations would get flirty, but I didn't see it going anywhere since she lived far away and she had a boyfriend. When the photoshoot we did at Gold's Gym hit the magazines, Tonya told me that her boyfriend said that we looked great together and that we should do a couples bodybuilding contest. Unfortunately, because of my pec tear, I had to pass.

A few weeks later, Tonya let me know that she had booked a commercial shoot for Sharper Image in San Francisco, and when the shoot was over, she would hop down to Venice to train with me at Gold's for ten days. I offered her my place to crash so she wouldn't have to spend money on a hotel. She took me up on it.

to the audience. They miss that vital connection. I'm not saying I'm the best, but my people always do well. Ask Dorothy, Mike Quinn, and Tonya!

When designing a routine, it's important that the mood, the tempo, and the movements are a reflection of the poser. Quinn's routine, for instance, must be powerful and forceful. Tonya's routine must be cute, seductive, and aggressive.

Aside from posing to music and flowing transitions, we spend a lot of time on the static mandatory poses. Competitors who overlook this will cramp on stage, shake during the poses, and lack the ability to isolate the muscles bringing out minute detail.

We work on the mandatories for hours before a contest. Holding each pose for forty seconds fully flexed. I start them with twenty second poses and increase the time, working up to forty seconds. This is hard work for the instructor who has to deal with the moods of dieting, irritable athletes. I push them anyway, like a Marine drill sergeant. They hate my guts, but they do it.

They know it's no fun, but it's necessary to win. The screaming matches I had with Mike Quinn and Tonya during these sessions still echo in my head! The important thing....it works!

Grooming is an aspect of preparation too often overlooked. Is your hair styled right for you? Is it neat and does it contribute to a good complete look? Unusual styles are too distracting for competition where general appearance can knock you down several places.

Women have to be even more careful. Too short of hair looks too tomboyish and detracts from that often-used term—femininity.

Long hair must be styled so it doesn't cover up impressive muscle. The right amount of make-up applied exactly right is vital for female contestants.

The color of your trunks or posing suit is also important. Your attire should go well with your complexion. It can't be too colorful as to be distracting or too bland that it fades into your skin tone.

COACHING

On the day of the contest, my job is not over. I now become the coach. Backstage, I psych my client, like a boxer before a fight. I work up their adrenalin and aggressive attitude before and during their routine. I'm always in the first or second row yelling myself hoarse. I want them to know their support system is there during the most important time.

While personal training, coaching, and posing instruction have become lucrative businesses in the bodybuilding world, it means much more to me. This is why I took no money from the champions I mentioned. I did it for self gratification. If, after reading this, you become interested in instructing, you are in for a lot of work. Work with results that are as exciting and rewarding as winning that First Place trophy yourself! ■

tonya knight
and rick valente

PHOTO BY PAULA CRANE

The photoshoot we did with Paula the day we met

column and she'd get some free publicity. Otherwise, it would have to wait a month till the next issue. It was quite late in the day when I phoned her, probably 5 p.m. When I hung up, I immediately told Bob Kennedy and Steve Douglas about the picture of Tonya and Rodney, and that we'd have it in time to go in this month's gossip. "Forget it Zulie," they both told me. "You know these bodybuilders. They always promise to send articles and pictures and never do, or it comes 3 months late. They miss photo-sessions, they don't show up for interviews. They're totally irresponsible and unprofessional. Just forget it."

Well to make a long story short, by the time I came into work next morning, the picture was there by courier. Not only did she send the picture of her and Rodney, but half a dozen slides of herself (one of which we are considering for our "Top Body" page), several cards and a professionally typed letter with a proper letterhead, about numerous things happening in her life. And she had it to us from Missouri to Brampton, Ontario in little more than half a day. Needless to say, her professionalism is a breath of fresh air compared to the typical lazy bodybuilders who never send us gossip about themselves, miss photo-sessions and interviews and then complain bitterly when they are not in the magazine. With her attitude, Tonya is going to win a lot of points with editors of muscle magazines all over the world.

Born in Kirksville, Missouri (hometown of another bodybuilding beauty, Penny Price), Tonya was an all-round athlete at Fort Osage High School where she played volley-ball, soft-ball, ran track and field and swam. She started weight-training with her boyfriend in a basement gym before she was 17 and joined a commercial gym a

Tonya Knight and Rick Valente.

month later. She took to bodybuilding instantly and almost immediately decided she wanted to compete. She progressed very quickly.

Remember back in Grade School when there always seemed to be someone who could skip grades and advanced much faster than the other people your age? Tonya Knight is like that. She seems to have the knack and the skill necessary to by-pass or skip the usual route necessary to go into competitive bodybuilding (and other activities too). Despite being only 17 and after only 5 months of serious training she by-passed novice, local and regional competition and went right to the 1983 Missouri State Championships.

Tonya Knight helps Rick Valente through a set of curls.

Despite her youth and inexperience, she won! At only age 17 and with less than half a year of training under her belt, she had qualified for the Nationals. It would take most people 3-5 years and she made it in 5 months. Amazing!

Nobody's life is all ups and for the next couple of years she had to pay her dues while she developed her body. In 1984 she finished a disappointing 11th place at the USA's. In 1985 she won the Gold's Mid-West Classic and then placed 6th in her class at the USA's. In 1986 she moved up to the Heavyweight class and finished a respectable 4th at the USA's again.

Then came her big break (what her critics might call a lucky break but you make your own breaks in life by being prepared when the breaks come). In May, 1987 Tonya was invited to compete in Tokyo, Japan at the World Amateur International Invitational (a pro qualifier) and won! She defeated Canada's Negrita Jayde. Once again, as she did in 1983, she was able to by-pass the usual, long, tedious and treacherous route to the pro's-winning the NPC Nationals and IFBB World Amateur Championships — and go directly into the pro's. And to do it before she was 21 years of age!

It is said that some are born to greatness while others have it thrust upon them. Such seems to be the case with Tonya. Upon her return from Japan, she was asked to do a screen test for **American Muscle Magazine** on **ESPN**. Although competing for the job against two highly experienced, articulate and intelligent (and not to mention, beautiful) women bodybuilders, **Carla Dunlap** and **Lydia Cheng**, Tonya won the job. Tonya's youthful enthusiasm and beauty were definite winning factors on her behalf. She had the looks, the body, the brains and the drive to go for the job and get it.

From the shows that I have seen when Tonya has been on, I have honestly been impressed with how well-spoken she is and how comfortable she appears on camera. Her success on American Muscle Magazine has led to many offers for this bright new star-promotional work, modelling assignments, TV and movie scripts, among many things. It's amazing she has time to train at all but like all highly motivated people, she sets her goals and priorities and makes the time to fit all things in.

It might sound strange but winning big bodybuilding contests is not a major priority with Tonya because acquiring the type of physique necessary to win pro shows (although within her capabilities) would limit her too much for modelling and roles for TV, movies etc. In an article in **Women's Physique World** she said, "I've always been very conscious about my size and I'll be even more now. I don't want to be something they don't want." She has always had a preference for a less-muscular physique and just doesn't want to outgrow or get too big to do the lucrative modelling and TV work that is now coming her way. She realizes she stands to earn far more from modelling and acting than she could ever earn as a bodybuilder and doesn't want to kill the goose that laid the golden egg just to ▸

How I Train and Diet to Win

In my current training routine, I train 4 days in a row and then rest one day. With this type of training cycle, I am not able to hit every bodypart twice a week but I train very hard and my body needs the extra recovery time. I've tried all sorts of training schedules and this is the one I have found to be the most successful for me.

Off-season

1st Day:	Chest, Biceps, Abs
2nd Day:	Back, Calves
3rd Day:	Shoulders, Triceps, Abs
4th Day:	Legs, Calves

Like most bodybuilders, initially I learned most of my bodybuilding knowledge from muscle magazines and from the bodybuilders I have met and spoken to. But now I feel I know what's best for me. People sometimes try to tell me to do certain things differently but I do it my way. I don't mean to say I know everything about bodybuilding but after 4 years of hard training, I know my body and I do what's best for me.

For example, I've tried doing triceps with chest but after doing a full-blown chest routine, my triceps are pretty much shot. I've also tried to train back with biceps and ran into the same problem. It would be fine if I was able to train twice a day on a double-split routine but unfortunately, this isn't always possible. When I train biceps after chest I'm able to train with intensity because my biceps aren't involved in any of my chest exercises.

I just love spending one whole workout dedicated to back because I'm really working hard to add some thickness there. If you think about it, there's a lot of muscles to be

Tonya's great shape and symmetry show through in this pose.

worked in your back (traps, upper and lower lats, middle and lower back). Last but not least, I've always trained legs alone because **I love to train legs!** My legs are probably my best bodypart because I enjoy training them so much. I set goals every leg workout and work hard to achieve them. I just love pain, I guess.

My calves are probably my most lagging bodypart but they're coming along finally. I ordered a course from Muscle & Fitness called "Maximum Calves". It's very scientific and it's working wonders. I can't tell you too much about it but I'll say this. It takes about 15 minutes to do this calf routine and in that 15 minutes, you never rest at all. The pain and burn is unbelievable but it really works. My calves have grown 1½ inches in about 3 months!

As for the exercises I do in each training session, that's difficult to say because I always change the exercises, the order of the exercises, the weight and the number of repetitions. The following will give you an idea of my typical workouts.

Chest
- Bench Press (barbell or dumbbell)
- Incline Press (barbell or dumbbell)
- Flyes (flat or incline)
- Cable Crossovers
- Pullovers (dumbbell)

Biceps
- Standing Barbell Curls
- Machine Preacher (my favorite machine in the world)
- Incline Dumbbell Curls
- Spider Barbell Curls
- Concentration Curls

Back
- Deadlifts (once every two weeks for about two hours)
- Chins
- Pulldowns (to front and rear/close grip and wide grip)
- Bent-Over Rows
- Seated Rows ▸

MUSCLE Go-Round

that were used to illustrate the article turned out to be bogus according to people who know about such things. Upon close inspection of the photographs it was noticed that one of the containers was labelled **Andriol 50**, when the real McCoy is known as **Anodrol 50**, and there never was a legitimate pharmaceutical called **Winston Depot**, according to a World wide drug text. Even the gang at **MuscleMag** were surprised. And then we got our hands on this little gem. A professionally produced counterfeit label for **Lilly's** growth hormone. Obviously created by a graphics studio, the label would pass the closest inspection. As they used to say on **Hill Street Blues**, "Be carefully out there".

Tonya Knight and Rick Valente plan to tie the knot soon.

Seems on again, off again, **Tonya Knight** and **Rick Valente** are on yet again. This time for keeps. The pair are living in Southern California and plan to wed real soon. Some guys have all the luck… meanwhile, Tonya is doing very well for herself thank you very much with engagements, no pun intended, all over the place. She just signed with the **Mobil Oil Company** to appear at the mega corps annual convention where she will be guest posing and doing the entire PR bit. Her take for the event is a whopping five grand a day. Gives a new meaning to all in a days work, don't it? But it does seem the major outfits are more than willing to shell out macho dinero to associate themselves with bodybuilding's premier ladies. Take **Marjo Selin** for example. She has been working with the **Mid West** steel company for some time now, with an impressive ad campaign that has become the target of criticism from some women that really should know better. **NOW**, a feminist lobby group, objected to the company utilizing a female body to sell steel, calling the ad sexist. Yet the obvious connection between the company's product and Marjo was that of strength, an area usually reserved for the male species. C'mon ladies grow up, will ya? Incidently, if you would like to see more of the aforementioned beauties, why not keep an eye open for the new video featuring Marjo and Tonya. Directed by our own **Robert Kennedy**, the video is in pre-production stages right now, and should be coming your way reel, I mean real, soon.

Rick Wayne's recent trip to the United States had nothing to do with a return to the **Weider** fold and his position as editor of **FLEX** magazine, contrary to some rumours travelling around the physique World. Ricky is quite content with his lot on the tiny West Indies island of St. Lucia where he is running successful magazines and a newspaper, and he tells us that he will remain there some time. Expect some articles from Ricky coming your way soon in **MuscleMag**…

Rumours of Rick Wayne's return to FLEX premature.

Remember our article **'Confessions of a Steroid Dealer'** published several issues back? That feature centered around the issue of fake steroids being distributed across America, and was an eye opening look at the entire black market. Well, even the drugs

Bogus drugs again.

HUMATROPE®

COMBINATION PACKAGE

HUMATROPE®

SOMATROPIN FOR INJECTION

5mg

FOR PARENTERAL USE ONLY

PROTECT FROM LIGHT

REFRIGERATE

A ready to print Growth Hormone label. The counterfeit market is flourishing.

And speaking of our 'Confessions' article we would like to point out an error that was printed regarding **Tony Fitton**. Due to a typo, it was reported that Fitton was involved in the sale of counterfeit drugs, when in fact he was only involved in the distribution of legitimate pharmaceuticals.

NATIONAL BODYBUILDING CHAMPIONSHIPS

SPECIAL ATHLETES MENU

Some promoters could take a valuable lesson from **David Levine** of **Great Lakes Gym** in Rochester, New York. At the recent **Niagara Falls Pro Championships**, which David had a hand in organizing, the official hotel, **The Hilton**, had a menu that was created with the bodybuilders in mind. The meals, with no fat or salt, were a big hit with the competitors. Now wouldn't it be nice if all contests featured such little touches.

Joanne McCartney and **John Terilli** have joined forces and are appearing as a guest pose duo all over the country. The pair competed at the **World Couples Championships** in Nice, France, where they placed a respectable fifth place. They received so many compliments about their routine that they decided to take their act on the road.

Well, all you folks in Southern California must be sighing with relief right 'bout now. That's after spending the entire month of May in appre- ►

Sept/MUSCLEMAG 9

Over those ten days, we solidified what we both knew—that we were meant to be together. When she went back to Kansas City, it was only to break up with her boyfriend and to get her things to make the move to Venice and live with me.

Once she moved in, we basically did everything together, from eating and training to hanging out. I shared with her my diet and love for sweet potatoes and showed her how to cook entire meals in the steamer. We also connected over music. I remember playing her Gregory Hines and Luther Vandross's song "There's Nothing Better Than Love," and we'd get lost in the beauty of their voices and lyrics.

Rick Valente and famed championess—TV commentator Tonya Knight are well armed for the sport plus media modeling field. (Photo: Paula Crane—courtesy Gold's Gym)

Tonya had her eyes set on the upcoming 1988 Ms. Olympia contest, so I started to help her train at Gold's Gym specifically for that show. She was a breath of fresh air, and even though I wasn't the one who would be competing, it felt great to pass on what I had learned during my six years at Gold's. I also introduced her to all my friends so she could meet people in her new city. And, to be honest, so I could show her off. Tonya felt really special to me. Looking back, I guess I was also letting the other guys know she's taken.

Helping someone else get ready for a show helped me in

more ways than I could have imagined. She gave me a purpose and a reason to get back into bodybuilding, which was obviously my burning passion. She really helped me rekindle my love affair that I had for the sport, and for this, she meant the world to me. I often look back and think that God put Tonya in my life, like the young man in the wheelchair, to help me through this phase of my journey.

The awesome thing about Tonya was that she loved bodybuilding as much as I did. That shared passion and interest was the bond that connected us and that made me fall in love with her—so much so that I had bought an engagement ring and popped the question, which was a first for me! She said yes, and just like that, we were engaged. It happened so fast that it was after the fact that I thought I better take her back east to meet Mom and Dad.

In Ansonia, Tonya fit right in with my family. That made me feel amazing, especially when Mom had given me a look like she was proud of me. All my old buddies liked her as well. It was a short but sweet trip. When we returned to Venice, it was all business in the gym and booking gigs.

The funny thing about being engaged was that I started to feel responsible for Tonya's well-being and safety. Maybe it was the Sicilian in me, but I hated the thought of her going to these auditions and casting calls when I knew Hollywood was full of casting-couch creeps.

Everyone back then had their story about being put in a bad position. Vultures were everywhere, and they took advantage of young people that were hungry to make it big, people who would do just about anything for their shot at being famous. This wasn't just an issue for women but for guys as well.

I even had an issue once with a guy who was a big-shot studio head. Apparently, he had seen me in a commercial and reached out to Derek about a film he wanted me to star in. Even though I wasn't big into acting, I thought, "Sure, let's see what this guy has to offer."

Derek arranged a meeting with the guy and me, and that's when things got really weird.

To start with, this guy had insisted that we meet for dinner in Beverly Hills, so he sent his driver to pick me up in a Rolls-Royce. Dinner was just the two of us and we mostly talked shop, so no big deal. After we ate, though, he said he'd like to take me back to his house on the corner of San Vincente and Ocean Avenue in Santa Monica so he could give me the script. And that's when shit went sideways because, as he was sitting next to me and showing me the script at his dining room table, he put his hand between my thighs. I grabbed his hand so fucking fast and bent his wrist backward.

"What the fuck are you doing?!" I yelled.

He looked at me like I was crazy. "Don't you understand how Hollywood works?"

"I don't give a fuck. I'm not into any of that!" I said. "I'm into women. I wouldn't do that no matter what you could give me."

"Okay, then get out of my house," he said.

I got up and left, slamming the door shut. I walked home to Venice, the whole way thinking about how fucked up this town can be.

Between my experience and hearing all sorts of similar stories from my male and female friends, it was only natural that I went with Tonya on her casting calls to make sure no funny business went down. I didn't want Los Angeles to eat her up or to change her sweet, innocent personality because I had seen it happen to a few friends of mine. I knew there were plenty of dark paths that could derail her from her dream and took it upon myself to shield her from negative influences and to keep her focused on her goal, which was the upcoming Ms. Olympia.

As the contest got closer, Tonya and I spent hours and hours in the posing room, making sure each of her mandatory poses were dialed in, that she hit each of the poses at just the right angle to highlight her best body parts. She was an incredible student and took suggestions to heart, wanting only to get better. We also had an absolute blast working on her posing routine, selecting the perfect song for her personality, and making sure all her movements were choreographed so she hit her poses in sync with the music. Tonya was an incredible poser.

At the contest, Tonya killed it during the pre-judging event and made jaws drop during her posing routine. When she was called out in the top five, it gave me butterflies in my stomach as if I was the one onstage. I could not have been prouder of her and for what she had accomplished since moving to Los Angeles. It was truly an incredible feeling to be a part of someone else's journey to one of the biggest stages in the sport.

Tonya took fourth place and a prize check at the Ms. Olympia, beating out some notable names in the sport. We continued training after that show, and in 1989, Tonya took first place in the Ms. International, which was a huge deal.

As Tonya started making a name for herself in the sport, one of the top female bodybuilders at the time started trashing Tonya behind her back. When word had reached Tonya about what this woman was doing, she was devastated. Being from a small town where everyone knew one another and was respectful, Tonya could not understand why this was happening.

I thought this other female bodybuilder was jealous of Tonya and maybe even felt threatened by her on a professional level. Whatever the reason was, I was not going to let this person continue doing this to Tonya. I was dying to give her a piece of my mind, but the best I could do was get the number of a guy who was supposedly on her business team.

It took a few tries, but when I finally got this guy on the phone, I introduced myself and then started questioning him to try to confirm who trashed Tonya. The more we talked, the more my hot Italian temper came out, and I lashed into the guy, calling him everything under the sun. I ended that call by saying, "Fuck you and the horse you rode in on!"

I then slammed the phone down and that was that. Or so I thought.

As you can imagine, this whole episode weighed heavily on Tonya. She was discouraged. So, I booked her on some shoots for a couple of clothing lines. After that, she started doing photoshoots for the muscle magazines. Things were starting to take off for her.

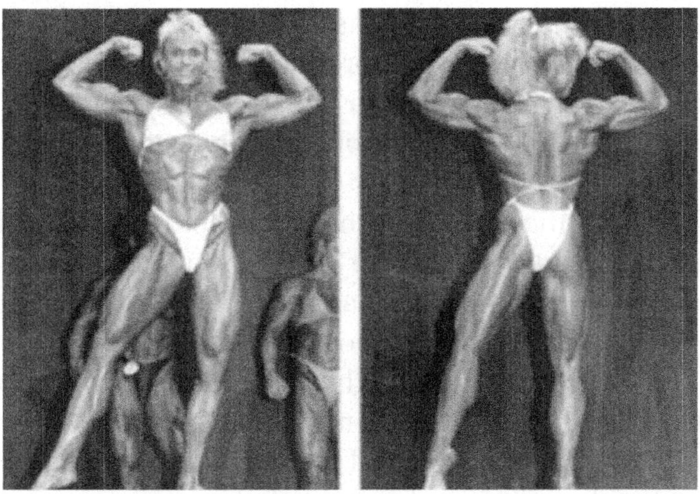

Around this time, I noticed that I started becoming a smaller part of her life. I think it was because we were at different stages in our lives. At the time, I was thirty, and she was twenty-one. Like any twenty-one-year-old, she wanted to go out with her girlfriends and have fun. I get it. I was exactly the same when I was her age.

Eventually, she moved out and got her own apartment. That ended our engagement. It broke my heart, but I understood. We went our separate ways and moved on with our lives. We were together for almost two years, and that's a time I will treasure forever.

After that, things went back to normal. I was auditioning and booking gigs, training clients, prepping contestants, and doing Gold's Gym openings. I wasn't the same guy as I was before because I couldn't lift the same amount of weight with the same intensity. I plateaued at a body weight that was a solid twenty pounds lighter, but all in all, things were good, and I was happy with my progress.

One day, I was at the gym working out when Derek came out of his office to tell me about a casting call he had just received. I hadn't seen Derek this excited since he approached me about auditioning for the Van Halen album cover, so I knew that whatever he was about to say was a big deal. And it sure was.

The call he got was from a producer looking for a host for a new fitness show that would air on ESPN. I knew ESPN was turning into a powerhouse cable channel and was aired all around the world, so I said, "Sign me up."

On the day of the audition, which was held at Gold's, the line of talented people trying out for the show wrapped around the block. I had thought the Van Halen casting call was huge, but this one brought in way more people.

As I inched up in line, I kept thinking about my life's journey, how I had been a student of fitness, and how I loved training others and watching them grow. I played out all my competitions in my head and everything I learned from my pec injury. I was thirty-one years old and thought I had something to share with the world.

I finally made it to the on-deck circle where I waited until a production assistant took me into the room, told me to introduce myself, and give a quick bio to the producer. After I did my spiel, the producer was smiling and sort of laughing at me. I wasn't sure how to take it, and then things got even weirder when the guy asked, "You don't know who I am, do you?"

I apologized that I didn't know him. That's when he reminded me.

"I'm the guy you said, 'Fuck you and the horse you rode in on' to and hung up on."

"Oh, shit," I thought as my hopes faded and my stomach knotted up. "Damn, I'll just turn around and leave now," I said, giving him a little smile.

"No, stay," the guy said, and laughed. "My name is John Traetta. Stick around. Your passion is pretty impressive."

He went on to tell me that he was a fan of mine as I was making my way up the ranks prior to my pec tear. John was a class act for not telling me to fuck off like I had told him. He didn't let his ego get the best of him, and I really respected him for giving me the chance to audition under the circumstances.

John was from New York and had a company, High Bar Productions (a nod to the sport of gymnastics), which specialized in the production, promotion, and sponsorship of national events and organizations. Over the years, he would do work for major brands, including the National Basketball Association, the United States Gymnastics Federation, the IFBB, and many others. He also managed a handful of select, elite athletes at one time or another, including Mary Lou Retton and Lee Haney.

John Traetta

During the audition, John had informed me that the show was a new concept called *BodyShaping*, which would feature male and female cohosts and a mix of high-profile guests working out on an exotic beach, wearing not much more than shorts or a bikini. I smiled and said that I was all in, then gave him my best audition.

I walked out of there thinking it went well and that John was a really cool guy. By then, I had grown pretty used to waiting to hear back after an audition, but this one was a little different, so I had done my best to try not to think about it.

Luckily, I didn't have to wait too long because Derek gave me the news that John had selected me and a few others to cohost *BodyShaping*. I was so excited to do a TV show on ESPN that I immediately called my parents and close friends to tell them the good news.

After the ink was dry on the contract, I confided in John that after my pec tear, I was worried that I'd be too small to book any serious bodybuilding or fitness gigs.

"The fact you didn't have as much muscle on you is the exact reason why we picked you," John laughed.

After hearing his words, I sat back and thought, "How crazy is that? My injury actually *helped* me!"

And so, as they say, when one door closes, another opens. I had gotten knocked down and I had gotten back up, but it took the help of a lot of people who I will never forget. I am truly grateful to everyone and could not have made it through that dark time without all their love and support.

As for Tonya, she was a true angel and a gift to me when I needed it most. I cannot thank her enough and was so excited for her when she won the 1991 Ms. International title without incident. What a champion she was!

A few weeks after I signed the contract for *BodyShaping*, John mailed me a plane ticket to Hawaii, where I'd meet the other cast and crew and get started. At that time, I had no idea just how huge the show would become, or how it would change my life forever. All I knew was that I was heading to one of my favorite places on earth and that the next "aloha" I would hear wouldn't be from an anesthesiologist before surgery but from a beautiful Hawaiian girl when I would get off the plane, just as that warm island air hit me.

This flight to Hawaii reminded me a lot of my flight as a young man when I left Ansonia to move to Fort Lauderdale. How that flight, like this flight, marked a big change in my life's journey. I had all the same feelings—excitement, curiosity, and that feeling of embarking on a new adventure where you're not sure exactly what is going to happen next, but you just believe that it's going to be incredible.

When my flight landed in Honolulu, there was a driver waiting to take me to the North Shore of Oahu and over to the Turtle Bay Resort. If you don't know, the locals call the hustle and bustle of Honolulu "Town" and the quiet side of the North Shore "Country," and nothing could be more accurate.

The North Shore is known as a mecca of its own: not for bodybuilding, of course, but for surfing. Much like a bodybuilder had to prove his or herself at Gold's Gym, surfers had been coming to the North Shore of Oahu to prove themselves for decades. As we headed through the town of Haleiwa and up the Kamehameha Highway toward the east side, I could really feel the energy of the place. The synergy of something that has a common purpose is a beautiful thing.

After driving for a while, we pulled into a large resort area, drove past a golf course, and arrived at the Turtle Bay Resort. It was an impressive place sitting on a beautiful piece of land that jutted out into the Pacific Ocean, with waves crashing all around it.

John greeted me and we headed off to meet the rest of the team in one of the conference rooms. As we walked down the hallway, I got butterflies in my stomach. These were the people who, like me, John had selected to carry out his vision for the show. I was about to meet my new teammates, and it reminded me of my first day of football practice in Ansonia as a kid.

Who would they be? What would they be like? Would we all get along? A lot of questions ran through my head. But when I rounded the corner and saw a small group of women and just one guy, a huge smile spread across my face.

"Oh, yeah," I thought, "this is going to be fun."

CHAPTER THIRTEEN

ESPN'S *BODYSHAPING*

"The most important thing is to try and inspire people so that they can be great in whatever they want to do."
—Kobe Bryant

TRAINING A CLIENT ONE-ON-ONE IN GOLD'S GYM and working with professional bodybuilders to get them ready for contests was one thing. Training and educating millions of people from all walks of life on a television show was an entirely different thing. From skinny people wanting to add muscle to obese people wanting to lose fat, as well as handicapped people and people recovering from surgery, educating the audience wasn't always easy. But from what I could tell, over our more-than-ten-year run, we inspired so many people to achieve their goals and live a healthier and happier lifestyle.

BodyShaping's story is a fascinating one that shows how creative people with similar ideas and passions seem to find each other. The law of attraction is a very real thing. But before *BodyShaping* was created, the landscape had shifted in a major way in order to make room for sports on television.

Back in 1979, the Entertainment and Sports Programming Network (ESPN) was founded during a shifting television landscape. Founders Bill Rasmussen, Scott Rasmussen, and Ed Eagan wanted to create a network that would show all types of sports all day long across all of America—a brand-new concept at the time.

The 1979 Men's NCAA Basketball Tournament was one of ESPN's first broadcasts. It was watched by 24.1 million people. The championship game, which featured legends Larry Bird and Earvin "Magic" Johnson, is still the highest-rated televised college basketball game in history.

On September 7, 1979, the first *SportsCenter* episode aired across the country. It lasted for thirty minutes and attracted an estimated 30,000 viewers. The first game that ESPN aired following that *SportsCenter* episode was the first game of the World Series for men's professional slow-pitch softball, between the Milwaukee Schlitz and the Kentucky Bourbons.

From there, ESPN picked up bigger and better sports, including deals with the major professional leagues, landing major college sports like football and basketball as well as lacrosse and gymnastics. All of this grew into what ESPN is today, one of the most famous and recognizable brands, the leader in televised sports, worth more than $50 billion.

Radio announcer Marty Glickman and gymnastics coach John Traetta formed High Bar Productions in 1979. Both men had been in the industry for years and witnessed the rise of sports on TV, so they were wise to team up and become a part of the revolution. They would go on to produce gymnastics and boxing programming for HBO during the 1980s.

It was in 1983 when John happened to be at Caesars Palace to produce a gymnastics show for HBO, where he just happened to pop into the Caesars World Cup, a high-level bodybuilding show at the time. The bodybuilding show also happened to be the focus of the movie *Pumping Iron II: The Women*. The film crew made the contest extra buzzworthy and even more of a spectacle to John.

MEET the Promoters
By Caroline McNamara
John Traetta Pulls It Off

It was at that event where John first met Cory Everson, who was one of the biggest stars of female bodybuilding and fitness at that time. John was so impressed and inspired by the bodybuilding contest and with Cory that he started to brainstorm how he could bring the fitness craze to the masses through ESPN.

It would take a few years to get it all together, but in 1988, John launched *BodyShaping* with Cory Everson, where she was the only host of the show. Within two years, though, John reimagined the show, deciding to replace Cory with a cast of a few hosts. And that's when John put out the casting call in Los Angeles and New York City, and by running ads in *USA Today* that started with, "Babe alert! Looking for talent for a fitness show…"

According to John, between in-person auditions and videos, he vetted over 6,000 people for the limited cast positions on the show. After sorting through all the self-tapes, headshots, auditions, and interviews, John selected Kiana Tom, Deprise Brescia, Mary Jean Traetta, Kendell Hogan, Jennifer Dempster, and me to be the core cast of the show, along with several others to fill in and help us out. Within a few weeks of finalizing the cast, John mailed all of us airplane tickets, and off to Hawaii we went.

Deprise Brescia, Kendell Hogan, Mary Jean Traetta, me, Jennifer Dempster, and Kiana Tom

Once in Hawaii, John didn't waste any time getting us on the set and in front of the cameras. We had a meet and greet one day and started filming the very next. John was a New Yorker through and through and wanted to get right at it without any rehearsals. Luckily, to John's credit, he assembled an initial core cast and crew that could rise to the challenge.

In choosing the cast, John was not only looking for pretty faces and amazing physiques but he was also looking for personality, enthusiasm, energy, and passion. A cast who could communicate and connect with viewers, think fast on their toes, and have the discipline to put in the hard work.

While writing this chapter, I got to hop on the phone and talk to several of the initial cast members who I had kept in touch with over the years. Hearing their voices and catching up was such an amazing experience. Like family, even though a lot of us hadn't talked in a long while, we picked right up where we had left off. They each shared their stories of how they ended up on *BodyShaping*.

Kiana Tom came in at five feet, six inches tall. She had an exotic look, with long black hair and a trim athletic body to compliment her boundless energy and drive.

Kiana Tom:

I was born in Hawaii on the island of Maui, to parents of Asian and Irish descent. As a kid, I fell in love with tennis, and it was my high school coach who suggested that I hit the weights to add some muscle to increase my power. Before that, I had never really worked out. I mean, I had always played sports, but lifting weights was something new. And I have to say that once I started to see that I could put muscle on my frame, I was hooked!

After high school, I went to college at UCLA, where I started picking up steady work as an athletic swimsuit model. I was majoring in broadcast journalism, thinking I wanted to be a news anchor, when I landed my first cover shot for Bicycling Magazine, which was a huge confidence boost, that maybe I could do this for my career.

Fast forward a little bit, and one day I got a call from my agent about "BodyShaping." It sounded like a cool gig, so I met with John here in Los Angeles. He explained the show and said all the right things, and before I knew it, I was negotiating my contract for that first season of the show. And I have to say, I was a pretty good negotiator because I made sure I got to have my very own hotel room without a roommate! But I did have to share it with the wardrobe department.

Deprise Brescia was five feet, seven inches tall, and had sparkling hazel eyes, Mediterranean looks, long brown hair, and a fit, model-perfect body to go along with her magnetic personality.

Deprise Bresica:

I was born in La Jolla, down in San Diego, and ended up going to college at California State University, Chico, where I majored in dance and theater. I started to do some modeling during college, and right when I graduated, I was fortunate enough to sign with one of the biggest modeling agencies, the Wilhelmina Modeling and Talent Agency.

I was getting a lot of work, but the funny thing was that I didn't hear about "BodyShaping" from my agent. It's more of a small world kind of story.

I was actually in Florida for the Venus International Swimwear pageant, and one of the judges happened to be Cory Everson. I ended up winning the show, and afterward, Cory said, "Hey, Deprise, you should audition for this fitness show called 'BodyShaping.'"

She explained the show to me and it sounded like a really cool thing to be a part of, so I went to the audition at Gold's Gym Venice. The line went around the block, and so when I got my offer letter from John, I was pretty excited!

Kendell Hogan came in at six feet, two inches tall, had an amazing smile, and a chiseled body to go with his fun-loving and cool demeanor.

Kendell Hogan:

I grew up in Chicago's South Side with my mom, and to be totally honest, I had zero aspirations to go into fitness as my career choice. I was the first in my family to graduate from college and wanted to use my degree to get a regular suit-and-tie type of thing. I got a job working at Lakeshore Athletic Club in Chicago just to get a free membership, but then one day, one of the aerobics instructors didn't show up to teach her class and my coworkers egged me on to substitute for it. I was outgoing enough, so I thought, why not? Next thing I knew, I became one of the regular aerobics instructors.

I had never really done anything like that and think I got my rhythm and moves from my mom, who always had music on in our house growing up. I remember she'd play so much Al Green.

Back then, I couldn't stand listening to him, but now he's one of my favorites.

Anyway, so check this out: One *day, I'm teaching a class when afterward, this guy walks up to me and introduces himself as John Traetta. He said, "I'm creating this fitness show and you should definitely audition for it." I couldn't tell if it was a scam or whatever, and so I kind of shrugged him off at first. John wasn't one to take no for an answer, and he got my phone number from the front desk and kept calling me up.*

It was my girlfriend at the time who told me that I should at least send in an audition tape. And so I learned a short step aerobics routine and mailed John the tape. I didn't think much of it until I got an offer from John to be on the show, but even then I was still hesitant because I had my college degree and felt like this was just a big departure from my game plan. But then when I told my mom about it, she was like, go for it, you can always fall back and use your degree if it doesn't work out. And so I went for it. Luckily it worked out.

Jennifer Dempster was five feet, six inches tall, had dark brown hair, olive skin, piercing eyes, and the lean, strong body of a dancer to go with her bubbly, sharp-witted personality.

Jennifer Dempster:

I grew up on Long Island just outside of New York City. I started dancing professionally at ten years old, touring as Clara in "The Nutcracker." At sixteen, I toured throughout Europe and the U.S., performing on Broadway with "The American Dance Machine," recreating hit musical numbers from Broadway shows. I wanted to go to college, so I left the tour and

went to Hofstra University, where I majored in communications. During college, I had the opportunity to work for SportsChannel (the other cable sports network) as a studio camera operator, stage manager, and teleprompter operator for "Sports Nightly" and the NHL.

Since I had stopped dancing and was in college just trying to figure life out, I ended up gaining about forty pounds. But through diet, behavior modification, and yes, by watching the ESPN lineup of fitness shows, including "BodyShaping" with Cory Everson, I got back in shape.

After that, I started to look for Broadway auditions, and one day, I was looking in a trade magazine called Backstage when I saw a casting for an untitled fitness show. And so I sent in an audition tape, dressed up like the women on Cory's show, which, by the way, also included a girl named Kiana at the time. Not long after that, I got the call to meet John, and he hired me to do a workout video as a kind of audition. And the next thing I know, I'm meeting my Step Aerobics teammate and new best friend, Kendell, on our connecting flight to Hawaii to shoot the new "BodyShaping." Crazy!

Mary Jean Traetta came in at five feet, six inches, had wavy blonde hair, and a great body to go with her easygoing and fun personality.

Mary Jean Traetta:

I grew up in the Bronx and met John because he was the lifeguard at the pool I used to go to in the summertime as a teenager. He had a great body and was always super nice and flirty with me. His favorite come-on was to make sure I had enough sunscreen on my back, which he was more than happy to apply on me. We hit it off, and when John started High Bar Productions, I got involved helping to produce gymnastic shows and hosting camps. Fast-forward a few years and when John came up with the idea for "BodyShaping," I thought, I love to work out—I should study up and get my personal trainer certification. So I did just that at the Aerobics & Fitness

Association of America. And the rest is history as they say!

Rick Valente is me, of course, and you know my story of how I got on the show. It started with my pec tear and losing some bulk, and ended with that crazy audition where John laughed at me for cussing him out on the phone because of the whole Tonya Knight issue. I've said it before and I'll say it again—I'm so grateful John was a true professional and looked past that phone call and offered me a spot on his show.

In addition to the cast, John assembled a great, tight crew. Doug Rutt was one of the show's directors. Sadly, Doug is no longer with us. Rest in peace. You were amazing!

Our lighting guy was a dude named Dave Jenkins. Our stage manager was Susan Hemond-Dent, who was an amazing athlete in her own right. (She crewed on the all-women's America's Cup sailing team in 1995.) And Larry Chong, who owned and operated West Coast Video Productions, provided all the cameras and technical gear for the show.

We also had an outstanding camera crew, which consisted of Kevin Murphy, Kirk Hepburn, and Jeff Muhlstock. Kevin was a freelance cameraman who John had hired to film another fitness show that John was producing called *Lee Haney's Championship Workout*. Kevin also filmed a *Flex* magazine show with Boyer Coe and did National Physique Committee filming for John. Long story short, within a few months after starting on the Lee Haney show, Kevin got a call from one of John's employees, who said they were going to start filming *BodyShaping* on ESPN and offered Kevin a job. He took it.

Our great cast and crew

BodyShaping was a thirty-minute fitness show where we educated the viewers about weight training, aerobics, and healthier lifestyle choices such as eating better, getting enough rest, and everything else fitness-related. With my bodybuilding background, I stepped into the role of the weightlifting instructor, while Kendell was the step and aerobics instructor. Kiana, Jennifer, Deprise, and Mary Jean all had a good grasp of both training methods and were able to do segments in either. Although I never taught any of the aerobics segments, it was common for me to be in the background as part of Kendell's class. Likewise, it was common for any of the others to be in a weightlifting segment to help demonstrate, teach, coach, or give me a spot.

One of the coolest things about *BodyShaping* was that each member of the cast wore a live mic, and so, at any given time, any of us could speak. This was a big change and set us apart from other popular fitness shows like *The Jack LaLanne Show* and *Getting Fit with Denise Austin*, where only one person spoke for the whole show. Our format allowed each of our individual voices and personalities to shine through, which let the audience get to know each of us on a personal level.

It also provided a lot of fun dynamics on set, including some friendly razzing and pushing each other to train harder, not to mention some flirting and joking. For example, on screen, Kiana and I hammed it up, putting a fun, flirtatious spin on our roles. We would wrap most shows with a little rivalry of who got the last word, and by far, she won out nearly every time by sneaking in a quick "aloha" as we would fade out. Our on-air chemistry made a lot of people think we were dating. We had a great working relationship, as well as a friendship that carries on to this day.

As for the actual filming of the show, it was not easy and often quite challenging. Now, look, I get it—it's a television fitness show. How hard can it be, right? I'm not saying we were laying bricks, working in a factory, or anything like that. I'm just saying that filming a show has its own difficulties and obstacles to overcome.

For starters, we shot three to five shows every single day for a total of seventy-two shows per year. Accounting for commercials, that meant we needed to have twenty-two minutes of solid content per show. But here's the deal—the show was totally unscripted, so the cast was completely responsible for filling every second of those twenty-two minutes with someone talking. This took a lot of improvising and quick thinking because, when you're on the air, a few seconds of nobody talking feels like an eternity. The pressure was on each of us to avoid that awkward silence and to keep the airwaves full of our voices. This was way easier said than done, even for a trained TV personality, let alone a bunch of fitness trainers and models with limited experience talking in front of the camera.

To make matters even more difficult, we also had to battle the elements—heat, humidity, and the scorching sun. This was because John chose to film at high-end resorts during their offseason, when the weather was hottest and there were fewer guests around. That meant we were shooting in Hawaii, Jamaica, or wherever in the dead middle of summer, during triple-digit temperatures and crazy humidity. And if the natural heat of the sun wasn't enough, our stage set was rigged with heavy-duty lighting, which turned the whole thing into a sauna that we had to work out in. I'd sweat so much that I'd drink gallons of water.

Tired after a day of filming in triple-digit temperatures

Not only were dehydration and fatigue big issues but so was getting sunburned. We all had our fair share of lobster-red skin, especially in the early days. One of the few exceptions to the heat was when we filmed in Jackson Hole, Wyoming, in November.

It was forty degrees out and super windy, which blew a few of the girls off their step more than once. If that wasn't enough, a horse (yes, a horse) had come by and knocked one of them off as well.

But the human brain and body are pretty resourceful, and we all learned to adapt over time. The learning curve, though, wasn't conquered as individuals. Nope. Instead, we all leaned on each other for support, guidance, and feedback so that we could improve our craft and elevate the show.

When we weren't filming, whether it was between shows or at the end of each day, the cast would get together to decompress and trade ideas about how to improve. Most of the time, we talked about different and better ways to present certain workouts and movements, as well as the on-set choreography, so we wouldn't get in each other's way and ruin a shot.

The transitions in and out of segments and various workouts were always something we worked on quite a bit as well—how to go from one thing to the next and make it look effortless. I was always so impressed with how everyone was receptive to learning and growing. I think a lot of that had to do with the fact that we all came from a sports or modeling background and always had coaches, trainers, or photographers giving us helpful insights.

When we'd be coaching each other, it wasn't a big deal, and no one had any ego in it. Of course, we would have disagreements and arguments, but they were short-lived, and we'd always move on right afterward, like a close-knit family.

The teamwork was not just limited to the cast but included the crew as well. It was such a unique show because, as Kevin the cameraman said, "The talent and the techs were in the same foxhole, and so we all bonded really quick."

I always remember how great the camera guys were, especially in the early days. As cameramen, they were essentially the eyes of the audience and therefore had that unique vantage to view us.

One day, Kevin saw that I was nervous and overthinking my delivery. So, he pulled me to the side and said, "Just pretend you're talking to me and not to millions of people watching the show."

From that point on, I tricked my brain into thinking I was only talking to one person.

Kevin did a lot of things that helped maintain a fun atmosphere while we were on set. I loved when he'd sing the old Dean Martin song "Volare" when I would walk onto the set, except he would sing it, "Valente, oh, oh, oh…"

We would all have a good laugh, and that would help set the tone for the day. Smart dude, that Kevin!

In turn, I shared my tips with the camera guys about which angles they should film us from to accentuate our muscles, as well as to help the viewers at home understand the correct form of a movement. This is a skill I honed over countless sessions in the posing room, getting ready for contests myself, and helping others. To present the human body in the most aesthetically pleasing way possible had been my number one concern for so long, and now that knowledge was paying off in a different way. All and all, it truly took a village. It was the group's collective efforts that led to the quality of the show.

On the individual side of things, I took it upon myself to work on my new craft. To do so, I watched a lot of tapes of the show to self-critique my performance, just like a boxer watches tapes of his fights to see where he could improve. The funny thing was that while we were filming, I thought I was a pretty smooth talker. But when I watched the videos, I thought, "Damn, I have some work to do!"

One of the first things I noticed that needed correcting was, like a lot of people, I used a lot of filler words and sounds like "uh" and "huh." Also, I was speaking improperly, saying things like, "Tuck in them elbows," instead of, "Tuck in your elbows."

I had to expand my vocabulary and my understanding of proper English so I could deliver my message in a way that would resonate not only with fitness buffs but with people from all walks of life. This was not an overnight process but something I had to work on over time. Awareness of the issue was the first step to becoming a better host of a fitness show for ESPN.

During that first season, I'd go to bed in my hotel room at the Turtle Bay Resort and lay my head on the pillow, thinking about the fact that I had barely graduated from high school. And now, I had the responsibility, along with the rest of the cast, to educate millions of people about proper and safe workout techniques. To inspire people from all backgrounds to get up off their couches and move their bodies. As a kid, I would have thought that this type of job was for someone who had gone to college. But, as it turned out, when you love something as much as I love bodybuilding, you read everything you can about the sport and you speak to everyone who has made a name for themselves. That's how you educate yourself. I created my own college and my own curriculum over the years.

Jim Bell

In order to be on this show, we all had to be certified as fitness trainers through the International Fitness Professional Association. It was run by a great guy by the name of Jim Bell. The books for those tests were so thick, but because I had been studying for what felt like was most of my life, I quickly absorbed the information and passed the tests.

While the passion we all had for fitness seemed to be translating to the camera, it was hard to tell what the ratings would be like once the show was released. Would our blood, sweat, and tears result in success? Would it attract viewers and advertisers? Would it resonate with people and get them off their butts? In short, the answer was a big, huge "yes!"

From the moment it first aired, *BodyShaping* was a hit. We

were all thrilled and excited that the hard work we put in was paying off. Receiving fan mail from the viewers meant the world to us and provided the drive and motivation to create the best fitness show possible. ESPN provided John with a bigger budget, enabling him to expand the scope of the show and bring on guests. It was in season two that John was able to hire supermodel Kathy Ireland to answer our fan mail on air.

Kathy Ireland was an absolute knockout who gained worldwide popularity by being in *Sports Illustrated*'s Swimsuit Issue for thirteen straight years, not to mention its super successful swimsuit calendar. Kathy had also been on the cover of all the big fashion magazines such as *Vogue, Mademoiselle*, and *Cosmopolitan.* Also, she had appeared on mainstream television shows such as *Melrose Place* and on the big screen in movies such as *Necessary Roughness*. In 1993, she started her own company, Kathy Ireland Worldwide, and over the years, she rolled out her own fashion and home lines.

Before Kathy joined *BodyShaping*, fans would mail letters (yes, actual letters on actual paper, not emails, tweets, or direct messages) and we'd each take turns answering a handful of the more on-point questions. I always loved reading the fan mail because the letters always included stories and thank-you notes about how we helped them out. When Kathy came on the show, we'd pick out the letters, write our answers to them, and then Kathy would read them on air. Having her on the show made it even more popular.

Around this time, John introduced new segments on the show and brought on other people to mix things up. One of my favorites was a guy who came to be known simply as Dr. Pete.

Dr. Pete Gratale

Dr. Pete, whose full name is Pete Gratale, was always into weight training, working out, and curious about how the body worked. That passion led him to graduate from chiropractic school in 1986 at the age of twenty-six. At that time, he had three specific goals: to have a successful chiropractic business by the time he was thirty; to own a Harley Davidson; and to be on a television fitness show. He would achieve all those goals, the last one coming directly through his relationship with John Traetta.

Dr. Pete first met John at a gym in New Jersey called the Health Spa II. He and his buddy Artie Grazioso worked out there, and so did John and Mary Jean. (Artie was another great guy who left us too soon. Artie, rest in peace. Thank you for the friendship!) Ultimately, Dr. Pete, Artie, and John became training partners, and it wasn't long until John asked Dr. Pete to make an appearance on *Lee Haney's Championship Workout.*

Lee Haney

If you don't know, Lee Haney was, and is, one of bodybuilding's biggest legends. He won the 1979 Mr. Teen America and ultimately went on to win eight Mr. Olympia titles between 1984 and 1991. Lee has always been an incredible ambassador of the sport, which is why President Bill Clinton appointed him to be the Chairman for the President's Council on Sports, Fitness, and Nutrition from 1999 to 2002.

As for Dr. Pete, John was thinking that he could add even more credibility to Lee's fitness show by having a medical professional on it to talk about the body, proper form, proper recovery, and how to avoid and deal with injuries. So, for Lee's show, John flew Dr. Pete out to Los Angeles, and they all met in Manhattan Beach. Long story short, they ended up filming the show, which ran for two seasons on ESPN, and introduced Dr. Pete to the world of television.

One of my favorite stories that Dr. Pete shared with me about Lee was the time Lee had just won his eighth Mr. Olympia title. After he won, they all went out to dinner to celebrate.

During dinner, Dr. Pete held up his champagne glass and offered a toast: "Lee, here is to you winning your eighth Mr. Olympia!"

Dr. Pete and Lee

Instead of clinking his glass, Lee said back to him, "That was a shitty toast, Dr. Pete. Let me do it." Lee then raised his glass and said, "Dr. Pete, here's to our friendship."

What a great guy and champion!

Once *BodyShaping* was off to the races, John called Dr. Pete and invited him to come check out the show. Dr. Pete accepted and John flew him and Artie down to Jamaica, the location of our set that year. When I was talking to Dr. Pete while writing this chapter, he told to me that he was kind of nervous meeting me because he thought that I might be threatened by having another dude on the show. That gave me a good laugh because the complete opposite was true. I was so excited to have another guy to train with that I welcomed Dr. Pete with open arms. Dr. Pete was a great fit and ended up working on *BodyShaping* for five years.

Over those years, Dr. Pete and I developed a great friendship, which extended beyond the show. One time, when we weren't filming *BodyShaping*, Dr. Pete came to Los Angeles so he and I could help Boyer Coe and Shawn Ray on a fitness show they were doing for *Flex* magazine. It was another show that John Traetta created and produced for ESPN. Dr. Pete stayed with me, and I somehow scored us floor seats for a Lakers game. Before the game, we went out for sushi and got to talking to a few girls, and before we knew it, we had drunk so much sake that we stayed with the girls and missed the entire game!

It was awesome having Dr. Pete on set because he would work his chiropractic magic on all of us, giving our sore bodies some much needed adjustments and treatment. He must have spent hours every week working on us, and he never charged any of us a dime. That's the kind of cast and crew we had. Everyone had each other's backs and did their part to keep things running full steam ahead.

Dr. Pete working his chiropractic magic on set

Living and working in close quarters with the cast and crew turned us into something like a platoon. Aside from the actual military, they say that restaurant kitchen staffs develop that kind of a tight bond. I think the same could be said for a television show, where everyone is living, working, and hanging out together for months at a time. The friendships we developed were strong and have lasted a lifetime.

In the beginning, I bunked with Kendell, while Jen and Deprise shared a room, and of course, Mary Jean and John had their room. The only person who had her own room was Kiana. In addition to filming the show, we also ate breakfast, lunch, and dinner together. We relaxed together. We blew off steam together.

One time, we were filming in Jamaica and went out for dinner and drinks at a spot called Rick's Cafe in Negril. Rick's Cafe was a famous spot known for its cliffs and cliff jumping. That night, after we got some liquid courage going, someone got the bright idea that we should all jump off the highest cliff into the water, which was a solid forty-foot drop.

Everyone was talking a big game until it was time to step up to the edge. Each one of us would take a look and think, "Damn, that's a long way down!"

Deprise went first, and when she looked down, she said, "I don't want to die in Jamaica!"

She tried to back out, but we egged her on. She swallowed her fear like a champ and launched herself off the rock and into the water below.

Artie, John, and Dr. Pete

Dr. Pete and Artie both busted their asses on the water, which felt like concrete from that high up. They could barely walk the next day and were sporting huge bruises. We all gave them a lot of shit for that, especially when they had to sit out that day's filming.

Jen also called in sick, but that's because she drank a little too much. When John asked us, "Where the hell is Jen?" we covered for her, telling him that she got food poisoning from the jerk chicken.

We also had a lot of fun on set to keep things light. When we filmed in Jackson Hole, Kirk got a hold of a jackalope, a stuffed rabbit with antlers glued onto its head. He would hide it on set for each show, and it became a fun game of who would eventually find it. Some shows we never saw it, but when we'd watch the tapes, someone would see the antlers sticking up in some obscure spot.

Stuff like that kept us loose and provided a good laugh during those long, tense days. For me, it also didn't hurt that we got to work with a great cast that featured beautiful fitness models. I never had any issues getting out of bed each morning and making it to the set no matter how early the call time was.

Me and Dr. Pete

Though we were having a blast, the fact remained that John had a show to run, and he ran a pretty strict set. There were times when he'd come down hard on someone for messing up (or for what he perceived as a mess up). Because I was the oldest cast member aside from Mary Jean, I'd take it upon myself to try to cheer them up.

Jen reminded me about this when she once broke a watch during filming. It was a watch that her father had given her, so she was pretty unhappy. Seeing her like that, I decided to run out and buy her a replacement watch. Jen told me how much that cheered her up. My mom used to do things like that all the time,

and I think that's where I got it from. I get a lot of enjoyment helping other people. For doing things like that, and because of my age, the cast members nicknamed me "Big Daddy."

Of the cast members, only Jen, Kendell, and I made it through the entire run of the show. From year to year, we were the ones that provided the familiar faces and the continuity. We also had some people leave the show and return years later. In one case, John agreed to let Deprise out of her contract because she had a scheduling conflict with a Michael Bay movie she was cast in. Years later, Jen went to bat for Deprise to get her back on the show, and John agreed to it. In fact, John had so much appreciation and respect for Deprise that he also hired her for another show he produced called *Co-ed Training*.

During the run of the show, the cast would change from one season to the next. Some of the other cast members that come to mind that I haven't mentioned yet are Carla Dunlap (a Ms. Olympia winner), Danielle Corley, Laurie Donnelly, Kimiko Tanaka, Keelin Curnuck, Sharlene Hawkes, Christian Boeving, Boyer Coe, Page Langton, and Linda Sobek. I know

I'm leaving a few people out, whether in front of or behind the camera, but just know we couldn't have done it without you!

Sadly, Linda Sobek was murdered on a photoshoot in 1995, which broke my heart. She was a talented Raiders cheerleader who still had her whole career ahead of her. Rest in peace, Linda. I will never forget you!

BodyShaping continued to grow in popularity to the point that it ran on ESPN three times per day, and once ESPN2 launched, it ran on there twice a day for a total of five airings per day. Crazy! At its height, we were getting over three million viewers per day, and it was the highest-rated fitness show in the world. It was so cool when the *SportsCenter* anchors like Craig Kilborn, Steve Levy, or Rich Eisen would wrap up the show with a shoutout to *BodyShaping*, which would air right after *SportsCenter*.

Not only was *BodyShaping* piped into houses throughout the United States, but it was broadcast all over the world as well. That kind of popularity led us to be featured on the covers of popular entertainment magazines such as *TV Guide* and on shows such as *Entertainment Tonight*, *Late Night with David Letterman*, and *The Tonight Show with Jay Leno*, to mention a few. On *Entertainment Tonight,* host John Tesh introduced a segment on *BodyShaping* by calling it "the number one fitness show in the world!"

In addition to the show, John Traetta was also a mastermind at cross-marketing. He started selling fitness equipment and videos to capitalize on *BodyShaping*'s great ratings. He created *The BodyShaping SuperPower Building System*, which consisted of four different types of supplements, an instructional video, and a nutritional guide that I did commercials for. He also sent us to QVC, the Home Shopping Network, trade shows, and anywhere else that sold stuff.

Once, Kendell and I did a tour of Target stores in the Midwest to promote *BodyShaping* and John's fitness products. The flyer for it had a picture of Kendell and me and read, "Come Rub Deltoids With Them—Tomorrow mingle with the stars of *BodyShaping*!"

I recall being in the studio one time at QVC pitching John's fitness products in front of the camera, and I could literally hear the phones ringing off the hook with everyone buying them up.

We always sold out.

With the show's popularity, my personal bookings increased during the parts of the year when we were not filming. I also got a big boost in my visibility in a way that I could not have imagined. One day, Kiana, Kendell, Jennifer, Mary Jean, and I were at a big fitness convention. The aim of the convention was to provide a venue in which all the stars in the fitness industry could interact with the public and meet up with sponsors as well as vendors. Everyone had their own booth, including us. We were giving away signed cast photos to the fans.

During our break, we took a walk to check out the other booths. As we were walking around, a guy came up behind me and grabbed me in a bear hug. When I turned around, I was blown away—it was fitness icon Jack LaLanne.

Jack LaLanne

"Jack LaLanne, I'm a big fan of yours," I told him, shaking his hand.

"I'm a fan of yours," he replied. "You're doing great!"

"Thank you, sir. That means a lot coming from you. Can I please get one of your pictures?" I asked.

"Absolutely," he said.

So, we walked over to his booth and he signed a photo for me. I still have it to this day.

Doing the show went beyond my wildest dreams. My initial goal of being a pro bodybuilder was to win the Mr. Olympia. Pop culture-wise, though, when I was a kid, scoring a cover shot was a fantasy of mine, so ending up on *BodyShaping* was insane. It took things into the stratosphere. The show benefited me in so many ways, paying huge dividends in the form of friendships and knowing that we helped people.

CHAPTER FOURTEEN

THAT RESTLESS FEELING

"The happiness of your life depends upon the quality of your thoughts."
—Marcus Aurelius

BEFORE *BODYSHAPING*, I HAD A DECENT number of fans. I had done so many magazine covers, commercials, and articles that featured me. I also booked that incredible gig to be on the Van Halen album cover. But my visibility pretty much stayed within the bodybuilding world. If I were at an airport and someone there happened to be into bodybuilding, they might approach me and say, "Hey, you were on the cover of that mag," which was super cool, of course. Otherwise, the general public didn't know me from the next guy, except for the fact that I looked like a bodybuilder.

Being on television around the world took what celebrity I had to another level. Not for the ego stroke, although that was always nice, but more for getting to meet people who the show had helped. Many times, a total stranger would come up to me and say, "Hey, you're Rick Valente from *BodyShaping*. I just wanted to say that I love the show! You guys helped me lose twenty pounds!" or "You inspired me to work out and now I feel great!" or "Waking up to work out with you guys makes my day so much better!"

Those conversations always ended with them thanking me for doing what we did, and me thanking them for tuning in and working out. It was such a rewarding feeling to hear people talk about what *BodyShaping* meant to them—to hear their success stories, to know that we were making a difference in people's lives and helping them reach their goals. That was the real payoff for doing the show.

BodyShaping also opened a lot of other doors for me through Derek Barton and my other reps, Jim Crabbe (William Morris

Endeavor) and Andy Wolf (World Class Sports), during the 1990s. In addition to doing more commercials, I also started to book television appearances.

Chuck Woolery wearing the Gold's Gym hat I gave him

One of my first was on *The Chuck Woolery Show.* I had trained Chuck at Gold's Gym. He made a name for himself hosting *Wheel of Fortune* and *Love Connection*, in addition to several other shows, and wanted to take a shot at doing a talk show. He invited me on one episode of his show, and we did a fun segment where I made him an egg-white omelet with tomatoes and spinach, and then I joined him with his other guests for a chat.

For that episode, the guests were Bruce Boxleitner (a famous actor of that time), Susan Anton (a famous singer and actress), Linda Blair (the famous actress who as a kid played the girl in *The Exorcist*), and Ronn Lucas (an amazing comedian and ventriloquist). At the end of the show, I presented Chuck with a Gold's Gym hat. This was my way of helping to market Gold's Gym. Chuck put the hat on while on the air. That show aired on November 29, 1991. Thank you, Chuck. It was a blast!

Me on "The Chuck Woolery Show"

I also made an appearance on the famous television show *Into the Night Starring Rick Dees*. Rick was a super famous radio show DJ who made the crossover to television with ease. On his show, I was part of a hilarious little bit where he was challenged to a game of "truth or dare."

Rick was asked, "Did you ever think of another woman while making love to your wife?"

"I'm not gonna talk about that," he answered.

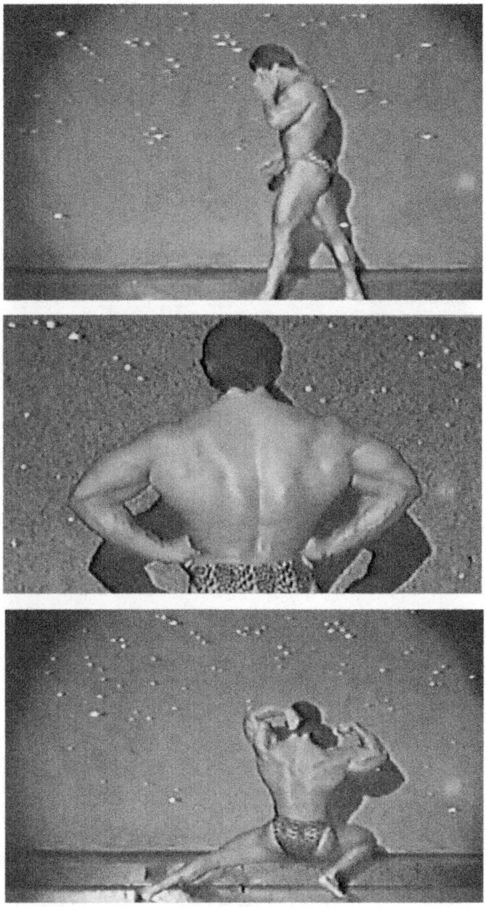

Me on Rick Dees's show

Rather than tell the truth and answer the question, he chose to take the dare. This meant he had to take off his clothes and do the show in just his "Fruit of the Looms." So, Rick went backstage and kept talking on his mic, and then I came out and did a little posing routine as if I were him.

I'll never forget how the crowd went nuts, clapping, laughing, and hooting. I loved being part of entertaining people. Thanks, Rick Dees!

I also did a spot on the long-running and super popular *Live with Regis and Kathie Lee* morning talk show (the same one that became *Live with Regis and Kelly* and is now *Live with Kelly and Mark*). On that day, the super famous, popular, and talented Suzanne Somers was guest-hosting. I did a posing routine on set that ended with me making my pecs dance up and down. Janice Ragain, Shawn Ray, Neal Spruce, and Tonya Knight also did their own routines.

Just before this show, I was on Suzanne's television special, and a few of us carried her on a throne above our heads like she was a queen. And so when I did the *Live with Regis and Kathie*

Lee show, Suzanne said, "There's my friend, Ricky!"

That made me feel so good. Thanks to everyone, and especially Suzanne for making that happen!

Unfortunately, both Regis and Suzanne have since passed away. These were two legends whose talent and charm will never be duplicated. They will forever be missed.

Tonya Knight

Neal Spruce

Suzanne Sommers, Kathie Lee, and Derek Barton

Derek Barton got me booked on another popular talk show of that era, *The Jenny Jones Show.* For that episode, Neal Spruce (a legend in the supplement world), Derek Barton, and I were on the show representing Gold's Gym and helping to bring fitness to the masses. We laughed, exercised, and educated the audience members and viewers. I even did a workout with Jenny. She was a lot of fun and made the audience laugh when she complimented my chest and demanded that I make my pecs dance up and down. Thanks, Jenny!

Another one of my favorite TV appearances was on *The Gregory Hines Show,* where I got to be on screen with my dear friend Gregory. His show ran for a few years in the late 1990s and featured himself playing a publishing agent who lost his wife and had to raise his twelve-year-old son alone. On the show, I played his personal trainer. I didn't have to act because I had trained Gregory for more than ten years, getting him in shape for movies and Broadway shows.

Me on "The Jenny Jones Show"

We had developed such a beautiful friendship, and the show was a true case of when art imitates life. Because of that, we had incredible chemistry on camera. It was fun being on set with one of the greats. What an amazing spirit Gregory had. Rest in peace, brother! I am so grateful for your friendship. Miss you!

Thank you so much, Derek, for working so damn hard and getting me booked on so many great TV shows. I had some of the most fun of my life when we were booking these gigs together.

Now, in addition to television shows, I was also fortunate to land some gigs for ESPN as a commentator for several bodybuilding shows that John Traetta produced. One that comes to mind is the 1991 NPC Men's Junior National Bodybuilding Championships in New Jersey, dubbed the Showdown at the Shore. My fellow commentators included the amazing and beautiful Carla Dunlap as well as Bob Papa, who was a great broadcaster and covered a lot of sports for ESPN and other networks. For that show, Carla did the interviewing, and Bob and I did the commentating.

Another is the 1993 Women's NPC Championship. I got to interview the competitors as they came off stage and was fortunate to interview Sue Price, the overall winner. She was so excited that she had won.

Commentating for the '91 Showdown at the Shore on ESPN

Working those shows and being that close to the action reminded me of what it felt like being onstage. What a rush!

Interviewing Sue Price after her '93 Women's NPC Championship win

I got to know Carla pretty well between her time on *BodyShaping* and our time doing the bodybuilding shows. I also knew of her from all her great successes as a bodybuilder, like her 1983 Ms. Olympia title that put her squarely on the map. What made her a champion onstage made her an amazing commentator and person to work with—hard work and dedication to the sport. She was a true professional and had a great personality. Anytime I heard that I was going to be working with her, I got super excited. What a blessing it was for me to cross paths with a legend like Carla. Thanks, Carla! And a big thanks to John and ESPN for these bodybuilding gigs!

Around this time, I met Dorian Yates at Gold's Gym. Dorian is a six-time Mr. Olympia, having won consecutively from 1992 to 1997. Needless to say, he's a major icon of bodybuilding, and meeting him at this time of my career was very inspiring to me.

One day, I was training at Gold's when Juliette Bergmann

and her boyfriend, Jim Lensveld, asked me if I'd be interested in doing a photoshoot at their home in the Netherlands. Juliette is a Dutch female bodybuilder who gained fame during the 1980s. She'd periodically train at Gold's Gym in the '90s with Jim and her sister, Liona.

Dorian Yates and me

Going to another country and doing a shoot sounded fun, so I said, "Hell yeah!"

They flew me and Bertil Fox to the town of Middelharnis. Like Juliette, Bertil had made a name for himself in the '80s and was still riding high. Being able to train with him was amazing. He was exceptionally strong. I believe he was getting ready for a competition. Anyway, Juliette and Jim put us up in their house, and they were very generous.

Jim and Juliette

The photoshoot they had planned was to be done in a barn. I was excited when I saw the woman who was going to model with me. She was Erika Mes, another successful and beautiful female bodybuilder. We shot some amazing photos together.

I did another photoshoot with Jim on a motorcycle on a country road. One of the pictures from that shoot turned out to be one of my all-time favorites. It's of me riding the motorcycle, flexing my right arm. Thank you, Jim and Juliette!

Rick Valente, Erika Mes

In the mid-'90s, the publisher and owner of *Muscle Mag,* Robert Kennedy, gave me an unheard-of eight-page profile in his magazine. I was so grateful for that.

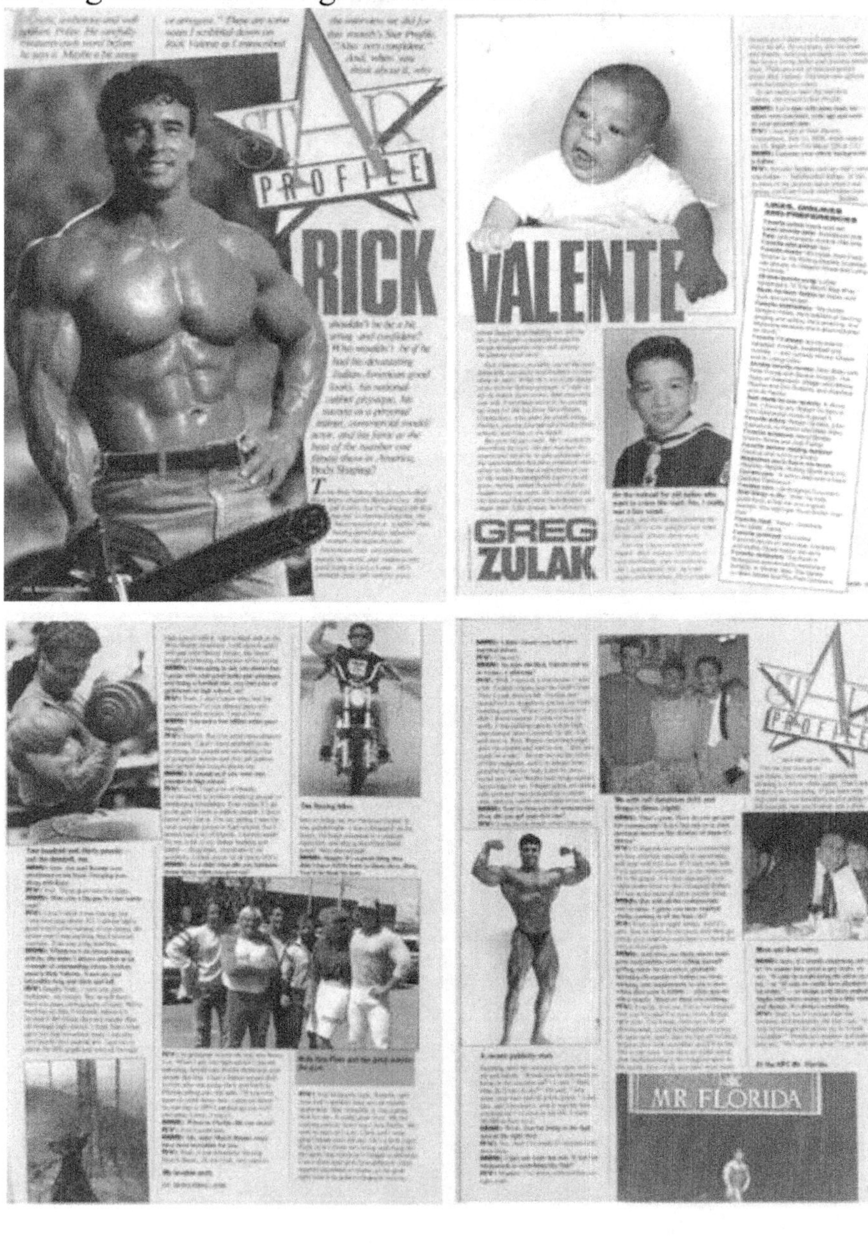

STAR PROFILE

RICK VALENTE

GREG ZULAK

STAR PROFILE

MR FLORIDA

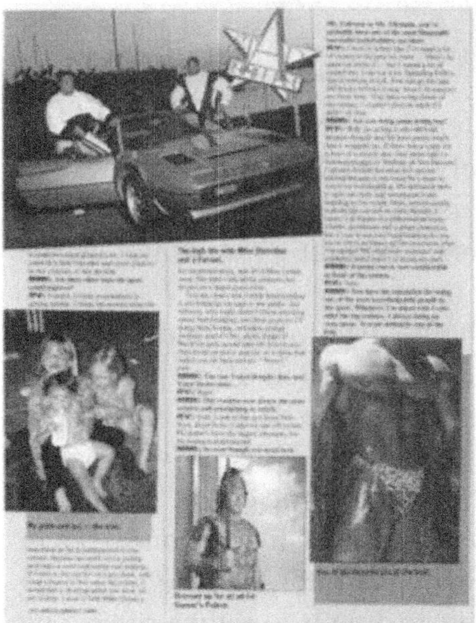

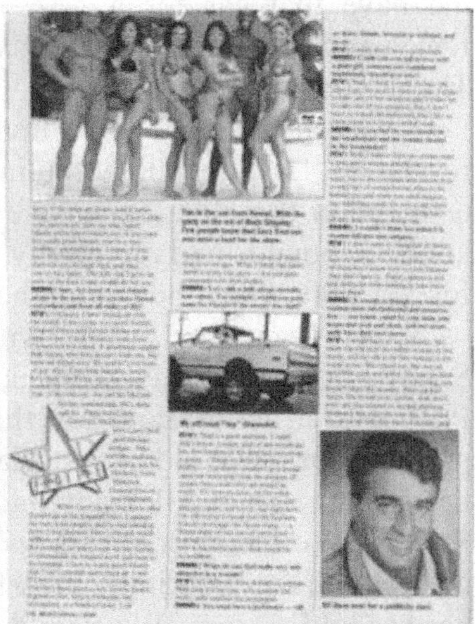

Robert was a very talented and creative man. He published other magazines, such as *Oxygen,* and was a *New York Times* bestselling author. I was fortunate to have developed a friendship with him. It broke my heart when I learned he had passed away. Rest in peace, Robert. You will be missed.

During the '90s, I'd have dinner on Christmas Eve at Joe Pytka's house. He had a hundred-year-old mansion designed by famous architect John DeLario and previously owned by Madonna. He was also a prolific car collector. One time, he got a Bentley but ran out of garage space for it, so he gave it to me! He let me have that car for a few years. Unbelievable. Thank you, Joe.

The Bentley Joe gave me

I was also lucky to be invited to parties at Joe's French restaurant, Bastide, which routinely made the list of the best, not to mention the most expensive restaurants in the country. Joe knew no bounds and reportedly once bought a rare white truffle for $35,000, which he put on the menu.

I once went to Bastide with the beautiful Sandy Taylor. Sandy is a very talented woman, having started off as a model, a Playmate, an actress, and now the head of the Brand Ambassador program for the Waldorf Astoria in Beverly Hills, as well as the head sommelier at Allegiant Stadium, the home of the Las Vegas Raiders. We met thirty years ago at a car wash and bonded over our passion for working out. A few days later, I started training her at Gold's Gym. We would go to lunch together often and loved hanging out with each other all day. We've remained friends to this day.

I'm so grateful to have met so many beautiful and talented women, just to name a few: Sandy Taylor, Monica Brant, Erika

Mes, Juliette Bergmann, Tonya Knight, Karen McDougal, Lisa Lyon, Kay Baxter Janice Ragain, Katie Arnoldi, Penny Price, Kiana Tom, Jennifer Dempster, Page Langton, Deprise Brescia, Mary Jean Traetta, and Lisa Lorio. We all did countless photoshoots, TV shows, commercials, and workouts together, and always had a blast in the process.

Sandy Taylor

Me and Sandy

Katie Arnoldi

Karen McDougal

Lisa Lorio

Penny Price

Monica Brant (left) and me

Mary Jean Traetta

Erika Mes

Page Langton and Tsianina Joelson

The most
beautiful
couple at the
banquet? Rick
Valente and
Tonya Knight.
Nordic

121
SHARKSKIN
BASEBALL JERSEY
Logo Embroidered
Black / Green
M / L / XL
11
ELVET LADIES
OODED JACKET
eopard / Dalmatian
/ M / L

Rick & Kiana:

rick valente & kiana tom:

HOW HAS BECOMING A TV CELEBRITY CHANGED YOUR PRIVATE LIVES?

WHAT IS IT LIKE ON THE SET OF BODYSHAPING BETWEEN TAKES?

BODYSHAPING'S Kiana Tom and Rick Valente talk to Powerhouse Magazine about some things you've been wanting to know.

This Q&A serves as the introductory feature that answers your questions about everything from diet and fitness, beauty and fashion, career and personal, to just plain curious queries from admiring fans. You name it, this is your column. Submit your questions for Kiana or Rick in writing to Powerhouse Magazine by mail or FAX. Then, wait for your next issue to arrive in the mail, or pick it up on the newsstand!

FITNESS

Sports And Games

CHAMPIONS

BODYSHAPING'S

One ON One

with rick valente

TV's #1 Rated Fitness Show

Rick Valente and Laurie Donnelly, BodyShaping cast members

The Star-Making Machine:

When your effort to rise to the top of one highly specialized field inadvertently propels you to celebrity status in a much broader category, don't ask questions. Just thank the academy.

What an amazing time that was. A street kid from the blue-collar factory town of Ansonia, Connecticut, and here I was hopping on private jets. I used to look up to drug dealers and motorcycle gangsters, and now I was hanging out with A-list celebrities and world-class athletes. I lost so many friends to drugs and violence because they had no hope, and now my circle of friends saw nothing but opportunity in front of them. I never lost sight of where I came from, so I had to keep pinching myself to make sure I wasn't dreaming.

What a great ride those years were, but like everything in life, nothing lasts forever.

When we'd received word that the ninth season of *BodyShaping* would be the last, I was sad to see the show end, but I looked forward to the next chapter of my life. We all wanted to make it one of the best seasons ever and help as many people as we could.

I was thankful for the incredible relationships I had with the cast and crew. So many of the folks from *BodyShaping* went on to continue their careers and excel in life.

Kiana left *BodyShaping* in 1995 and went on to be the face of her own successful fitness show, *Flex Appeal*. She also had a successful run as an actress, scoring some major roles in big films such as *Universal Soldier: The Return* with Jean-Claude Van Damme. *Playboy* had always courted her to do a centerfold spread, and just before settling down, Kiana agreed to bare all, appearing in the May 2002 edition. She now has an awesome athletic family and is very active in the fitness world, and she loves to write cookbooks. Kiana always had that amazing entrepreneurial spirit, and she isn't slowing down anytime soon.

When we spoke recently, Kiana said: "We had such amazing chemistry working together on *BodyShaping*! So many fun times hosting the shows and motivating millions! Such a blast working together, Rick!"

And I feel the exact same way about her. Thank you, Kiana!

Deprise went on to continue her acting career, landing roles in all sorts of movies, television shows, and nationally televised commercials. She seemed to find her true calling after *BodyShaping* as a mixed medium artist, creating incredible paintings and other styles of artwork. She now has her very own gallery, "The Deprise Brescia Art Gallery," in Paso Robles, California, on the Central Coast, and is critically renowned, having grown a loyal fan base.

Deprise pretty much captured my exact feelings when she said, "To know that we had a positive impact on someone's life that inspired them to take care of themselves or get over something in their life is an amazing feeling. By far, that and the friendships that we developed were the biggest gifts of the show."

Exactly! Thanks, Deprise, for everything!

Jennifer continued her TV career, hosting on a variety of networks including QVC's Q2, Fine Living, and RSN. She is now a contributor on CBS New York and is still acting in movies and commercials. She currently coproduces the podcast *Fowler, Who You Got?*

In the late '90s, Jennifer met her husband, ESPN/ABC sportscaster Chris Fowler, at an ESPN Christmas party. Chris is an amazing host and commentator for college football and Grand Slam tennis. He also happens to be a kind and generous guy who I got to know over the years. I was lucky enough to get invited to Jen and Chris's wedding. Kendell and Deprise also attended. We all had an absolute blast. All because of *BodyShaping*.

To this day, Jen and Deprise are just like sisters, and Jen and Kendell are still best friends. How cool is that?

"Nowadays, you can find any type of fitness show you want to on the internet," Jen said, "but back then, *BodyShaping* was really the only thing like it. I am so grateful to have been part of something so unique and special. And to have worked with and made lifelong, deep friendships with such inspiring and wonderful people. In addition, Kendell, Rick, and I made it all the way through. What a run we had!"

It was such an honor for me to work with Jen, Kendell, and everyone else on *BodyShaping*, developing lifelong, incredible friendships. Thanks, Jen, I'm so grateful for the time we spent together and that we are still friends!

Kendell took his momentum from *BodyShaping* and became a highly sought-after fitness presenter and instructor, doing tours around the country to teach other fitness professionals. From there, Kendell went on to his current position at Crunch Fitness as its West Coast Director of Fitness, overseeing more than one hundred gyms. He also runs his own consulting business to help celebrities and others produce their fitness videos and shows. Among many A-list clients, he counts Jillian Michaels (creator and host of the super popular show *The Biggest Loser* and others) as one of his favorite success stories. Kendell is still in amazing shape and continues to inspire so many people to reach their fitness goals to this day. Rock on, Kendell!

"We all grew up so much on the show," Kendell said. "We'd take care of each other, getting up each and every day to do a tough-ass job. And we kicked ass doing it, making some good, educational, entertaining TV!"

Well said, Kendell. I feel the same way, brother!

Once *BodyShaping* was over, Dr. Pete settled into his chiropractic practice in Teaneck, New Jersey. He has now been in practice for thirty-three years and is married with two teenage kids. His daughter is excelling at ballet, and his son in basketball. Dr. Pete credits *BodyShaping* and all the visibility and publicity he got from the show with helping make his business so successful.

"The show was like family and we were like brothers," Dr. Pete told me. "We'd get done with the day and unwind, smoke a cigar, and talk about all of life's craziness. You know, to this day, people still talk to me about *BodyShaping*. It has always been one of the coolest things I've ever been a part of. It was huge!"

As for the camera crew, Kevin, Jeff, and Kirk, they were the best at what they did. After *BodyShaping,* Kevin went on to do hundreds of shows and sporting events, including the Olympics. Kirk went on to film all sorts of shows, specializing in big events like the NBA All-Star game and the Oscars.

Likewise, Jeff went on to film countless television shows and movies, including some of the biggest blockbusters such as *Captain America: The First Avenger*. In fact, in 2020, Jeff was nominated for camera operator of the year by the Society of Camera Operators—a huge deal. Congrats, Jeff!

Each of these guys has huge filmographies on IMDb. And to this day, Kevin and Jeff remain best friends.

You may remember my friend Lyle Alzado. It was Lyle who took me to the Raiders' physician when I tore my pec. He was an amazing football player whose talent is still unmatched today. Throughout his career, he accomplished nearly a thousand tackles, 112.5 sacks, and 24 forced fumbles in 196 games, according to ESPN. He was also named to the All-Pro team three times and was a two-time Pro Bowl selection. He also appeared in nine movies throughout his career, including the horror movie *Destroyer* and the comedy *Who's Harry Crumb?* He also was a boxer who held an exhibition match with Muhammad Ali in 1979.

Lyle Alzado

He was a standup guy and a good friend to me and many others at Gold's Gym. So, you can imagine our dismay in 1991 when we learned that Lyle was battling a brain tumor. He was a tough son of a bitch, and we thought that if anyone could pull through, it would be him. Sadly, it wasn't to be. By the spring of 1992, we knew he wasn't going to make it.

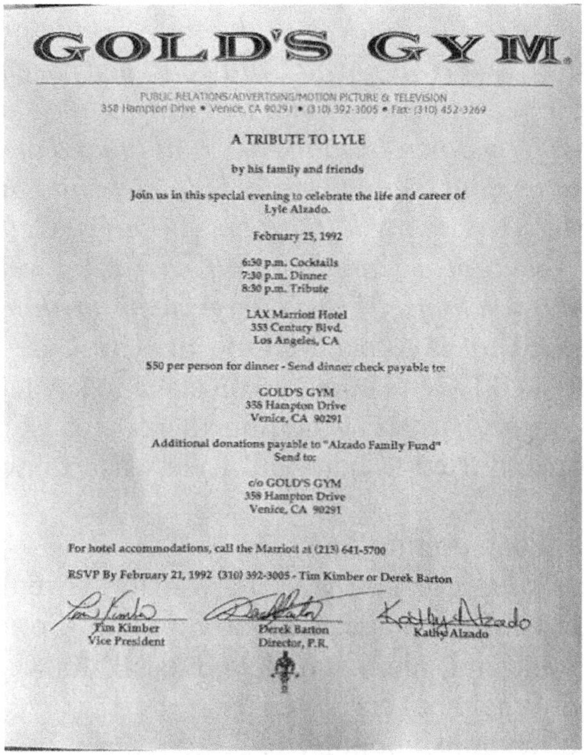

GOLD'S GYM

PUBLIC RELATIONS/ADVERTISING/MOTION PICTURE & TELEVISION
358 Hampton Drive • Venice, CA 90291 • (310) 392-3005 • Fax: (310) 452-3269

A TRIBUTE TO LYLE

by his family and friends

Join us in this special evening to celebrate the life and career of
Lyle Alzado.

February 25, 1992

6:30 p.m. Cocktails
7:30 p.m. Dinner
8:30 p.m. Tribute

LAX Marriott Hotel
353 Century Blvd.
Los Angeles, CA

$50 per person for dinner - Send dinner check payable to:

GOLD'S GYM
358 Hampton Drive
Venice, CA 90291

Additional donations payable to "Alzado Family Fund"
Send to:

c/o GOLD'S GYM
358 Hampton Drive
Venice, CA 90291

For hotel accommodations, call the Marriott at (213) 641-5700

RSVP By February 21, 1992 (310) 392-3005 - Tim Kimber or Derek Barton

Tim Kimber
Vice President

Derek Barton
Director, P.R.

Kathy Alzado

Derek Barton had arranged to stage a tribute for Lyle. As I was preparing to write my thoughts on Lyle, I asked Derek about what he put together in honor of Lyle. Here's what he recalled from the tribute and from Lyle's eventual funeral:

Since I was very close to Lyle, I arranged that tribute at the LAX Marriott before he died. I was the MC. I had Pete, Ed, and Tim's full support, and they paid for everything. We called all of Lyle's family and friends to be there, as well as his doctor, who was taking good care of Lyle. At one table I had O.J. Simpson, Marcus Allen, Jeff Goldblum, and Howie Long. I put my brother Jack and his wife there as well. He was in awe.

Anyway, as the MC for that evening tribute, I would bring up various people to say a few words about Lyle. It was very moving. I believe Lyle was the last to come up and thank us all. As you recall, he was frail but appreciative to all who were there.

When Lyle passed, Tim and I flew to Oregon along with Al

Davis, the owner of the Raiders at the time. At the grave site, it was just us three and Lyle's wife Cathy and her parents, and the minister. There was a magical moment during the service when two love doves flew down from the sky and landed on his casket. They looked at us, and then the male, Lyle, flew into the heavens.

And I looked over to my left at Tim, Al Davis, Cathy, and the parents, and they got a tear. They all saw it as well. And the minister was beside himself. He'd never seen anything like that.

I was blessed to have been sitting next to Lyle that night. When Derek asked Lyle to come up on stage to say a few words, Lyle was having a hard time getting there because he was so weak. I got up and tried to help, but Lyle wasn't having any of it.

"No, Rick. I can do this," he said.

"God bless you, bro. You're still a warrior," I replied.

Lyle made it to the stage without any help. From there, he thanked everyone and said that he loved us all. As we listened to him, we couldn't help but cry. Even to this day, I often think about Lyle.

A giant bronze bust of Lyle is on the wall in the third room at Gold's. Pete, Tim, and Derek put it up shortly after he passed away. When I'm at the gym, I love looking up at it. Lyle, I'll never forget you.

There's someone else I'd like to mention who was a fixture at Gold's Gym throughout the '80s and into the '90s: Don Ross. Don was a pro bodybuilder, wrestler, trainer, and writer who became well known during the 1970s.

By the time I had arrived at Gold's in 1982, Don was like the unofficial mayor of Gold's

Gym. He was always in there, and if he was in there, you could hear him. Don was very personable and would answer any question you had. But what made him so memorable was that when he spoke, it was like he was doing a wrestling promo.

For instance, I heard someone ask him if red meat was bad for you. Don answered with such fervor that I never forgot it. When he spoke to you, he was entirely focused on you—his eyes would get wide, and he'd be making these big gestures with his hands.

"Are you kidding? Red meat's the best thing for you!" he said. "When you eat a steak, your whole body sucks up all that protein, like it's thirsting for it. Your body loves beef protein and gets more out it than chicken, fish, or any of that stuff. Yes, eat red meat. Eat a lot of red meat. Make THAT your steroid."

Don Ross and me

I always appreciated his enthusiasm and deep knowledge of health. Unfortunately, Don passed away in 1995. It hit all of us really hard. Rest in peace, Don. I'll always be grateful for your friendship and all the things you did for me.

Losing two legendary friends in such a short period of time reminded me how fleeting life can be and that you must make it a point to appreciate every minute of it.

As the late '90s wore on, I felt a shift in myself. I was constantly thinking about all the people I had lost during that time. I became very depressed and unhappy because I kept thinking about things that were depressing. What we think about becomes our reality.

More and more I was being visited by an old enemy. And that

enemy came in the form of an itchy, restless feeling that I hadn't felt since I was a teenager back in Ansonia. Back when I would run around with my friends burning off angst and extra energy by partying and getting into fights. Only this time around, I was pushing toward my fortieth birthday and was too old to be feeling restless and acting destructively.

It had been a long time since I heard that little voice in my head that was drawing me to destructive behaviors. I was caught up in my negative feelings, not aware of the consequences of life. I wasn't thinking about how at any moment, something could happen that would force me to be fully present.

It was like I had gone back to that desensitized feeling. All the loss I had dealt with made me turn inward and act destructively. It should have made me feel more present, like at any moment, I could be the one dead, too—but it just pushed me to keep following that voice in my head.

It was the combination of all these things that made me finally call Bobby LeVine and move down to Fort Lauderdale. That was back in 1978, and now it was late 1998 when I said to myself, "There's got to be more to life than this."

My gut was telling me that it was time to switch things up. And if my gut wasn't talking loud enough, my actions were speaking volumes.

Since I no longer had to work every day, I didn't have much in the way of responsibilities, kind of like a teenager. So, what did I do? I started hanging out with my actor friends, partying all night, and doing cocaine. Needless to say, when you're living this lifestyle, it's going bite you in the ass when you least expect it, and that's exactly what happened next.

It was a Friday night in 1998, and I was hanging out with my friend David at a strip club he owned near LAX. That night, I got to talking to a couple of women, and at closing time, they asked me if I would drive them home. So, like any gentleman would have done, I said, "Yes, of course."

After the last call lights flashed on, the two girls and I walked out of the club and got into my black Fleetwood Cadillac. Before we drove off, we lit up a big joint, and I put on some music to match the mood. We were laughing, joking, and carrying on, and I thought, "Damn, this is going to be a great night."

We were driving down the street, and before I knew it, I heard the *whoop whoop!* of a squad car and saw the red and blue lights flashing behind me.

"Oh, fuck," I thought to myself.

I pulled my car over and my mind started racing, trying to figure out how I could talk my way out of this. My Caddy was filled with pot smoke, and did I mention that I had a few tabs of ecstasy and a vial of cocaine in my pocket, as well as an unregistered 9mm handgun tucked in my waistline? Yeah, this was a really fucked-up spot I put myself in.

You're probably wondering why I was carrying a gun. Well, that story highlights one of the downsides of being on television. Along with all the love you get when you're on TV, you also get some hate. At a certain point, I was receiving death threats from disturbed individuals. I knew from growing up in the street that you can't ignore this shit, because sometimes it's for real. So, to protect myself, I started carrying a gun.

As I sat in my Cadillac, I knew the female cop walking toward me wouldn't have any sympathy for my situation. As soon as I rolled my window down, I knew it was over. A cloud of pot smoke rose out of the car. You didn't have to be a bloodhound to know what was going on.

"Get out of the car and put your hands on the hood," the cop said.

I was caught red-handed, and I knew it. So, I followed her order and got out of my car and made my way up to the hood. As I did so, I noticed another squad car pulling up. I was so fucked.

It seemed like my whole life flashed in front of me. I was high and had an unregistered gun on me and a pocketful of drugs. This was not going to end well. I'd be in all the magazines, news shows, and probably my hometown newspaper as the TV fitness guy on ESPN who got arrested on his way home from the strip club. As tough as it was to earn the pride of my father and family and to get to where I was in life, I had just thrown it all away. What a huge embarrassment I'd be to my parents and to everyone else who helped me along the way. Worst of all, I'd be an embarrassment to myself.

I cringed, thinking to myself, "What the fuck are you doing, Ricky?"

And then a miracle happened.

The other cop who pulled up shined his flashlight right in my face.

"Hey, Rick Valente. I'm a big fan," he said. "Where you headed to?"

"Just down the street, sir," I said as respectfully as possible.

That cop then took the other cop to the side, and then he returned to me after they talked for a minute.

"Get back in your car and I'll follow you home to make sure you get there safe," he said.

"Yes, sir. Thank you, sir," is all I said.

I got back in my Caddy, and I'd never driven so slow and carefully in my whole life. After that stressful situation, the night was over as far as I was concerned. I took the women home and then went back to my place.

It was the next morning when the seriousness of what happened really started to sink in. I realized that I was privileged way beyond what I deserved, and not everyone is as fortunate when they screw up. But I have to say, what a fucking wake-up call it turned out to be. Since then, I have not done cocaine or any hard drugs ever again. I am forever grateful for what you did, Mr. Officer!

It was time for me to reassess the direction my life was going. I had to be honest with myself, which is not easy to do. You have to admit to yourself that you're doing things the wrong way. In other words, you have to set your ego aside and look at yourself as objectively as possible. It's a challenge to change your thoughts and behavior.

More than anything, it came down to needing something to focus on. Something that inspired me, that made me wake up and feel excited, like the way bodybuilding had done when I was a kid. But what would that be? Would it be another passion? I wasn't sure what the answers were. The only thing I knew was that I had self-destructive tendencies, and if I didn't have something positive to put my energy into, my life was going to continue in the wrong direction.

And so, for the first time in a really long time, I stepped into a bookstore.

CHAPTER FIFTEEN

MASTERING THE MIND

"If you correct your mind, the rest of your life will fall into place."
—Lao Tzu

WHAT IS ADULTHOOD ALL ABOUT? I think the answer to that might depend on who you ask. I mean, when you're a kid, you look up to your parents and other adults and think, "Man, once I'm that old, I'll have life all figured out." But once you're actually an adult, you kind of think, "Wait, this isn't exactly what I was expecting."

Not that adulthood is a letdown or anything like that. The same challenges you face as a kid, you face as an adult, but in a different way. Here I was, forty years old, still trying to discover myself. Still wondering, still searching for that ultimate sweet spot in life. And in doing so, I was still pulled to the dark side, making bad choices when I got bored.

By this time in my life, I had been blessed to know a lot of different people from all walks of life, from janitors to billionaires and everyone in between. The thing I noticed about money was that it did not appear to make people happy. No matter how many material things they had, they never seemed content. I found that amazing and came to the realization that while money could solve a lot of problems, it could not buy you happiness. So the question became, what *could* bring you happiness?

I had been doing *BodyShaping* for the better part of a decade, and I started asking myself, what am I going to do once the show is done? I knew I wanted to change things up. Find a new passion, a new project, a new idea to explore. Something that would make me happy and proud. Looking back on it, I really do think life is a lot like training your muscles. If you do the same workout over and over, your muscles will get used to it and stop responding. You have to keep them guessing. Same goes for life.

I knew *BodyShaping* wasn't going to last forever. Times change, and in show business, the only constant is that there is no constant. It's unpredictable. Just like life. As crazy as life can be, I always felt better about myself when I was making proactive decisions rather than reacting to whatever curveball life threw at me.

I always knew there was a powerful connection between the mind, body, and spirit, but I was also aware that I didn't truly know that much about it. I had used my mind as a bodybuilder to learn all about the body, different training techniques, nutrition, posing, and rest. And of course, I used my mind for the discipline and all the tricks it takes to get your body to push through the pain, to push through the plateaus, to lift more weight, to get more reps. And yes, I had used my mind while training others in the gym and on *BodyShaping*. But I had never taken the time to just focus on training my mind and my thoughts. There's a saying that the teacher appears when the student is ready to learn. That was me. I was ready to learn.

This curiosity led me to challenge myself to exercise my mind, to work it out like I had worked on my body all those years ago. To figure out why I made the decisions I made. Instead of me judging others or having others judging me, I was ready to be the judge of myself.

Like training the body, there's no one-size-fits-all when it comes to the mind. You could take classes or go see a therapist. I chose to do my studies with books, just like when I was a kid and ordered the Charles Atlas book to start bodybuilding. Only now, I was setting off to strengthen my mind.

As I was getting ready to go on this journey, I reflected—what was it about bodybuilding that made me love it so much? My bodybuilding journey started with a problem and a need. The problem was that in my neighborhood, weak people got beat up, and therefore I needed to get strong. Once I started training in my basement gym, I began to see results. And when I saw those results, it fueled my burning passion even more.

There happened to be another benefit of spending time in the gym apart from just building muscle. If I was in the gym focusing on my body, then that meant that I was not out on the street getting into trouble. Put more generally, if I was focusing on something positive, I was not doing something negative. That felt good to me. You see what I'm getting at? If I gave my mind something positive to focus on, that meant it would not be focused on negative shit, like the anxiety and paranoia from my bad choices.

It was a hot summer day when I opened the door to the Barnes & Noble bookstore in Marina del Rey. The air conditioning felt nice, and the smell of books hit my nose.

"How are you doing?" a cute clerk asked as I walked in. "Can I help you find anything in particular?"

"Actually, yes," I said. "Can you point me to some books that deal with the mind and human behavior?"

I followed her to the nonfiction area, where she pointed out a few sections where I could find everything I needed. Those sections were philosophy, psychology, and self-help. There was no shortage of books to choose from. My only challenge was where to start.

Fortunately, my Barnes & Noble tour guide suggested a few to begin with, and then she let me be. As I flipped through them and looked around at all the others, I couldn't help but see the comparison between the bookstore and the gym. In the gym, there's all sorts of free weights, benches, and machines to work any muscle from any angle. Likewise, in the bookstore, there was every type of book that could help you work out any part of your mind, from any and every angle.

That day, I bought a few books to get me started. Titles like *The Power of Now*, *The Alchemist*, and *The Power of Positive Thinking*, just to name a few.

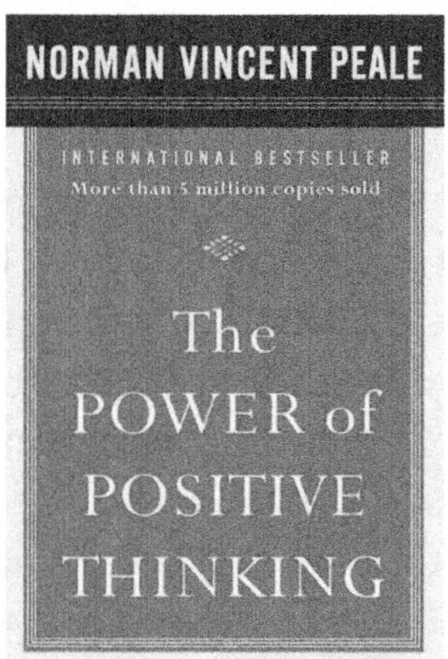

I had my work cut out for me, but I felt excited. I had that burning feeling in my stomach once again. Was it the same feeling that I had when I fell in love with bodybuilding? Not exactly. At least not yet. Instead, it was more like the feeling I got when I was nineteen years old and my parents took me to the airport to get on the plane to move to Fort Lauderdale. Just like that adventure, I was about to go on a wild ride.

Okay, look, I'm not going to repeat everything I've learned from the books I've read. The lessons they've taught me have filtered into this book, from the very first chapter all the way through to the end. That said, here are a few of my favorite lessons that I've learned:

1) The mind is far more powerful than any muscle.

2) If you can control your thoughts, you can do anything.

3) Thoughts create your feelings, and your feelings create your actions.

4) Live in the moment.

5) Nothing is guaranteed, not even tomorrow, so do it now.

6) In the face of adversity, the one thing you can control is how you respond to it.

7) You get back what you give.

8) The law of attraction is real. Relationships truly are everything.

9) Be generous, be humble, and be compassionate.

10) Be grateful for every day you wake up because every day is a gift.

There are of course countless others, but these are the ones I keep coming back to when I find myself feeling challenged.

Over the years, studying the mind and human behavior has become a passion of mine. It's helped me navigate this ever-changing world. More importantly, it's helped me navigate myself. In a way, it reminds of karate—how you could use your opponent's energy and movement against them. When someone runs at you, you can simply step to the side and use their momentum to shove them into a wall, using very little of your own energy (or a mirror, like I once had to do to a wacko stalker guy at Gold's Gym).

To be able to understand and exercise your subconscious mind is a powerful thing. For example, if something happens and I find myself in an angry and negative place, I challenge myself to think of three things I'm grateful for, no matter how big or small, and it always calms me down.

First, I'm grateful I woke up. I'm blessed to have another day. Second, remembering to live in the moment and enjoy whatever

I'm doing. Third, I'm so happy about the relationships I have. Doing this dissolves the anger and negativity right away. Same goes if I'm overthinking something and mind-fucking myself.

It's difficult for your brain to be angry and happy at the same time, or negative and positive all at once. Darkness can't exist when there's light. For me, as a kid, it was cool to have muscles and try to outmuscle my problems. But as an adult, I found my mind to be a far more powerful tool in life. If I could override my subconscious thoughts and demons when they were trying to sabotage me, I could set myself free of my destructive tendencies. I could channel that energy into something good.

Now, on a practical, day-to-day level, I love to start off each morning by simply thanking the universe for what I have. From there, it's green tea and breakfast, where I read or listen to an audiobook instead of watching the news.

One of the biggest challenges we've all had to face in our lifetimes was the COVID-19 pandemic. We were all impacted by this disease in one way or another, whether it was sickness, death, or simply having to deal with being in lockdown. This pandemic tested us every which way, and it just so happened that I was working on this chapter during lockdown. In an interesting way, the lessons I was trying to highlight in this chapter became useful to me as we faced this unprecedented event.

The books I've read and studied helped me with the difficulties of being on lockdown while facing an uncertain future. I live by myself, so the isolation was tough to deal with, especially for my mental health and well-being. It was during this time that I discovered an amazing audiobook on Audible. It's called *How to Train Your Mind* by Chris Bailey. He breaks down meditation into bite-size chunks and provides an easy-to-digest entry into this extremely beneficial mental exercise. He also provides a lot of great statistics and useful information that explains why meditation is so helpful.

I highly recommend Chris Bailey's book and encourage you to take on a meditation practice. I loved listening to it and doing his meditation exercises while out on a walk—as you will hear if you listen to his book, not all meditation has to be done sitting still.

Chris Bailey's book helped me during a tough time, and it will be something that I will return to for the rest of my life. We never know what this world has in store for us, but one thing we can control is ourselves. If we take the time to build up a strong mind, then when adversity does strike, we can better respond to it.

No matter what is going on in my life, I look at each day as an opportunity to create a new project and spread some happiness—be the positive energy in the room, the smile that makes someone else smile. If I can accomplish that, then it makes me feel good. Isn't that what life is all about?

Of all the things we can do to make others and ourselves feel good, one of my favorites is giving. Whether it's with time, a thank-you, a compliment, or a gift, you're letting someone know, "I see you and I appreciate you."

One of my favorite things to give people is a book that I found helpful and enlightening in my life. If the person already has it, I tell them to pass it on to someone else. It's a fun little thing I like to do.

There's a cool saying that goes something like this: "Whatever I keep, I lose. Whatever I give away is mine forever."

I think it means we are gifts to the world, and if we keep everything for ourselves, no one will know or remember us. And if that happens, did we even really exist? If you love something with passion, share it with people, and they'll always remember and appreciate you.

Speaking of giving and gratitude, here's a few stories that show how everything is truly connected, and that the power of the universe bends in your favor when you're open to it and in a positive state of mind.

The gratitude I have for Mom and Dad cannot be measured. I would always let them know how thankful I was to be their son and for allowing me the space in their basement, and life, to chase my passion. They were amazing parents who loved and respected each other. I had a front-row seat to their incredible relationship, where I got to see two people in harmony who loved to share and give. They showed their kids what it was like to be unconditionally loved.

I also felt like I owed them a little something for all the heartache and worry I put them through as a kid. I always remember how worried Mom would get when Chas would be gone for days, and even though I didn't disappear like he did, I'm pretty sure Mom got more than a few gray hairs from my antics.

The thing was, once I left Ansonia in 1978, my life was a whirlwind, and, as they say, time flies. While I'd talk to my parents every week on the phone and send them small gifts, like a box of desserts from Ferrara Bakery, I always wanted to get them something bigger, something really cool. Something that would say, "I am so grateful for you two and love you so much." When you want to give a gift that says something as important as that, it's not how much the gift costs; it's about making their souls smile.

Dad's Gift

Looking back at it, even though I gave Dad's gift to him in 1999, I see now that it all came about from a series of events and relationships going all the way back to the 1980s. That was when a dude from Connecticut named TR Goodman called me up one day out of the blue and asked me, from one Connecticut kid to another, if he could visit me in Venice to check out the scene. After we talked for a bit, I said, "Hell yes! Come on out!"

TR grew up in Connecticut like me, except he was from a rural farming town called Suffield, in the northern part of the state near the border of Massachusetts. He was an amazingly gifted athlete who played ice hockey and lacrosse. He ended up going to Trinity College, a private school in Hartford, Connecticut, on a hockey scholarship, and was so good that his coaches picked him to be the team's captain.

TR ended up getting a degree in economics and got an office job in Hartford. But having a boss and falling in line didn't sit well with him. He had seen his dad play that game at a bank and saw how his dad kept getting passed over for promotions. After witnessing that as a kid, TR decided he never wanted to depend on anyone for anything. And that's when he called me to see a different way of life.

Soon after that call, TR flew out and stayed on my couch. It was the very next morning that I took him to Gold's Gym Venice and his eyes just about popped out of his head. I always loved taking a newcomer to Gold's Gym, especially someone like TR, who was as passionate about working out as I was. Seeing their joy and amazement would never get old.

That day, TR and I had an amazing workout. In between our sets, I introduced him to some of my friends. TR seemed to fit in right away, and a group of us ended up grabbing lunch at the Firehouse afterward for a post-workout recovery meal. Over the next few weeks, he stayed with me. We worked out every day together, and I could tell he had the Gold's Gym bug just like I had.

In addition to Gold's Gym and all the incredible workouts we did together, two other things left a huge impression on TR. The first was taking him to meet my good friend and famous commercial director Joe Pytka so he could see what the energy was like working in a creative studio. TR was floored when he saw not only how hard Pytka and his team were working but also with how much fun they were having. Also, TR loved the fact that everyone was wearing jeans and T-shirts—which was completely opposite of the East Coast's dressing in a suit mentality.

The second thing that left an impression on TR was listening to my answering machine one day when I was out on a shoot.

"I was just sitting here on the couch and all these girls were leaving message after message to hang out with you," TR told me when I got home. "Los Angeles is way better than Hartford!"

After his trip to Venice, TR returned to Connecticut and invested in himself by opening his own gym. A few years later, his gym had done so well that a bigger gym came along and made an offer to buy it. TR cashed out, and he packed his bags and moved to Venice, where he started his personal training business called Pro Camp in the early 1990s. He smartly set up shop right next to Gold's Gym.

Because TR was so passionate about hockey and fitness, he developed a unique and highly effective training system that targeted hockey players during their off season. This in turn led him to score his first pro hockey client, Alan May, who played for the Washington Capitals. From there, TR landed other superstar players such as Chris Chelios, Mario Lemieux, Rob Blake, Rick Tocchet, Jeremy Roenick and many others.

TR's workouts became so legendary that he ended up building one of the most impressive client lists I've ever seen, which includes pro athletes from every sport. He also trained A-list actors and directors such as Ray Liotta and Peter Berg, as well as famous musicians and notable people from other professions such as the famous architect Frank Gehry.

Chris Chelios and TR Goodman with the 2002 Stanley Cup

In talking to TR about our journeys, he told me: "You know, Rick, looking back, I see how you really shaped my life. You showed me that a kid from a small town in Connecticut could leave and do something with himself. It was as if your example gave me permission to do the same. It gave me the courage to go for it. I don't think I realized it at the time, but I do now. Thank you, brother!"

TR's words made my heart smile and damn near made me cry. To me, that's what life is all about—helping others. I had so many people help me make the move and support me along the way. Where would I be if Bobby LeVine hadn't given me his business card and told me that if I ever wanted to get out of Ansonia to give him a call? To TR's credit, and I guess mine, too, when we were presented with the opportunity to change things up, we decided to jump for it. I can say, fortunately, it seemed to have worked out pretty well for both of us.

In the 1990s, when I wasn't away filming *BodyShaping*, I'd be at Gold's Gym working out at about the same time TR was running his Pro Camp training sessions. I would get to know the players and the other guys he was training, including the actor James Caan. I had met "Jimmy," as he was known to his friends, at Gold's Gym before he became TR's client.

As a lot of you probably know, Jimmy had some great roles in movies like *El Dorado* with John Wayne before he scored his iconic role as Sonny Corleone in *The Godfather*. And when Jimmy got his chance at the plate, he knocked it out of the park. For doing so, he got an Oscar nomination for Best Actor in a Supporting Role. My dad loved that movie, and he also loved Jimmy, whose character shared my dad's nickname.

To us Italians, watching *The Godfather* was the best. As a kid, watching it with Dad was incredible. As an adult, hanging out with Jimmy was insane.

Derek Barton and James Caan

Back then, Jimmy had a place on Speedway near the Venice pier, not too far from Gold's. Speedway is an alleyway that is one block east of the beach, between Venice and Marina del Rey. Needless to stay, there's some high-end, highly sought-after real estate on it.

On most days after our workouts, Jimmy, TR, and I would grab lunch at the Firehouse with other friends, like the great guy Jimmy Hart, and then we'd hit the beach or ride bicycles on the boardwalk. Sure, we were working on our tans, but we were also out there meeting girls. After a little of that, we'd head over to

Jimmy's place and throw some steaks on the barbecue and have a little cookout with whoever was around and whoever we met. If we weren't doing that, Jimmy loved to ride motorcycles. So we'd hop on our bikes and head up the coast to Malibu or wherever.

And if we weren't doing that, we'd hop on a private jet and go to Las Vegas for a night or two to check out a fight or some other event. Hanging out in Sin City with those guys was wild. The food we ate. The clubs we got into. The VIP treatment we were given. Crazy.

Me, James Caan, TR Goodman, and Jimmy Hart

Those years represented a special time for me. I was living the life. I mean, TR and I would eat Thanksgiving dinner over at Jimmy Caan's house. Are you kidding me? It got even better when Jimmy invited TR and me up to the Playboy Mansion every once in a while for parties, like the famous Halloween blowout, or to watch movies in the theater.

In 1971, *Playboy* magazine bought the Playboy Mansion, which sits just north of Westwood near Bel Air. Hugh Hefner lived there from 1975 to 2017. Jimmy was one of Hugh's best friends, so when Jimmy and his wife, Sheila, (his son, Scott's mom) went through a bad divorce, Hugh decided to help Jimmy get over it by writing him a "prescription" to come live at the mansion, for "medicinal purposes," of course. As far as anyone knows, Jimmy is the only guy other than Hugh to have lived at the mansion for an extended stay, which lasted from about 1980 to 1982. The "prescription" seemed to do the trick.

Anything and everything you've ever heard about the Playboy Mansion is pretty much true. As much as Gold's Gym was the place to see and be seen in the fitness world, the Playboy Mansion was the place to see and be seen in the celebrity and socialite world. Going to it with TR and Jimmy was a special thing. At that time in my life, it was like being a kid in a candy store, much in the same way Fort Lauderdale had been when I was nineteen.

During one of my Sunday calls home, I told Dad about how I got to hang out with TR and Jimmy at the Playboy Mansion. Dad couldn't believe that his son was partying with "Sonny" from *The Godfather*. I guess, in a way, I couldn't really believe it either. It was one of those "pinch me" moments. And then it hit me.

Here's the deal—I can count the times on one hand that I've asked someone for their autograph. I hated bothering people and didn't want to use them for that. But with Jimmy, I couldn't help myself. Not for me, but for Dad.

When I had approached Jimmy to see if he would sign one of

his headshots for my pops, he said, "Of course."

The coolest part was how Jimmy signed it:

To Sonny,

What did you do with this kid of yours?

My best always,

James Caan

Mom's Gift

Mom's gift had a lot to do with the fact that I was training my billionaire client, Gary Winnick, who I met because I was good friends with his former bodyguard/trainer, Dennis Alexio. Like I've said, so much in life comes down to relationships.

Now, in addition to training Gary, I also doubled as his bodyguard when he'd go to parties or travel. This in turn meant that I'd be meeting a lot of important people, and the last thing I wanted to come across as was some dumb "muscle head."

To beat the stereotype, I took it upon myself to study up on whoever I was going to meet at the event I was going to. Say, for instance, Michael Bloomberg, Bill Clinton, George Bush Sr. or Jr. would be attending, I would read up on them to find out about their professional lives, as well their hobbies and passions outside of making money. My thinking was that if I got the opportunity to shake their hand, I could strike up a conversation with them.

For example, if I knew someone was into sailing, I'd read up on sailing and then say something like, "Hey, I read where you really enjoy sailing. What kind of boat do you have?" And before I knew it, they'd be off and running, telling me all kinds of stories about their passion.

I found through studying the art of conversation that people open up when they talk about what they love to do, just like how I open up when I talk about bodybuilding. I also discovered that by reading more books and keeping current with world events, they would find me interesting as well—I could bring something to the table. What I learned was that passion, in and of itself, is contagious. People love to talk about theirs and they love to hear about yours, even if the passions happen to be totally different. For me, it also didn't hurt that almost everyone is curious about eating right, living well, and working out. Also, most of the high-rollers, dignitaries, and other important people I met had seen *BodyShaping*, or were at least aware of it.

One of the side benefits of getting to know this crowd was that I was getting a great education on investing in the stock market. I guess being open to this sort of thing had something to do with getting older and maturing. I knew I couldn't work forever and it would be nice to have some "passive income," where my money was making money while I got to live my life. How cool is that? Save up, invest, and then if everything works out, one day down the road, you get a nice payday. To me, real success is having the financial freedom to do as you please. To have enough money to be able to feel secure and to give some away.

The gift I'd end up giving Mom had to do with investing in a company that had such a huge initial public offering that it spun off enough money that I could save some and spend some. Not spend on me, mind you, but on Mom. I wasn't sure what to give her, but I knew that if I thought about it hard enough and kept my ears open, something would reveal itself. And soon enough, it did.

The same year I cashed those stocks in, I went home for Christmas. It had to have been about 1998 or so. My brother, Chas, was married and living in Florida with his wife, Sophie. He had been drug-free and out of trouble for a while, which made me very happy for him. He was in a stable relationship with a good woman, and together they ran a couple of small businesses.

Mom and Dad hadn't changed much. We had always kept up our Sunday phone calls, so I was up to speed on all their goings on. Mom had her church and volunteer activities, and Dad hung his wallpaper by day and played cards with his buddies at night at the St. Sebastian Italian Club. He still went to his cabin in Maine during deer hunting season. They seemed to be happy and in a good place in their lives.

On that trip home, Mom and I happened to be watching TV in the parlor when a commercial came on for a Chevy Malibu. Mom saw the sleek ad and the beautiful sedan.

"Someday, I'd love to have a new car like that," she said, and smiled.

Bingo.

She probably meant it as a throwaway comment and nothing more, but my ears perked up and the light bulb went off. Before I knew it, I was down at the Dworkin Chevrolet dealership that Bobby LeVine used to work at. I met one of the sales agents and was so grateful that he recognized me as the bodybuilder from Ansonia who had a show on ESPN. He ended up giving me a great price on a brand-new, top-of-the-line, silver, four-door Chevy Malibu, which I paid cash for.

I drove off the lot with a huge smile on my face. Nothing like that new car smell.

I took the long way home, passing by my old school, Ansonia High, where Mr. Germe let me teach weightlifting to other students. I drove through the projects, thinking about all the trouble I got into with Jimmy Vane, the drugs and the petty bullshit crime we'd do. All the near misses and close calls and how some of my friends weren't so lucky—like Jimmy. I drove past his old house. I thought about what could have been if he had just made it down to Florida to visit me before he overdosed.

I cruised past the old YMCA that I used to train at. Thinking about the time I spent there put a smile on my face.

One of the last places I drove past before going home was

our church, Holy Rosary Catholic Church, on Father Salemi Drive. I spotted the St. Sebastian Italian Club and the parking lot where they would hold the Holy Rosary Italian Festival. Did my journey really start because I saw some dude get his ass beat right in front of me? Maybe it did. How crazy is that?

After taking the tour of my hometown, I drove up the hill toward my parents' house. When I was a kid, we did that drive in Dad's station wagon. He'd be smoking his Camels and listening to Frank Sinatra. I have to say, the brand-new Malibu smelled a whole lot better.

I pulled up right in front of our house and laid on the horn—*HONK!* Dad was the first one to come out. Not because he expected me to be delivering a brand-new car but because he thought some yahoo was making a ruckus.

I remember he threw his hands up and said, "What?!" And then he recognized that it was his son in the driver seat.

"Get mom!" I yelled at him.

And so Dad went to get Mom, and when she came out of the house, she was a little confused.

"What's Ricky doing in that car?" she asked Dad.

I got out, being sure to keep the door open like a valet would do. "Hey, Mom, Merry Christmas!" I said.

Mom was so surprised and overcome with happiness that she started to cry. "Nobody's ever done anything like this for me before!" she said.

But in true Mom fashion, she was more concerned about me and whether I could afford it. After I reassured her that I was good, she finally got in it and gripped the wheel. Dad and I watched her adjust the seat and get the mirrors just right.

"Well, what are you two waiting for? Get in!" she said.

I jumped in the back seat and Dad took shotgun. And off we went.

Spoiling Mom after all the years that she spoiled me, and everyone else for that matter, made me feel really good. She was always that angel on my shoulder, that voice in my head telling me to ease up or walk away to help me make a better choice. As we drove around town, we passed by Holy Rosary again, and I thought, without Mom and her positive influence on me, I'm pretty sure things would have turned out differently.

Mom with her new car

When we got home, I told Dad to wait in the parlor for me. I then went into my room and dug into my suitcase. It was time to give Dad his gift. And so I walked out and handed him a simple manila envelope. Compared to Mom's car, it didn't seem like much, but when Dad opened it up and slid out Jimmy Caan's headshot, he couldn't believe it. Jimmy had actually signed two photos for my dad. Unbelievable.

Dad read out loud what Jimmy had written on one of the photos: "To Sonny from Sonny, how ya doin? Love you, bro!" I got a huge kick out of watching Dad's smile and how excited he got.

"Sonny from *The Godfather*? Are you serious?!" Dad said.

He thanked me more than a few times, and then he went downstairs into his woodshop and built a custom frame for it. He hung it in his office at home, and anytime one of his buddies would come over, Dad would show off his one-of-a-kind, autographed headshot of James Caan.

We wrapped up that day with an amazing Italian meal with my cousin Mark and his family, along with other relatives. It was a day I will never forget.

If your parents are still alive, God bless you. Stop what you're doing and send them some love and gratitude.

Life is crazy, and having a strong mind to help you through it is the most powerful weapon in your arsenal. Jobs, money, and even people come and go. Here's the reality of living: As soon as we're born, we are all on this journey, and eventually we will leave this earth. Some sooner. Some later. As long as you're alive, each day you wake up, you're going to have to deal with yourself, and that means dealing with your thoughts and your emotions.

This is why learning about and understanding human behavior is the key to unlocking so much more potential in ourselves than a gym ever could. The more books you read (or listen to) and the more time you spend strengthening your mind, the better you can handle whatever life throws at you. Because, to be clear, life is going to toss a lot of shit your way. On the flip side, it's also going to bring you amazing opportunities and triumphs. Whether an adversity or a victory, how you respond to it is the most important part. If you're coming from a place of gratitude, then I think you'll handle anything with humility, kindness, and compassion for yourself and for others.

The mind-body-spirit connection can only work if your mind and spirit are as strong, if not stronger, than your body. Makes sense if you stop and think about it. But maybe that's how life goes. When you're young, you feel invincible, and you're not really stopping to think about it, let alone study it. We're so busy trying to fill ourselves up from the outside with things like money and experiences that we often overlook the fact that everything we need to make us happy is already within us.

It just takes exercising your mind to help figure this out. It also takes living and being confronted with the fact that life is truly so short.

Although I had been around a lot of death as a kid in my neighborhood, it wasn't until I got older and started to have friends pass away from illnesses that I thought about my own mortality. We are not on this planet forever, no matter how big and strong we are. One of the examples of this, unfortunately, had to do with my dear friend Gregory Hines.

It was early 2003 when I got the news that broke my heart. Gregory had gone in for a routine checkup. He was feeling fine and looked amazing, except that his bloodwork revealed some abnormalities. After a few more tests, his doctors diagnosed him with cancer of the liver.

Look, I'm not going to rail against Western medicine or anything like that, but what I know was that once Gregory got his diagnosis and started chemotherapy, his health fell off the cliff. It was like one day he was fine, and once his treatment started, he never got out of bed again.

It was on August 9, 2003, when the man who entertained people with dancing, acting, and singing—putting so many smiles on faces—died. I had known him for more than twenty years and was fortunate to train him for some of his best roles. The news devastated me.

I've had so many friends pass away, going back as far as I can remember. Each one is heartbreaking, but when someone as pure and loving as Gregory dies so young (he was fifty-seven), it makes you question everything. Why him? Why now? How could this happen to such a great person? I did my best to understand that those thoughts were normal when someone was taken from you.

But still, Gregory? Damn, damn, damn!

As best I could, I tried to deal with my broken heart by thinking of all the great memories I had of Gregory. I could go on and on about him, but more than anything, he really inspired me to always be a giver, whether with time, money, or even a compliment. I loved how he entered a room and lit it up with his incredible energy. Nowhere was this more true than at his funeral, as crazy as that might sound.

On that somber day, we all gathered at St. Monica Catholic Church in Santa Monica to say our goodbyes. The church was filled with his close friends, his family and children, and those who simply wanted to pay their respects. I ended up sitting next to Gregory's father, Maurice, who I was lucky enough to have met on several occasions before that day. He reminded me of my dad, and I was grateful that I had the opportunity to develop a nice friendship with him over the years. I kept thinking that, of all the things in life, one of the most painful things must be for a parent to have to bury one of their kids.

When I teared up, it was Maurice who leaned over and said to me, "Handle it."

I couldn't believe how strong he was, like a rock. Needless to say, it was a sad, gut-wrenching day. But then something happened that proves there has to be more to life once we pass away. During his time here on Earth, Gregory had always been quick with a joke or an impromptu performance to put a huge smile on your face. And guess what? Today would be no different.

During the priest's eulogy, as if choreographed by Gregory

from heaven way up above, a little girl got up and started to tap dance around Gregory's casket. I immediately got goose bumps, and as the little girl kept tap dancing, other dancers got up and began tap dancing as well. And before I knew it, there were about a dozen people up there dancing around the casket. When the rest of us got into it by dancing, clapping, and stomping our feet, it was the most amazing thing I've ever been a part of. The energy was unbelievable, and it was so very true to who Gregory was as a person.

In a way, I think it was Gregory's way of letting all of us know that it was going to be okay. More so than his acting and singing, dancing was Gregory's gift to the world. And it was something that we could continue doing in his honor, knowing he'd be looking down and smiling at us. In that instant, during that slice of time, our sadness was replaced with love and hope. Our tears of despair were replaced with tears of joy. By far, it was the most heart-wrenching yet loving funeral I had ever been to. Leave it up to someone as talented as Gregory to pull that off.

Gregory, if you're reading this up above, just know that I miss you every day, brother! You still live on with me, your family, friends, and fans, in spirit and in heart! Love you!

Gregory's death served as a reminder that when we leave this earth, people will remember us and judge us by how we treated other people. Gregory's funeral proved that. Over the next few years, I had whittled my crazy work schedule down to training just one client. By the time 2007 rolled around, I felt like I had things pretty much under control.

In the seven short years since *BodyShaping* had ended, I had transitioned mentally, learning so much about myself through the books I was reading. Those books really helped me understand human behavior, including my behavior. Having that knowledge helped me deal with any adversity in my life and helped me understand why people behave the way they do, including myself. I was in a good, happy place. I was living in the moment and not taking anything for granted.

You might recall my routine. My Monday-Friday schedule looked like this: Wake up. Eat six egg whites. Wait fifteen minutes, and then eat a cup of steel-cut oats with a whole cup of blueberries, along with a cup or two of coffee. After breakfast, ride my Harley to Gold's Gym, train one body part, and finish with forty-five minutes of cardio. Post-workout, lunch at the Firehouse, where I'd have a flank steak, egg whites, and a yam. After all of that, I'd go home, take a power nap, and then around 6 p.m., I'd head up to Bel-Air to train Gary Winnick.

Gary's home was one of the most luxurious homes in America. When he bought it in 2000, it was the most expensive home ever sold in the country. The home sits on nearly nine acres next to the Bel-Air Country Club, also making it one of the biggest pieces of property in Los Angeles. The amazing home was complete with a full-sized basketball court, tennis court, massive pool, and perfectly landscaped gardens. You name it, this house has it. It's so big that Gary and I used to walk the perimeter of the property twice a day and get all our steps in for the day.

Gary Winnick and me

I was grateful that Gary had enlisted me to design a gym for the house. He gave me the resources to fully realize the perfect gym. With a few treadmills, exercise bikes, weightlifting equipment, and everything you could possibly need, it was the perfect gym that

Gary could train in without ever having to leave home. It blows my mind to think of all the time we shared in that incredible gym.

I was fortunate to work for Gary for thirty-three years. Over that time, I'd developed a deep relationship with him and his family. Gary, his wife Karen, and his three sons, Adam, Alex, and Matt, always treated me like family. They always made sure to include me in all their holiday and birthday dinners, as well as dozens of vacations. It was like having a second family. I'm very lucky to have such gracious people like Gary's family in my life.

On the weekends, during the daytime, I loved riding my Harley up the Pacific Coast Highway to Malibu to grab lunch at Nobu. During the evenings, if I wasn't on a date, I'd watch sports. I love sports—the energy, fire, and competition—and so I made my townhouse my man cave. With three big flatscreen TVs, I never missed a second of the action. I even put up a heavy bag so when I'd watch boxing or MMA and get all pumped up and start screaming, I could release that adrenaline with a roundhouse kick and an overhand right.

Things were going pretty well for me until I got that punch that knocked me the fuck out—that call from Dad about how Mom fell and broke her hip and had to be rushed to the hospital. I still get sweaty palms when I think back to hearing Dad's shaky voice when he told me, "Get your ass home right now. I need you."

I think it's easy to negotiate with yourself in life. To put ideas and projects on the back burner, especially if they are passion projects with no boss or deadline breathing down your neck. But when I had to take care of my parents—my own flesh and blood—at the end of their lives, it really made me realize that after they go, I was next up to leave this earth. In other words, the time to do things is now. Not tomorrow. Not next week. Not next year.

CHAPTER SIXTEEN

EXPLORING NEW PASSIONS

"You'll never get bored when you try something new. There's really no limit to what you can do."
—Dr. Seuss

THROUGHOUT MY LIFETIME, I'VE PROVEN TO MYSELF time and time again that doing nothing drives me crazy. When I'm bored, I revert to the self-destructive tendencies I mentioned in earlier chapters. I'm pretty sure I'm not the only one who feels this way or that this happens to. That's why the thought of getting older and "retiring" is not all that exciting to me.

Look, I get it, I don't want to work forever either, but I definitely need a project or two to focus my energy on. That's my sweet spot. When I have something to work on that I'm passionate about, it makes me feel young at heart and gives me a new mountain to climb. All the studying, researching, and learning that goes into a new project keeps me in the moment and makes me forget all the world's craziness.

So as 2008 got going, I had just buried my older brother Chas and was helping Mom and Dad with the aftermath of Mom's broken hip. With her decline, Dad's physical and emotional health went downhill as well. I was bouncing back and forth from Los Angeles to Ansonia every month or two to help them out as much as possible, as Mom went through four failed surgeries, not to mention tons of appointments and inpatient stays at hospitals and convalescent homes. It was a roller coaster ride, to say the least, and it took its toll on Mom and Dad big time.

Back then, I was forty-seven and had been out of the entertainment industry for about eight years. When I wasn't back east with my family, my days were open and my evenings were spent training my one client. I was truly blessed to live a low-stress, fairly carefree life. I made enough to cover my bills, to help my family, and to have a little fun from time to time. But even so, it wasn't all that satisfying to me. I kept itching to do something else, to try a new project. Looking back at it, I think it was something about Chas passing away and seeing how fragile life can be that made me challenge myself to get going on a new venture.

When I began the process of figuring out what new thing I wanted to dive into, I started with what I knew, and I knew that I loved bodybuilding and I loved Gold's Gym. And that's when it hit me that it would be awesome to create documentary videos about the people who had influenced me over the years at or around Gold's Gym. I felt like it would be a natural fit to step behind the camera since I had spent so many years in front of it.

Now, to make sure this was something that I'd be into, I did a very simple test that consisted of only two questions: Was it the last thing I thought about at night before I went to bed? Was it the first thing I thought about when I woke up in the morning? The answer to both was a big "yes," so I came up with a game plan to become a documentary filmmaker.

I also thought it'd be cool to create a website to host the videos so people could go to the site and see them. That way, bodybuilders and workout enthusiasts could watch these videos and learn some history about the people and techniques that helped shape the sport. Keep in mind this was in 2008, and at that time, you couldn't put videos on Facebook, and the whole YouTube channel thing hadn't taken off yet. Oh, and Instagram? That didn't come out until 2010.

To get going, much like I did with bodybuilding, the first thing I did was buy a book about making documentaries. I also started asking guys in the industry, like Joe Pytka, a lot of questions about what equipment to buy and techniques to use. Luckily, I wasn't starting completely from scratch, as I had picked up a lot of useful info over the years doing all those commercial shoots and being on the set of *BodyShaping*.

Once I got my bearings, I figured out I needed three cameras and a tripod for each of them, along with lights, microphones, and rigging (ropes, clips, etc.) to be able to film my subjects in an interview setting. After buying all that, I had to find some help to operate it all. Like everything in life, it takes a team to get things done the right way. Think of it like a football game. You need different players to fill the different types of positions on the field. A quarterback can't block, and a lineman can't throw. But you need both, right?

For me, I had more of a director's mentality and lacked the technical skills, so I needed to hire a videographer and an audio engineer on the front end to capture the images and the sound for me. (This part of filming is called "production.") On the back end, I needed an editor to sit down at the computer with me to weed through all the video in order to put together a nicely packaged final product. (This part is called postproduction or, as they say in Hollywood, just "post.")

To assemble my team, I asked around and got referrals for the best available people. This was Los Angeles after all, which meant the best ones were constantly working, and so that became a challenge in finding the right people for the job. But like any team situation, you learn to roll with the punches and figure out who you like to work with, which was, to me, a combination of professionalism, skill, and above all, attitude and energy.

Now, the name of the game when you're interviewing a person about their life is to capture them from just the right angle to create whatever emotion you're hoping to achieve. This is why you need at least three cameras, two positioned on either side of the subject and one pointed straight at them. That way, you have all the angles covered and can decide which one works best in post-production.

Apart from all the technical stuff, I also had to learn how to treat and handle my subjects in a way that would make them feel comfortable opening up and talking about their lives. I had been in their shoes a number of times with the camera pointed at me, but it's always different when you're the one asking the questions instead of answering them. My goal was to not only get their factual biography but also to get their emotional journey. I wanted them to tell me all about their biggest fears and challenges, and how they were able to persevere and overcome them. To accomplish this, I would do as much research about them as I could before I sat them down. Once I got them in front of the camera, I would ask a few targeted questions, and then I would let them talk.

It was an amazing feeling to see them start off a little shy and then later on open up to the point where they'd be telling me some deep stuff about their lives. In so many of these shoots, they would tell me about some difficult moments in their life and would get emotional and start to cry, and that would make me tear up. It was truly a powerful and moving experience to guide someone through their life's journey, and a huge honor.

When the interview would be over, I'd give my subject a homework assignment, which was to send me as many photos and videos as possible that would help "show" their story. Once I'd receive their photos and videos, I'd work with my editor to weave in what they sent me so that their voices would narrate their stories over the images of their lives on the screen. In the videos, I'd do my best to bounce back and forth between them talking and the stuff they sent me. As Pytka once told me, you don't want to have a "talking head" on the screen more than five to ten seconds at a time because the viewer will get bored. Makes sense, right? Mixing things up, just like in life, keeps us interested and engaged.

The amazing thing about making these documentaries was realizing how similar they were to working out, that there is no one-size-fits-all solution. It took a lot of trial and error (not to mention money) to develop the craft. All the tinkering and adjusting, and all the learning and focus it took to figure out what worked for me and what didn't. Getting into the nitty-gritty details and techniques of filmmaking was fun and a great way to focus my creative energy.

Now, for my very first video, I stayed close to home and produced a clip featuring one of my best friends and one of the best trainers I know, Frankie Cassavetes. I met him back in 1985 at Gold's Gym. Frankie, who is a highly decorated Marine, worked for the Marine Corps at Camp Pendleton, where he trained other Marines. At that time, he started coming up to Los Angeles to help his buddies Tony Palermo and Danny Ringwood open their restaurant called Teasers, which was the first restaurant on the now-famous Third Street Promenade in Santa Monica. Each time Frankie would come to LA, he'd pop into Gold's Gym for a workout.

Frankie Cassavetes

We hit it off right away because Frankie was (and still is) an animal in the gym. He's notorious for working out at 2 a.m. He also loves boxing like I do, so we soon became friends. A few years later, Frankie met TR. They hit it off. When Frankie retired from the Marines in 1995, he joined TR's Pro Camp as a personal trainer.

Apparently, this change in career came at a tough patch in Frankie's life, and it was TR who really helped him find his footing.

As Frankie put it, "TR got me through some things. I'd take a bullet for that guy. I am who I am today because of him."

That's what good friends are for, right?

Over the years, Frankie and I had so many great

conversations about life and about training. The funny thing was, in his early years of training at Pro Camp, Frankie treated everyone like they were in the military, which typically didn't sit well with paying clients and especially not well with A-list athletes and actors. We got to talking about how he could better serve up his lessons, and it dawned on me that Frankie might really like an amazing book I had just read. That book was *Think and Grow Rich* by Napoleon Hill.

Gilbert Coppage, me, TR Goodman, and Frankie Cassavetes

It was written in 1937, but its lessons never got old. To Frankie's credit, he read the book and really worked on changing his training technique and communication style. He was still a hard-ass, but he found ways to sweeten his message. To this day, Frankie remembers an important lesson from that book, which is: "Q1+Q2+MA=C." That translates to "Quality of work+quantity of work+mental attitude=your compensation." (Keep in mind that the word "compensation" means any result, not just monetary.) Over the years, I'd end up giving Frankie several other books about human behavior, and he'd give me some of his favorites.

Fernando Vargas (second from right) and Frankie (far right)

With his new approach, Frankie's career really took off and he ended up training all sorts of A-list celebrities such as Denzel Washington, Justin Timberlake, Ray Liotta, Amanda Seyfried, and Robert Duvall, to name a few.

I once was doing a video of Frankie training Ray Liotta in the Pro Camp gym. Frankie was having Ray do a boxing-inspired workout, during which Ray was telling us how hard it is to lose the weight he sometimes has to gain for a role. In turn, Frankie was telling us why boxing is such a great tool to shed those extra pounds.

They were pretty serious about it when all of a sudden, out of nowhere, Robert Duvall appeared and jumped in front of Ray and started shadowboxing him! I couldn't believe my fucking eyes! There I was, doing my best to keep the camera still while Ray and Mr. Duvall are sparring and Frankie's yelling, "Mr. D!" over and over, sounding just like Dick Vitale. Everyone cracked up, and Mr. Duvall kept the laughter going with his quick-witted wisecracks. It was one of those spontaneously beautiful and fun moments that I was so glad to get on film. You could see just how much love and admiration those guys had for each other. A truly incredible slice of time!

Frankie not only had a knack for using boxing techniques to train non-boxers, but he also made quite a name for himself training professional boxers such as Ben Foster and world champion Fernando Vargas. In fact, Frankie and Vargas became such close friends that Vargas selected Frankie to be godfather to all his kids. Frankie now trains all of them.

Of all of Frankie's training successes, helping his brother Nick Cassavetes lose more than a hundred pounds might be one of his most meaningful accomplishments. I got to tag along for the ride with my mics and video cameras to make my very first documentary.

If you don't know, Nick was born to the very talented and famous director John Cassavetes. If that wasn't enough good genetics, his mom, Gena Rowlands, was an amazing actress. As they say, the apple doesn't fall too far from the tree. Nick's acting credits are long, but he really excelled with directing, which includes credits such as *The Notebook*, *Alpha Dog*, *John Q* and many other amazing films. Of all his movies, *The Notebook* really hit home for me because it featured an older couple with the love and affection that reminded me so much of

Nick Cassavetes

my parents. When I was back in Ansonia one year, I watched it with Mom and Dad. They also loved it, and I might have even caught my pops with a tear in his eye as he watched.

Now, if there's any downside to making movies and being a crazy in-demand director like Nick, it's that working out and eating healthy often go right out the window. Chalk it up to stress, lack of time, or whatever, but Nick ended up eating a lot of junk food and, of course, gained a ton of weight.

Frankie knew the best way to motivate Nick, who's a hypochondriac, was to exaggerate how out of shape he was. Frankie told Nick he "was one pork chop shy of a heart attack." That got Nick's attention. But what really got Nick motivated was a night of drinking when he made a $100,000 bet with Tobey Maguire that he could get ripped in six months. Hey, whatever works to get your ass in the gym and to get disciplined!

Enter Frankie.

Nick and Frankie

Nutrition-wise, the first thing Frankie did was go into Nick's kitchen and throw away all his junk food. He then got Nick eating only natural, whole foods, and by doing that, Nick lost twenty pounds right off the bat. From there, Frankie put Nick on a 2,500-calorie daily diet that consisted of four meals and four shakes per day. After a few weeks of that, Frankie then put Nick on my "steamed food only" diet.

Workout-wise, for the first three months, Frankie only had Nick rehabbing old injuries to his shoulders and hips. Nick had a few surgeries on those joints and still needed to give them some attention before jumping into a full-on weight training and cardio program. Once Nick finished rehabbing those injuries, for the next three months, Frankie put him through Pro Camp's hockey circuit.

After changing his eating habits, training regularly, and staying disciplined for six months, Nick took off his shirt and was shredded. What a transformation! Anything is possible. It just takes effort and consistency over time. Or, as Napoleon Hill said, "Q1+Q2+MA=C."

It was awesome to see brothers helping each other out. For them to come together as a team and accomplish such a positive result was truly incredible and inspiring. For me, not only was it a great experience in making my first film, but I gained a new friend in Nick. We bonded over sports and similar stories about our dreams being derailed by injuries. For me, it was my pec tear. For Nick, who is six feet, five inches tall, it was an injury that ended his dream of playing pro basketball. At the time of that injury, Nick was playing for the big-time hoops school

Syracuse University on a scholarship. With his hoops aspirations derailed, he moved to New York City to study acting and film. And the rest is history.

Over the next three years, I'd make dozens of these videos, learning more and more about filmmaking with each one. I was also learning a lot about the people I was lucky enough to interview. It was incredible hearing about their journeys and seeing how we are all so similar yet unique in our own ways.

It was in 2011 that I made one of my favorite videos. It was about a man named Floyd "Shad" Meshad who runs the National Veterans Foundation. Similar to Frankie, I met Shad around 1986, and we've been friends ever since.

Shad Meshad

I've always admired our military heroes for so many reasons, one of which is because my dad served in the military. They put their country before themselves and go off into battle to secure our freedom. They are the true warriors and don't get nearly enough recognition nor the support they deserve. That's why I was so drawn to Shad's story, not only because he's a war hero but also because he continued to be a hero for veterans once they returned home. His consistent, positive, and upbeat attitude also drew me to him. He's one of those guys who is always looking forward. If there's a problem, he doesn't complain about it. He figures out how to solve it.

Shad went to college in the early 1960s, where he signed up for the Reserve Officers' Training Corps (ROTC), thinking that, once he enlisted in the Army, he would go in as an officer. From there, he got his master's degree in psychiatric social work from Florida State University and ultimately went into the military as a mental health professional. By then, it was 1969, and the Vietnam War was raging not only in Southeast Asia but also back in the States, as American citizens had turned against the war and protests were happening everywhere.

Now, as all of this was going on, Shad, who was working in the States at the time, felt like he was sitting on the sidelines instead of playing in the game. So when an opportunity presented itself for a mental health counselor to go to Vietnam, Shad took it. Not many people would have done the same.

Once in Vietnam, Shad saw many horrific injuries and deaths, including having to bag over 360 of his fallen soldiers. It obviously had a huge impact on his life, which is recounted in the four short documentaries I did on him (they total about twenty minutes). You can check them out on my YouTube channel.

What you'll also see in the videos is how Shad returned after serving in Vietnam and went to work at the Department of Veterans Affairs. There, he treated vets when they returned from hot military zones. Not an easy feat by any stretch. After a few years working for the VA, Shad started his own nonprofit to do similar work, the National Veterans Foundation. You can learn more about it at nvf.org.

As you'll see in his documentary and from his website, Shad and his team do everything and anything they can to help vets, from handling those who are suicidal to hitting the streets to reach those who are homeless. As Shad points out, "They're not going to walk in our door, so we go out and get them."

It was an honor to be able to interview Shad for three hours given that he was always super busy with prior commitments.

After that, I had given him his homework assignment, which he really took to heart, sending me tons of videos and photographs.

When I showed him the finished product, he was floored. We spoke about it recently.

"I was so happy to sit and talk with Rick, and that he heard my entire story," Shad said. "I couldn't believe he actually used almost everything I sent to him. I was super impressed and loved it!"

Way before I did the documentary on him, I had met Shad when he changed gyms and started going to Gold's Gym in 1986. He had just received a medical retirement from the VA and wanted to get back into shape.

"I was emotionally, physically, and mentally exhausted, and needed to work out to boost my spirits and make my body feel better," according to Shad.

When Shad arrived at Gold's, he met up with Derek Barton. Derek introduced Shad to a bunch of the guys, including myself.

Shad's initial impression was like everyone else's back then: "It was a gym that was more like a night club. It made it so much fun to work out," he said.

Shad and I hit it off immediately as I quickly learned that he loved motorcycles and was there to train with specific goals in mind, which I admired. Over the years, he asked me all sorts of questions about bodybuilding and different techniques, and I asked him all sorts of questions about life (Shad is about fifteen years older than me) and veterans.

"I learned so much about working out with Rick," Shad said. "He helped me reach my goals and always included me when he was working out with others. I also enjoyed his thoughtful, curious questions about my life and line of work. We are friends to this day, and I love our talks when we get the chance to have them."

Jay Leno and Shad

Helping a good friend like Shad put on muscle and get healthier inspired me. I know it seems like I was helping him, but in a way, doing that helped me so much more than anyone could imagine. Nothing makes me happier than sharing my passion with others, so when Shad had asked me and other people from the gym to help him raise money for the National Veterans Foundation, we said, "Hell yes!"

Over the years, we wound up doing about half a dozen fundraisers for Shad. I got to meet and work with Ray "Boom Boom" Mancini and so many other celebrities and athletes such as the Doobie Brothers, Lyle Alzado (who would also be one of the NVF's spokespeople), Robin Williams, Michael Landon, Bob Hope, James Garner, Oliver Stone, Willie Nelson, Jay Leno, and my good Italian goombah, James Gisondo, who I knew from Gold's. (So many on this list are not with us anymore. Just another reminder to live every day to the fullest!)

Oh, and another fun thing about doing these fundraisers—a few were held at the Grotto at the Playboy Mansion, which always got a nice turnout.

All of this goes to show just how special Gold's Gym was. It was truly an amazing community. We had each other's backs and would rally behind someone's cause at the drop of a hat. I'm very fortunate to have met so many great people there, including my friend Shad.

Shad, me, Nick Cassavetes, and Ray "Boom Boom" Mancini

The website for my documentaries never took off because, at the time I created it, Facebook and other social media sites started allowing users to upload their video content for free. It was a case of bad timing. I won't lie and say I wasn't disappointed, because I was. But I was grateful for the opportunity to produce documentaries about people who were passionate about their work. Their enthusiasm made what they did that much more interesting.

Some opportunities did arise out of the work I was doing. I almost got a TV show going with Joe Pytka that was going to focus on a trainer at a gym, like the one I did on Frankie Cassavetes. In this show, we would teach the viewer new workout techniques while giving the trainer, his or her clients, and the gym a spotlight. Unfortunately, as we were developing the show, Pytka landed a great gig that would be filming in Europe, so the show was never pitched. Nonetheless, it was so much fun and such an honor to roundtable the idea with a Hollywood legend like Pytka.

I was beyond blessed that so many amazing people let me into their lives. Here's a few more of the people I interviewed:

ZABO

Irvin "Zabo" Koszewski became known in the 1950s as a bodybuilder with a ten-pack of abs. He won the Mr. Los Angeles in 1953, a few years before I was born and thirty years before I would win it. Zabo was best friends with Joe Gold and one of the first members of Gold's Gym, as he helped Joe get the gym off the ground. He was so old school and loyal that he stuck with Joe when Joe opened up World Gym. He was part of a group of bodybuilders that us younger guys looked up to, who we called the "original crew."

When World Gym shut down, I helped bring him and the other old-timers over to Gold's Gym and got them free lifetime memberships. Over the years, we watched fights together, and any time we went out to eat, he always demanded to pick up the tab. The times I paid for him, he made sure to get the next one. Just a classic, old-school guy. He was a great joke teller, too, and just such a fun personality to be around.

Zabo and me

Zabo was inducted into the International Federation of Bodybuilders Hall of Fame in 2007. He passed away in 2009 at 84 years of age. It's not often a bodybuilder gets a big write-up in the *Los Angeles Times*, but they did one for Zabo. He lived a great life, and I was so lucky to have been his friend. Rest in peace, legend!

RIC DRASIN

Ric Drasin was a bodybuilder, professional wrestler, personal trainer, actor, and stuntman. He had a huge fan base because of his wrestling and the crazy shit he would do in the ring. Google his name and check out his old clips. He was an absolute showman and entertainer. One of the best to ever do it. He also happened to be the guy who designed the Gold's Gym logo with the baldheaded bodybuilder, as well as the World Gym gorilla logo. Such a talented guy.

Ric 70's

2001

Ric passed away in 2020—way too young. His big smile and big heart are missed. RIP!

SHAWN RAY

Shawn Ray is one of the most consistent bodybuilders in the history of the sport, and one of my best friends. He placed in the top five in twelve Mr. Olympia contests from 1988 to 2001. The insane discipline it takes to stay in peak shape over a dozen years is all you need to know about Shawn. He is by far the hardest-working bodybuilder in the industry.

Shawn has a podcast, keeps up a huge social media presence, promotes shows and events, and does commentating for bodybuilding contests all over the world. We met at Gold's Gym in the early '80s and have been good friends ever since. He's a true inspiration for all of us. Shawn is the man!

BARTELS' HARLEY DAVIDSON

Bartels' Harley Davidson is a legendary Harley dealership in Marina del Rey. I've been a loyal customer for years, having bought five bikes there. The guys at Bartels', Bill Bartels and his son Ron, and Forrest Nolin always gave me a great price and took care of me. Whenever I wanted to sell a bike, I'd take it there and they'd sell it. They are the only people I trust to work on my bikes.

Ron and Bill Bartels

My five bikes from Bartels'

Hanging out with the crew is always an amazing experience. They really love what they do, and when you're around passionate people like Bill, Ron, and Forrest, you get filled up with all that incredible energy and inspiration. Thanks, Bartels!

GINA CLARKE-HELM

Gina was a beautiful professional model. At the age of twenty, her agent wanted her to take a job doing some nude modeling for world-renowned sculptor Robert Graham. Gina turned it down. Posing nude felt exploitive.

However, about a year later, she was looking through an architectural magazine when she came across a profile on Robert Graham's house. In it were photos of his sculptures spread throughout his home. The quality of his work convinced Gina to reconsider posing for him.

For the next ten years, Gina was Robert's muse. He made countless sculptures of her in various styles. In time, Robert was commissioned to create a sculpture to be erected in Windward Circle, a roundabout in Venice. His subject was Gina. The sculpture he created features Gina's hips and torso twisting at an angle. If you ever find yourself in Venice, check it out. It's amazing. Rest in peace, Robert.

Today, Gina runs her own business, Malibu Seaside Chef, through which she works as a private chef, serving movie stars,

CEOs, musicians, and professional athletes.

When my website didn't take off, I needed another project to sink my teeth into. That's when I called up my cousin Mark and said, "Hey, you want to start a clothing company with me?"

Okay, so this might sound a little out of the blue for me, but the idea came about because I wanted to spread positivity in the world. You see, in the 1990s and early 2000s, there was a handful of companies, like Life is Good, that sold clothing with positive messages along with unique art on it. Each time I saw someone wearing that type of clothing, I felt better about life and the world. It was truly uplifting to me. So, I thought, why can't I do that?

Mark and I had a few weeks of conversations as we figured out the business model and approach. Then we started our very own clothing company called Sugar Feel. Our idea was to create hats and T-shirts with positive words and messages on them like "Grateful," "Blessed," "Think Positive," "Unstoppable," and so on.

We needed someone who could design and produce the clothing, so I called my friend Steve Paris. Steve designs and manufactures a lot of sportswear for Gold's Gym. He was happy to work with us and gave us a good deal. Thank you, Steve.

For most businesses, and especially clothing, you need a solid website and marketing campaign to get customers and drive sales. One of the most effective ways to do that in the clothing world is to put your products on good-looking, vibrant, young men and women and photograph them. This meant we needed a photographer and models, both of which would cost us a lot of money. And that's when it dawned on me I could be a photographer, and I could recruit Gold's Gym members to be our models.

Mark, who is a successful small-business owner (he owns and operates his own jewelry store in Connecticut), agreed with me that this would help us save a lot of money, which could then be used for other parts of the business. And with that, off I went to my local camera store to shop for a camera. After asking the experts at the store a million questions, I left with my very first big-boy camera, a Nikon 800. I also bought a tripod, a few different lenses, and some flashes.

After that, I read a lot of books about photography techniques, and I also watched a lot of YouTube videos. I then practiced with still-life objects and nature, as well as with my friends. Once I had my technique pretty dialed in, I then started talking to potential models at Gold's Gym, and as I suspected, there was no shortage of young men and women who needed some extra cash for an hour or two of their time.

Similar to bodybuilding and filmmaking, the goal with photography is to photograph your subject at the best possible angle, with the best lighting, and depth of field. This is more complicated than it sounds. Luckily, with my digital camera, I didn't have to worry about the price of film. The only downside was having to comb through hundreds of photographs after each shoot. But that's the fun of it, not only trying to take the perfect photograph but figuring out the best ones to use.

With our website in place and our first batches of hats and T-shirts ready, I started photographing the models wearing our clothes at various locations throughout Venice. My favorite places to shoot them was in front of any one of Venice's cool murals, buildings, or sculptures. I always tried to keep the session to one hour, and afterward, I'd give them a $100 bill for their time. I remember being in their shoes in my twenties, when every dollar mattered, so I hoped this helped them out as much as it helped us with our website.

We launched our Sugar Feel website and tried to get our products out in the public through marketing and giveaways, but unfortunately, we never hit the high numbers you need to make real money. I learned that it takes a marketing expert and a substantial advertising budget to make money in the clothing industry. It also takes a huge social media presence and all that goes along with that. I gained a lot of respect for the people and companies that do this sort of thing successfully.

I never considered the documentaries and Sugar Feel to be failures because I had a blast doing them, I learned a lot about the people I interviewed, and the models had a great time. I know it's cheesy to say, but the truth is that the real victory is trying something new, not whether it works out or not, or if it makes money. It's hard to think of it that way sometimes, especially in our world where so much of our self-worth is associated with our wealth. But I know I'm always happier when I do things for myself and not for the sole sake of making money.

It's funny how certain things you do still have an effect on people. In 2015, Dr. Pete, my friend from *BodyShaping*, called me up to tell me that the International Chiropractors Association Council on Fitness and Sports chose me, Dr. Pete, and Kiana to receive their Pioneer of Fitness Education award. I was honored to hear the news, and even more so when I found out that Arnold Schwarzenegger would be presenting the award to Kiana, Dr. Pete, and I at his annual bodybuilding show, the Arnold Classic.

The Arnold Classic is one of the bigger annual shows that attracts the top names and sponsors. Arnold started it in 1989, and over the years, it has seen some of the greats win the top prize, including my good friend, Shawn Ray, who won in 1991.

And so, in front of a crowd of the sport's biggest stars, Arnold presented Kiana, Pete, and I with the ICA Council on Fitness and Sports Lifetime Achievement award.

Me, Kiana, and Dr. Pete at the Arnold Classic

It was an exciting and rewarding moment that marked a lifetime devoted to fitness. But the best part about getting the award, like a lot of events in life, isn't the thing itself but that the event serves as a reunion, where you get to see friends from all over the world that you hadn't seen in a long time.

You never know who you're going to run into at these events. While backstage at the Arnold Classic, I ran into former Mr. Olympia and good friend Lee Haney. After the show, we all went to Mitchell's Steakhouse—Dr. Pete, Kiana, my cousin Mark, and a few of our other close friends from back in the day. We ate, drank, and caught up on everyone's lives while doing a fair amount of

Me and Arnold Schwarzenegger with my ICA award

reminiscing on years gone by. And while we were there, I ran into another person I didn't expect to see, Ric Flair. We'd been friends for years, and it's always a pleasure seeing him. Thank you, Arnold and Dr. Pete! Much love!

Now I want to address the moment that brought me here in the first place, to writing this book. Back in 2014, Gold's Gym asked me and eight-time Ms. Olympia Lenda Murray to give a seminar at the gym covering our bodybuilding careers. A lot of gym members showed up and asked questions about training and how to reach their goals. Lenda and I used our decades of experience to answer their questions.

Me and Lenda Murray

It felt great to give back to the community at Gold's. Eddie Giuliani was there in the front row, and though he was a legend, even he had a lot of questions for us. We had a lot of laughs, reminiscing about what the gym was like during the '80s and '90s. I'll always be grateful for Gold's Gym.

That day of sharing stories got me thinking a lot about my life, and that led me to my next idea, which was to put my life's journey down on paper. I had recently read Chuck Zito's autobiography, *Street Justice*, as well as *The Good Son: The Life of Ray "Boom Boom" Mancini* and *The Magic of Lifting Weights* by Rick Newcombe. Those books were among the many that motivated me to write my life story.

Some of my favorite books

My good friend Colton Simpson's book, *Inside the Crips,* is especially one of the most inspiring memoirs I've ever read. It is in fact so influential that it is required reading for students at the University of Michigan and Harvard Law School. Colton and I met in 2007 at a party in Malibu, and I'm proud that we've been friends ever since. His uncle, Van Cotright, has also been a great friend of mine for thirty-four years. You have to read Colton's book if you haven't already. It will blow your mind!

Part of the motivation to write a book was to share my story so others could learn from it. The older I was getting, the more I realized that once I was gone, the only thing left of me would be

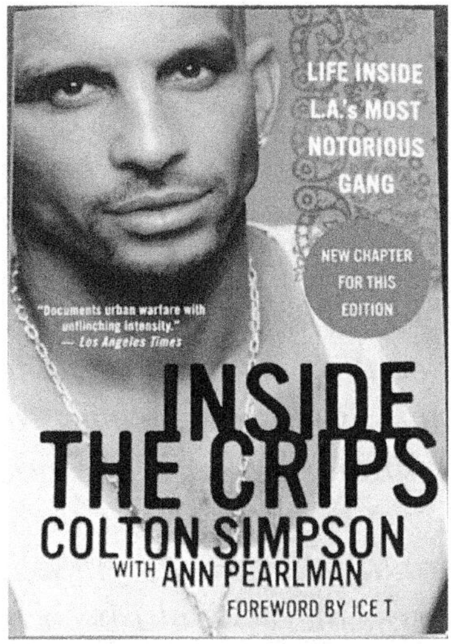

other people's memories and opinions of me. And that's why I wanted to do this book, to tell the story of my life's journey in my own words. It's something I think everyone should do, too, by the way.

To write this book, I knew I needed a writer that I would click with and who would be willing to go through all the chapters of my life. I had been listening to an audiobook, *The Secret*. *The Secret* is about the law of attraction, how your thoughts attract people or things into your life. Whatever you're trying to accomplish, just by thinking about it in a positive way, you will make it happen.

As I drove to the gym for my daily workout one day, I thought to myself, "Today, I'm going to meet a writer." That person ended up being Wendell Wellman.

Here's Wendell's version of how it happened:

I first became aware of Rick Valente during the glory years of Gold's Gym, the late '80s. The gym was like a larger-than-life Renaissance painting—fabulous colors, propulsive energy, massive, sculpted bodies, and celebrities who acted like fans. No elitism here. Everyone simply shared the joy of pumping iron. Even so, for me, Rick just stood out. Part of it was his look, the thick shock of dark hair, and the handsome face. Part of it was his pictures hanging on the wall in the gallery right alongside the giants of the sport. Rick's

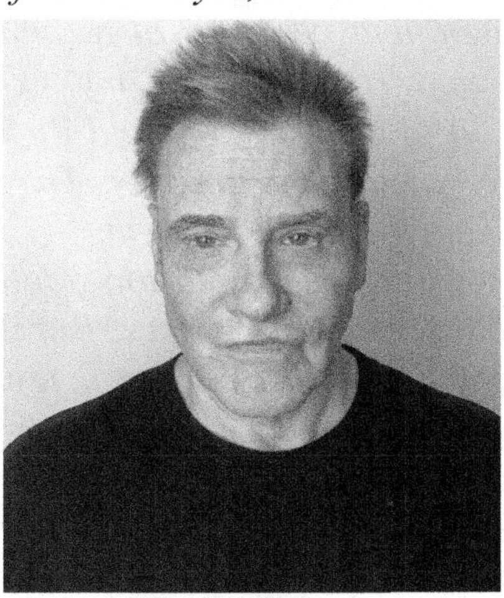
Wendell Wellman

pictures were more like movie posters, as opposed to the usual flex and pose. But mostly, it was his manner and his perpetual smile.

Most of bodybuilding's biggest stars could be seen in the gym in the morning, like Mike and Ray Mentzer, Mike Christian, Lee Haney, Charles Glass, and on and on. Most of them were pretty humorless, intense, letting out an occasional primal roar after executing some bar-bending bit of fabulousness. Not so with Rick. Rick just seemed to be having more fun. He was always grinning while going about his work. He was approachable. He never seemed to get through more than a set when somebody would come up to him looking for tips or wanting to talk. At times, there would be a cluster of people, and always included in the number were some of the gym's most attractive, cutest girls. Maybe it was the actor in me, but I was always fascinated to watch this. He was obliging, gracious. He would allow the conversations to continue even as he did his set. After a while, I nicknamed him "The Mayor," even though we had not formally met. I would tell people, "That guy is The Mayor. The Mayor is having a board meeting."

A very unique woman and friend of mine, Cathy Sassin, took a job at Gold's as a nutrition expert, trainer, and gym executive. Like Rick, Cathy was a spectacular athlete. She was also (and still is) the longtime best friend and roommate of my ex-girlfriend. Let's call her Lilly. In a bit of irony, Cathy and Rick grew to be great friends, training and hanging out together. They were constantly joking; they were like two kids in the gym.

I never knew if they were dating. They were both too adult and discreet to reveal anything about their private lives. But it didn't matter. My girlfriend and I had just broken up a few months prior, and I was missing her every day. Even so, Cathy would drag me out of the house on occasion to cheer me up. And now, here's Cathy hanging out with Rick. I figured sooner or later, Rick and I were destined to meet.

Cathy left the gym a short time later and joined an adventure racing team, competing all over the world. Eventually, she was hired by ABC, CBS, and ESPN to do sports commentary on extreme sports. But this served as an icebreaker.

Several months later, I walked up to Rick and said, "We know a couple of ladies in common."

"Oh, wow," Rick said, after we talked about it. "Cathy is a great lady."

The funny thing is, I had dinner with Cathy shortly before she moved. I asked her about Rick, and she just laughed, "Rick's a great guy."

Rick and I began to get to know each other over time, a conversation here, an anecdote there. Rick showed me a video platform he was creating, and he wanted my feedback on it. On another occasion, I went up to him and said, "If you ever have time, I'd love to pick up a tip or two on self-defense."

The following morning, he came up to me and pulled out a brand-new SABRE stun device and a pepper spray, and handed them both to me without saying a word. That's Rick.

The turning point was one morning in 2015 when I was working out using the arm bar. Rick approached me. "I'm trying to put together this book about my life," he said. "I've been paying a writer I met to work with me, but I don't feel like he's getting my voice."

"I teach writing off and on at StoryBoard at Fox Studios," I said. "Maybe I could take a look."

"I thought you were just an actor," Rick said.

"I do both. There are a lot of students in the class. Maybe I can find you somebody to work with you, if this doesn't work out."

I read the material. I realized the writer was very good, but he was doing a kind of Hunter S. Thompson, Gonzo journalism thing, the writer as star. It wasn't what Rick wanted. However, this began our relationship. I presented the opportunity to the Storyboard group the next time I spoke, and four writers volunteered. Rick interviewed every one of them, and chose one to work with. Like most things in life, the first time you try something, it generally doesn't work out. The writer called Rick and dropped out of the project. He had gotten a new job in Long Beach.

But after several months, I got an unexpected phone call from Scott Burnell, the leader of StoryBoard. "Is that writing situation with the bodybuilder still available? Craig Bealer just called and said he's interested. He said he almost volunteered at the time, but he was too busy with a law case."

Boom! In my heart, I knew this was it. Craig was one of the sharpest minds of all the forty or so writers at StoryBoard. He would always sit in the back and make very insightful comments. He would come up and talk to me after class.

Craig Bealer

The three of us began to meet at the Firehouse in Venice. After a few conversations, I could tell that Craig and Rick could work together. I volunteered to look at the chapters as they forged ahead. But as it evolved, I haven't had to do much of anything. Rick and Craig made a great team. Craig wrote with a clean, muscular edge, fitting Rick's personality. They found Rick's voice and navigated the story of Rick's fantastic life.

For me, I've gained two friends. To quote Rick, "I'm grateful."

Once Wendell hooked Craig and me up, we started meeting every week. And guess what? Like bodybuilding and the other passion projects I pursued, we went through a period of learning and researching, and then lots of trial and error, until we found our process and rhythm. From there, it was simply a matter of rolling up our sleeves and getting at it. Just like the gym, in so many aspects of life, there is no shortcut or substitute for plain old hard work.

CHAPTER SEVENTEEN

EVERY DAY WE WAKE UP IS A BLESSING

"No matter how good or bad your life is, wake up each morning and be thankful that you still have another day."
—Rick Valente

I had big plans to make this last chapter all about the gratitude I have for the life I've been blessed to live. For the people I've been lucky enough to meet and the ones I've become friends with. For being able to play in my passion and all the doors it opened for me. For Gold's Gym and all it's done for me over the years. But before we get to all that, we have to talk about the fact that all our lives were motoring along when all of a sudden—boom!—COVID-19 came along. A global pandemic turned the world completely upside down.

Life is challenging enough, with all its demands and stresses, right? Whether it's our jobs, friends, families, finances, or whatever, there never seems to be a shortage of things to worry about. And then, out of nowhere, a microscopic virus you can't even see is out there making people sick, putting them in hospitals, and for far too many, ending their lives way too soon.

There was not one person on the planet that the virus didn't impact in one way or another. We went through shutdowns, lockdowns, mask mandates, travel restrictions, vaccine mandates, reopenings, more closures, new strains of the virus, and along with those, more vaccines and boosters. Nothing made sense, and everyone's emotions were running out of control, from being scared and confused to having tons of anxiety, anger, and depression. Everyone was worn out and on edge because none of us knew what was going to happen.

As COVID-19 raged on, I couldn't help but think back to the Mike Tyson quote in the first chapter: "Everyone has a plan until they get punched in the mouth." COVID-19 was a collective punch to all our mouths.

Not only did the virus impact our daily lives, but it took an already divided country and made it even more divided. Everything turned political. If something bad happened, it was the other side's fault. Everyone was looking for someone to blame, but it seemed like no one was trying to work together to find a solution. The divisive politics filtered down into all our lives, too. You couldn't say anything without someone taking issue with you.

People used to respect each other. They'd listen to what you have to say and then reply however they might. But during the pandemic, everyone was so strung out that no one had any issue with snapping, even at a total stranger, for the littlest thing. I have never seen so many bouts of road rage, even for Los Angeles, in my entire life as I saw during the pandemic.

A glaring example of what I'm talking about happened on live television in front of millions of people worldwide. I'm talking about the 2022 Academy Awards show, when Will Smith walked onstage and slapped Chris Rock, which made all our jaws drop. I'm no expert, but I bet that slap wouldn't have happened if there hadn't been a pandemic. It's like the virus took away our capacity to deal with stress and emotions.

Another thing that added to the weight of the pandemic was that homelessness and crime levels went through the roof. I'd lived in Venice and Marina del Rey for over forty years, and I've seen it go through all sorts of changes. It seems like every few years, a new group of people come and go. I've seen it filled with hippies, coked-out yuppies, gangbangers, hipsters, and currently, techies—*and lots of homeless people.*

To be fair, the homeless issue was bad enough before the pandemic. So bad, in fact, that Third Street, which runs behind Gold's Gym, was completely overrun with tents. And since the pandemic, it's gotten much worse, with homeless encampments lining the front and side of the gym.

On one hand, I feel bad that people have to live that way.

Whether it's mental health issues, substance abuse issues, or whatever, no one should be without shelter. And on the other hand, I'm angry that our government, on a local, city, county, state, and national level, can't figure it out. I know it's a complicated problem, but I'm still at a complete loss that politicians and the so-called experts haven't found at least a partial solution to it.

Homeless encampment near Gold's Gym

And don't get me started on the news. No matter what channel you pick, it's a never-ending cycle of death, destruction, and despair. It feels like they want us to be confused and scared, so we tune in to see if they have any answers for us. Most of the time, they don't. Tack on global warming, drug overdoses, crime, and the threat of World War III (Russia invaded Ukraine while I was writing this chapter), and it's no wonder all of us are at our wit's end, feeling completely overwhelmed. The fearmongering they dish out is insane.

I'd turned off the news, but pretty much every day, I'd have a friend calling me up to rant and rave about this or that. Or when I'd log onto my social media accounts, there it would be, right in my face. It was so hard to tune out the negativity. As best I could, I tried to redirect their energy and remind myself and others to take a deep breath and think of three things to be grateful for, starting with waking up that morning.

Another way we were impacted was the sports shutdown. I depend so much on watching a game or a fight as a release. It's my favorite thing to do when I'm not at the gym or on my motorcycle. So, when all the leagues and fights stopped and no live sports games were airing, I really had to challenge myself to remain calm and find something else to do.

Luckily, mavericks like Dana White got the UFC back up and running as fast as he could so we'd have something to look forward to each week. With proper protocols in place, he forged ahead and showed other sports that it was possible to keep playing. I think they knew the country needed something to root for and believe in, and sports is that thing. Soon after the UFC started again, the NBA and MLB followed suit with abbreviated seasons, and the NFL as well.

Speaking of escapes, exercise has always been my number one go-to. It's my happy place. The one thing that, no matter what is going in my life, I can get completely lost in and makes the world's problems melt away. It's the very definition of living in the moment. When you're under the weight of the bar, counting out reps as the lactic acid builds up, there's nothing else going through your head except getting that bar up so it doesn't come down and crush you. Try doing high-rep sets, like fifty to 100 reps, and I promise that you'll be so focused on the movement and counting your reps that your brain won't think about anything else.

But guess what? Because of the pandemic, Gold's Gym had to shut its doors. I know that doesn't sound like a tragic thing, and it really isn't in the grand scheme of things. But it did take the one thing away from me that I loved—the ability to go to my gym, see my friends, and work out.

To put things in perceptive, I had been going to Gold's Gym to work out six days a week for over forty years. When it shut down, I got a taste of what life is like without having the structure of my workouts to look forward to.

Gold's Gym is not only where I work out, it's also my home away from home. Even an individual sport like bodybuilding can be a social activity. I missed seeing and talking to my friends face to face, and I really missed grabbing lunch with them after a good workout. With its doors closed, I had to spend the majority of my days at home like all of us. But that didn't mean I just had to sit there.

National Guard officers outside the shuttered Gold's Gym

We humans are good at adapting and evolving. And so, instead of dwelling on it, I reminded myself that I have the power of choice. I've read so many books that hammer home the point that we each have ultimate control over how we spend our time. I could either sit around my house and mope, or I could replace my gym workouts with something else. And so I challenged myself to get back to basics, go on walks, and to do workouts like I used to do when I was twelve years old back at my parents' house in Ansonia.

For my walks, I used my phone to track my steps, making it a point to challenge myself to walk a certain amount of steps each time. I started with 5,000 steps. Then, after a week or so, I went up to 10,000 steps. And after a week of that, I challenged myself to do 20,000 steps. Unfortunately, after a week of that, my knees started bothering me, forcing me to take salt baths at night and get back down to 10,000 steps.

By making a fun, goal-oriented game of it, I stayed motivated to keep doing it every day. Not only was I burning a lot of calories and fat (walking is by far one of the best things for that), but one of the cool byproducts of goal-setting is that our brains are wired to reward ourselves with a hit of dopamine when we achieve those goals. It's literally a natural high to reach a goal.

My favorite thing about walking is that you can either enjoy it with a friend or significant other, or you can listen to an audiobook (like *The Secret*) or a podcast (like *How to Train Your Mind*) or rock 'n' roll music to distract you from your thoughts and expand your mind. Another great option is listening to music that you love, makes you smile, and puts you in your happy place.

My home workouts got me in great shape

Walking gets you out of the house into some fresh air, burns up fat, and lets you work on your mind, body, and spirit all at once. What an amazing activity!

As for my home workouts, I pretty much copied what I did as a kid. I hung a pulley in my garage and did biceps curls and triceps pushdowns on it. I did squats, push-ups, two-chair dips, lunges, crunches, and pull-ups. You name it, I was doing it.

I became a competitor with myself, constantly pushing myself to do more and more each day. One day, I did 450 pushups broken down into three sets of 150, where I'd do fifty reps with my hands straight forward, fifty with them angled forty-five degrees, and fifty with them angled at about ninety degrees. Between each set of fifty, I'd walk up and down my flight of steps. What a burn that was. It gave me as good a pump as I've ever had. Between the walks and my home workouts, I got into fantastic shape during the pandemic, at the young age of sixty-three, no less!

Walking and working out provided me with much-needed stress relief during the pandemic, but I have to say, sometimes even that wasn't always enough to keep my brain from spiraling. I once read somewhere that humans have 60,000 thoughts per day. If we're stressed out and inundated with crazy news and energy, those 60,000 can all too easily be negative thoughts.

That's a tough place to be, and one that can really go downhill fast if you're not on top of it. Think of it this way—no one would sign up for getting punched 60,000 times a day, but we let our brains do it to ourselves if we're not careful.

I'm not saying to live inside your head all day long, but if you're aware of an angry or negative thought, you can catch it and control it. It takes work.

When things seemed to get too crazy and my thoughts started running wild, I had to really work at staying positive. Here are a few easy, helpful ways to flip a negative thought or mood:

- Set a timer and smile for sixty seconds straight.

- Create a voice or character in your head that says, "Shut up" or "Go away" (or an equivalent word or phrase) every time a negative thought pops in your head.

- Watch a lighthearted TV show or a cartoon that is sure to make you laugh.

Smiling and laughter truly are the best medicine. And you can't do that if you're constantly having negative thoughts. So catch those thoughts and cancel that shit right away! There are all sorts of other things you can do, but the three things above are easy ways that help me stay sane and positive-minded.

Another thing that helped me out during the pandemic was CBD oil. Unlike drinking, which usually comes with a hangover, CBD oil is an easy way to take the hard edge off of reality. It helps my brain turn off and allows me to get a great night's sleep so my mind, body, and spirit can reenergize.

Stress is exhausting. It's important to carve out the time to reset. Like a muscle, our mind and spirit also need to shut down to rebuild and come back stronger. If you really want to relax, you can also take a hot lavender Epsom salt bath at night just before going to sleep. Listening to an audiobook, podcast, or relaxing music is another great way to unwind.

The point of talking about mind and body so much is that our subconscious mind will always try to sabotage us, so it's important to have a game plan in place when your brain goes to negative town. The more techniques you have at your disposal, the better you will be able to catch those negative thoughts. You'll also be able to open up the valve and release the stress so you don't hold it all in and then blow up on a friend, a loved one, or a stranger.

It all goes back to bodybuilding for me. You want bigger pecs? A better ass? Flatter abs? There are all sorts of training techniques you can do to achieve those goals. But you have to do them. You have to put in the work. Same goes for your happiness and mental well-being. There's so many great books to help you get there. Or if you prefer, find a great therapist to help with your mind and spirit. Either way, you have to train your mind and spirit as much as your body. I set aside specific time to do so each day. You can do a few minutes, an hour, or even more. The point is, like the gym, put the work in and the results will follow.

Everything is an opportunity to learn and grow. The COVID-19 pandemic was no different. One of the biggest lessons it served up for me was just how important it is to live in the moment and have gratitude for everything in our lives.

Sometimes it takes something as big as a pandemic to make us realize that every day we wake up is truly a blessing. Every day is a gift. Now, if we could apply that thought to our lives even when there isn't a pandemic, I think the world would be a happier place.

Another thing COVID-19 taught us was what's important in

life. And it's not the material things. It's not our cars, or our clothes, or whatever thing we can buy at the store. I have way too many shoes, leather jackets, and watches, and they all just sit there.

I recall when my dear friend Bobby Scura (the guy who owned the auto body shop across from Charmer's Market back in the day) was getting older, and he sold his big house in Malibu and downsized into an apartment in Santa Monica. I was a lot younger back then and couldn't believe he'd give up his amazing pad and so many of his material things.

Bobby's Malibu home

Years later, Bobby ended up getting cancer, and I spent a lot of time bedside talking with him. It was so sad to see his decline, but I stayed with him until he passed away. I'm so grateful for those deep conversations with my good friend. I learned so much from him and how he realized, after a lifetime of acquiring material things, that none of that stuff mattered. What is important is our health, and the people we develop relationships with in our lives.

As I get older, I now understand that the number one goal in life is to be happy. Happiness, though, is a tricky thing. From day to day, week to week, month to month, or even year to year, that target can change.

Bobby Scura

As a kid, riding motorcycles, working on cars, and playing football lit my fuse. And then karate and bodybuilding came along. I left Ansonia because it didn't have what I needed to thrive. So, I moved to Florida, and it made me happy until I knew I had to be at Gold's Gym in Venice Beach to continue chasing my bodybuilding dream.

Now that I'm in my sixties, my happiness has more to do with being grateful and living in the moment than any singular place or thing. That said, I always want to be learning and trying new things, taking on new projects and climbing new mountains. As a bodybuilder, it was all about searching for a bigger and better contest to win or a bigger and better magazine to land a cover on. But if you focus solely on the destination, you miss the best part—the journey. The part of life where you're moving toward something is always the most exciting and rewarding. That's my sweet spot.

Part of the "being happy" equation has a lot to do with addressing the problems and worries in our lives. Almost everything has a solution or a fix. I have to remind myself that if something needs improving, I have to take action and figure out how to make it better. All of this, though, starts with a question I ask myself regularly: "Am I happy?" If the answer is no, I'll remain unhappy unless I do something about it.

Currently, I'm not happy with where I live. I feel like California today is not the California I came to love. It's changed, or I've changed. Doesn't matter. Either way, staying in California is emotionally taxing, and that means I will have to take action—either a reframing within myself or I'll have to pack up and move.

Ultimately, when it's time to make a life-changing decision, I recommend visualizing your life with and without making the choice. Take a moment and really think about it. See yourself in the future, in your solution. Make a vision board, if it helps. You know I'm a big fan of that. The one I made as a kid with all my favorite bodybuilders has stuck with me for a lifetime. I think about that vision board quite often. It's been a guiding light in my life that reminds me that if I continue to attack each day and each workout with passion, good things will happen.

Speaking of vision boards, once I arrived at Gold's Gym, I became good friends with one of the guys I put on mine—Robby Robinson. His chiseled, perfectly symmetrical physique landed him in all the magazines, and that's how he ended up on my wall in Ansonia.

Robby was born in 1946 and turned pro in 1975. He took the bodybuilding world by storm in his first year, winning the Mr. America, Mr. World, and Mr. Universe titles. From there, Robby would become known as "The Black Prince."

When I moved to Venice and started going to Gold's Gym, Robby was thirty-four years old. Fast-forward and Robby still has an incredible physique at seventy-eight, not just for his age but for anyone. He continues to crush it in the gym, and he loves to compete with whoever he's working out with. His competitive fire has never faded. Just recently, we were training arms together, and he was pushing me so hard it felt like it was 1985 all over again, when

Robby Robinson

we were getting ready for a show.

I will always be grateful for the forty years of friendship I've had with Robby. It's always fun to work out with him and then have lunch and talk about life. Robby eats cleaner than anyone I've ever known. Whenever I would take him out for his birthday, he would never eat cake, so I would get him an orange with a candle on it. He'd always love it. I've never seen him out of shape.

Me and Robby

Another example is one of the sport's true icons, Eddie Giuliani, who passed away while I was working on this chapter. He lived to the age of eighty-seven and had a high quality of life, all because he took care of himself with regular workouts. Eddie always had a smile on his face. He was always fun to talk to or have lunch with.

Eddie Giuliani

Eddie worked and trained at World Gym for twenty-eight years. When it closed in 2004, I got him and as many of the old timers from World Gym as I could into Gold's Gym. The manager at the time, Josh, gave them all free memberships. I really respect him for doing that. Eventually, Eddie was inducted into the Muscle Beach Hall of Fame in 2012. At the ceremony, he was inducted by his good friend, Al Pacino.

Joe Gold was renowned for building his own gym equipment. So, when World Gym closed, I spoke to Josh about grabbing some of that old gear and bringing it to Gold's Gym. Josh thought it was a good idea. We got a truck and drove it to World Gym. There, I loaded it with some of Joe's equipment. There was a multi-station machine and a set of beautiful chrome dumbbells, along with a custom rack for them.

Me and a World Gym employee the day we cleaned out Joe Gold's equipment

Once I brought all of this to Gold's, Josh had everything put in storage behind the gym building, where it rests today, only now it's all rusted and in need of restoration. They have had that equipment for twenty-one years now. Why on Earth that equipment isn't in the gym where it belongs is something I'll never understand.

I also wish that the gym would hang pictures in honor of the amazing A-list celebrities who worked out there and are no longer with us. People like Dennis Hopper, Gregory Hines, Jimmy Caan, Ray Liotta, Chuck Woolery, Carl Weathers, and Tonya Knight. Gold's also hasn't honored any of the Mr. Olympia winners since 2018 with their photos on the walls. I think such a simple gesture like hanging some photos would go a long way in showing some respect to these legends.

Thinking about this old equipment that has been left to rust reminded me of the subject of aging. It's not a subject any of us really like to talk about because you have to acknowledge the reality that we will all leave this earth eventually. It can be a scary thought, but one we must come to terms with.

I don't want to get too morbid, but listen, all of us are going to pass on, and the sooner we realize that, the sooner we can get back to living. One thing we can do to make the process of aging easier, in addition to working on our minds, bodies, and spirits, is to plan and prepare for when we do leave this planet.

The way I see it, aging doesn't have to be a negative thing. It's part of being born and something we should all embrace. What you don't want to do is wait until the last minute to do all those things you should have already prepared for.

When my parents were in their late seventies, they had a variety of health issues, making it impossible for them to continue living on their own. It was up to me to make arrangements to get them into an assisted living facility. But that wasn't all. I had to oversee every aspect of their lives, not just the health issues but financial ones as well. And it wasn't like there was a manual for how to go about doing this. I was learning on the fly during an emotionally difficult time. From tying up financial loose ends, deciding what to do with their house, and figuring out how to pay for their care, which was $13,000 a month, it was tough to handle.

My parents lived at the assisted living facility for the next two years, until they passed away. Even though they were gone, there were still a lot of things I needed to take care of. Did they have a burial plot picked out? What would they have wanted on their headstones? Did they have life insurance? I had to be on high alert because so many people saw me in a vulnerable position and tried to take advantage of the situation.

Hopefully, you can learn from my experiences, and maybe it will encourage you to have a conversation with your aging parents or, vice versa, with your kids. Remember, this is a very deep conversation, and it's important to approach it from a place of love, compassion, and empathy.

As for the logistics, do not assume everything is in order. Communicate about it. Ask the questions that need be asked and have the discussions that need to happen. I highly suggest consulting with a family lawyer or other consultant to help prepare for this phase of life, but that said, here's a list of topics to get the conversation going:

- Are there any medical directives?
- Is there a power of attorney?
- What is the health insurance situation?
- Where do they want to live, and in what kind of place (whether a house, apartment, assisted living facility, nursing home, or other)?
- What and where are all the assets and property (including bank accounts, stocks, life insurance, real estate, etc.)?
- What debts and liabilities are there?
- What is the plan to pass along assets? Through a will, trust, estate, or other?
- What are the wishes for a final resting place (burial, cremation, other)?

- If there's a tombstone, what should go on it? If there's cremation, do they want their ashes spread, and if so, where?

- Do they want a funeral or end-of-life party?

This is not a complete list, but it is a good starting point to get you thinking and talking about all the logistics. The point is, if you map it out, it takes away the stress and leaves everyone at peace, knowing things will be taken care of. And to be clear, this has as much to do with the person passing on as it does for the people left behind.

Life has a funny way of coming full circle, which is something you can't even begin to understand until you get older. When I arrived at Gold's Gym in 1982 with just a duffel bag and $400 in my pocket, I had no idea that it was the beginning of a lifelong journey. I had goals and a game plan, of course, but I didn't know what was in store for me. All the twists and turns. All the setbacks and triumphs. All the friends and relationships.

Mike Ryan and me, wearing a shirt Mike made me

Gold's Gym became my family. From the amazing trio of owners, Tim Kimber, Pete Grymkowski, and Ed Connors, to the men who helped build the company, Derek Barton, Neal Spruce, Paul Grymkowski (international president of financing), and Rich Minzer, and to all the managers over the years including Jeff Fee, Gary Siegrist, Tom Wilson, Darin Laniham, Mike Ryan, Kenny Flores, Mike Summers, Andy Lambert, Matteo Baker, Josh Fuglsby, and Jeff Suender. Gold's became a home away from home. A place where everyone flocks to work on their body, not to mention their mind and spirit. It is truly a special, one-of-a-kind place.

Due to the COVID-19 lockdown in 2020, GGI Holdings, the company that owned Gold's Gym, filed for bankruptcy. Fortunately, one of the most successful gym owners in Europe, Rainer Schaller, bought the gym.

One of the first things he did was invite some of the guys who had been training there for years to meet him at the gym. He was an amazing guy, very funny, loved the history of Gold's Gym, loved Harley-Davidsons, and was always asking me questions about motorcycles. He let me, Ray Liotta, Frankie Cassavetes, and TR Goodman train at the gym while the lockdown was still being enforced. It was fantastic.

Rainer and I developed a friendship, and every time he'd come to town, we'd sit outside and smoke a cigar together. Then, we'd grab lunch. Rainer was always trying to give me Gold's Gym clothing. In return, I would buy him cigars and lighters.

Rainer and me

Rainer had big plans for Gold's Gym. He renovated the front entrance and expanded the lobby so that it included a sitting area where trainers or clients could wait for their next appointment, or members could read or make phone calls before or after their workouts. He also updated some of the equipment. Rainer wasn't thinking about Gold's as merely a gym but as something that had its own culture as well. He started shooting a documentary about the history of the gym, which included interviews with many of us who had been there for years. He even wanted to start a Gold's Gym podcast. Furthermore, he brought back some of the old clothing designs and created new ones with Steve Paris.

Rainer had a tremendous amount of respect for the history of Gold's Gym and that of its creator, Joe Gold. March 10, 2022, marked what would have been Joe Gold's hundredth birthday. In his honor, Rainer put on a huge event at the gym with food, drinks, and contests. I hosted a discussion with people who either knew Joe or had been a part of Gold's Gym for decades. Jim Arrington, TR Goodman, Will Harris, Rico McClinton, Robby Robinson, Mike Ryan, Val Streit, and Mike Torchia all spoke at the event.

Joe Gold's hundredth birthday event

As we shared our stories about Joe, a common theme was that his vision of providing a space for serious bodybuilders paved the way for so many of us. It gave us a place to get off the streets and channel our energy into something positive.

As we talked about Joe, his gym, and what he meant to us, I

kept looking over at a wall that has one of Joe's famous quotes on it: "That's the object of going to a gym, having fun."

Rainer was the creative force behind Joe Gold's centennial celebration. He had a vision for something that included all of us. Seeing that kind of enthusiasm was amazing. It reminded me of when Pete, Tim, Ed, and Derek were running the gym.

Unfortunately, Rainer's life was cut short. While traveling in Costa Rica, Rainer, his girlfriend, and their children were killed in a plane crash. I broke down when I'd heard about it. I felt so bad for everyone on that plane.

A few months later, Rainer's staff wanted to honor him. They held a memorial inside Gold's that was open to all the gym members. Those of us who knew Rainer were asked to share our recollections of him, expressing our love and respect. Almost all of us cried as we spoke about him. To lose such a creative, successful, and happy man was a devastating loss.

Rainer and his girlfriend Christine

Among the people who spoke at Rainer's memorial were Sebastian Schoepe, Silke Hensel, Jeff Suender, Nikki Garcia, Joe Garcia, Julian Schmidt, Erica Berritz, Colin Thomas, Matt Radmamovich, Jarrad Hogue, Simeon Panda, Steve Paris, TR Goodman, Frankie Cassavetes, and Mike Ryan.

Once everyone was done reminiscing, the gym manager, Jeff Suender, hung a large photograph of Rainer in the first room.

Rainer was a special and creative man. He will be missed. Thank you, Rainer, for everything you did for us. Rest in peace.

In loving memory of Rainer Schaller

Over the forty-three years I've been at Gold's, I've changed a lot. When I first showed up, I was the young guy who people were helping out. Now, I'm the old guy who is the one helping out the next generation. It's crazy how that works when you have a passion for something. You go from being a kid to becoming an elder, a mentor.

Nowadays, I get about as much of a rush from helping someone with their workout than I get from my own workout. There's nothing like giving your time, expertise, and knowledge to a young person who has that same fire and passion that you had when you were their age. And the gym is a perfect place to do just that because, every year, there's always a new group who wants to take their physiques to the next level.

Me and Jake

I've recently started working out with a young guy, Jake Hines. He came to Gold's Gym with the goal of competing in fitness and physique contests (similar to bodybuilding but without as much bulk and with an emphasis on movement). It's been a blast working out with him. I get to share my knowledge and experiences, and in turn, I get to see the world through his youthful eyes. That's one way to stay young at heart, right? Interact and become friends with younger people. He did his first show in May 2022, and it reminded me of when I did my first show.

While I wrote this final chapter, the new owners of Gold's interviewed me for a documentary they're doing about the gym. What an honor and a privilege it was for me to be involved in a documentary that tells the story of the place I love. That was another full-circle moment.

I was also blessed to attend the 2024 Gold's Gym Hall of Fame ceremony, where Tim Kimber, Ed Connors, and Pete Grymkowski were inducted for their legendary ownership of Gold's from 1979 to 2000. These three men played a major role in making Gold's Gym the Mecca of bodybuilding, so of course it was a huge honor to be there to support them.

Ed, Pete, and Tim

Looking back on my life, I have to say Joe was right. The object was about having fun, about being happy. I've been so blessed to play in my passion for so long. And although this book is coming to an end, it doesn't mean that my journey is. My life, passion, and pursuits continue. I'm going to move on to the next chapter and, God willing, the next, and the next, and so on.

I keep photos of my parents, my brother, and Jimmy Vane near the door in my townhouse to remind me to live in the moment and get the most out of the day. Life's short. Spread positivity and put a smile on someone's face. I've lost so many friends and family over the years, and I try my best to honor them by living as full a life as I can, since they're not able to. And although no one knows what happens after we pass away, I hope to reunite with my parents, my brother, and all my friends I've lost.

So, I have to talk about what happened to Jimmy Caan after his last back surgery. Jimmy was eighty at the time, and this was the third surgery. The surgery went as well as it could have gone, which wasn't great. One of his legs was almost numb as a result of the surgery, and his lungs were filling up with fluid. To make matters worse, he developed an infection and ended up staying in the hospital for a year. His weight had dropped from 180 pounds to 140 pounds.

By the time Jimmy had arrived home, he was so weak that he couldn't even turn over in bed without assistance, never mind walk. His assistant, Mike Kijanski, hired two caretakers, Andrew Sajjabi and Patricia Aber, to assist him in taking care of Jimmy. But Jimmy really was a tough guy, a fighter, and he was determined to get back to Gold's Gym and regain what he had lost.

Three days a week, Mike, Andrew, or Patricia would pull Jimmy out of bed, get him onto a wheelchair, and take him to Gold's Gym. There, TR would work with him for hours, stretching his muscles and using an electric muscle stimulator.

From there, he was able to get Jimmy walking again and have him push a sled loaded with weights to strengthen his legs. Over the next year and a half, Jimmy worked his way up to pushing over a hundred pounds.

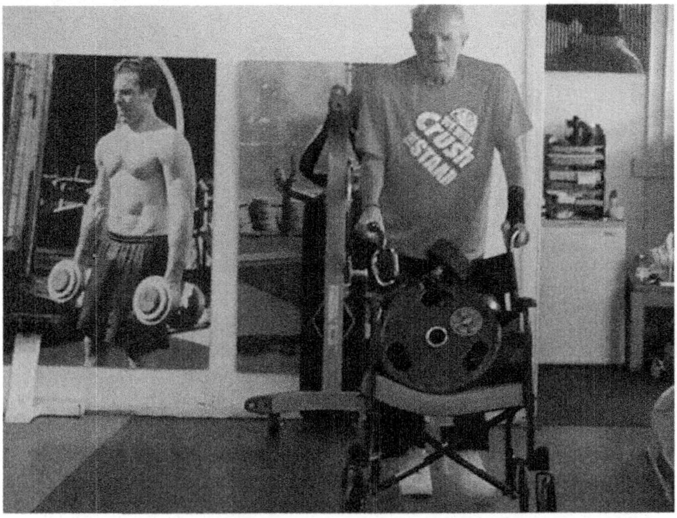

Jimmy Caan working out

During Jimmy's workout, I would train two of his sons, Jacob and Jimmy Jr. Once everyone was done working out, we'd all go out for lunch at the Firehouse. Jimmy would always brag about his sons.

Me with Jimmy Jr. and Jacob Caan

Jimmy and I also loved watching UFC fights on TV and in person. If we ever saw great fighters at Gold's Gym, we would have lunch with them, too, and talk all about fights and how to hit guys in the face and stomach. Ha, Jimmy loved doing to that to all of us! God bless you, Jimmy.

In July 2022, Jimmy passed away. That was a hard one to take, but it happens to all of us. TR, Frankie, Steve Paris, and I were at his memorial, along with celebrities Al Pacino, Joe Pesci, Brad Pitt, Elliot Gould, Chuck Zito, Kathy Bates, and many others.

TR Goodman, Shawn Ray, James Caan, and me

After the memorial, I reached out to Jimmy's assistant, Mike Kijanki, to see if there was anything he wanted to say about Jimmy from his perspective on Jimmy's last few years.

Jake Caan, Wallid Ismail, Jimmy Caan, me, Eric Albarracin, and Deiveson Figueiredo

Here's some of what he had to say:

Jimmy didn't allow a lot of people into his inner circle, but he told me Ricky and him clicked instantly. I heard great stories of epic workouts and sleepless nights at parties all over Hollywood, Vegas and countless other cities over their thirty-plus years of friendship.

When they wrapped up their training session, we would all head to lunch as a family. As I look back on those moments, those lunches with Ricky were just as helpful if not just as important as the physical workouts. As I would sit there and listen to two friends reminisce and share stories, I couldn't help but notice how much love and compassion Jimmy had for Ricky, and I'll cherish those lunches for the rest of my life.

Having people like Ricky and TR in his corner, who wanted nothing from Jimmy other than to push him to his limits and make him the best possible version of himself, meant more to him than they could possibly ever know, which is why I took the time to share this little bit about my best friend and boss James Caan.

What Mike wrote really touched my heart. Thank you, Mike.

Me, Jimmy, and Mike Kijanki

Over the past couple of years, I've lost dozens of friends. Overcoming the death of someone you know is never easy. It doesn't matter how old you are or the number of times you've been through it, grieving is a long process that takes its time.

Two months before Jimmy died, Ray Liotta passed away in his sleep. His passing was so sudden and difficult for me to understand.

Often, Ray and I would leave the gym at the same time. As we'd walk to our cars, we'd have conversations about working out, life, and whatever was on our minds that day. I miss those conversations. Rest in peace, Ray.

It's easy to get depressed and let your mind be flooded by negative thoughts, especially when you lose a lot of friends in a short period of time. What's helped me are all the books I've read regarding the grieving process. When you think about a friend or loved one who has passed, it's important that you remember the good times you were fortunate to have had with them. This way of coping has been a tremendous help to me.

Just as I thought I was getting a good handle dealing with grief, my friend Gary Winnick died. I was Gary's trainer for thirty-three years. Over that time, we developed a great friendship. He was a very wealthy guy and was very generous. Whenever we'd go to Beverly Hills so he could go shopping, whatever item he was buying, he'd insist on buying me one, too. If he was purchasing a suit, he'd buy one for me. Sneakers, watches, wallets, you name it—he made sure to get one for me. Even if I'd protest, telling him I had enough sneakers, he would have none of it. If he was getting a pair, then I was, too.

James Caan and Ray Liotta

Also, for many years, Gary had two great floor seats for the Lakers games at the Staples Center. Whenever he was out of town or didn't feel like going, he'd give the tickets to me. I always took a friend with me to the games—TR, Sandy Taylor, or I'd go with one of Gary's sons. It was always fun. Thank you, Gary, for treating me like a family member.

On the Friday night before Gary died, we had a great talk about how blessed we were to be alive and to be grateful every day we wake up. We agreed that I would come up to his house and take a walk around his nine-acre property (something we'd been doing for the last twenty years). Then, we would go downstairs to the beautiful gym he allowed me to create, and I would take him through a workout. And as always, we would grab lunch afterward.

Gary and me in one of his beautiful cars

So when I got up there at nine o'clock on Saturday morning, like I always do, it turned out Gary had passed away that morning. I was shocked. The whole family was in shock.

His funeral was held a few days later. It was amazing that 500 people from all over the country attended. A lot of family members and friends went up to the podium to reminisce about Gary. All of them cried. It was a testament to his character that so many people loved and respected him.

Gary showed me a life that I probably never would have seen. We flew around the country in a private jet. He was a car guy. He would buy some of the most amazing cars—Bentleys, Rolls-Royces, Lamborghinis, Ferraris, Porsches, Mercedes, Land Rovers, etc. And whenever he bought one, he'd take me for a drive in it, and then he'd let me drive. It was so much fun.

Gary Winnick and me

Thank you, Gary, for all the amazing things you shared with me for thirty-three years.

It's important to acknowledge the Gold's Gym family members who have also passed away. In doing so, we show our respect for who they were and how they touched our lives. Here's some love for many of the friends I've had at Gold's who have since passed away. Rest in peace. You'll always be remembered.

Kay Baxter—October 3, 1945, to May 6, 1988
Pete Grzymkowski Sr.—Passed away on April 28, 1989
Michael Landon—October 31, 1936, to July 1, 1991
Lyle Alzado—April 3, 1949, to May 14, 1992
Don Ross—October 6,1946, to June 2, 1995

Art Zeller—1930 to 1999
Mike Mentzer—November 15, 1951, to June 10, 2001
Ray Mentzer—August 3, 1953, to June 12, 2001
Gregory Hines—February 14, 1946, to August 9, 2003
Charles Bronson—November 3, 1921, to August 30, 2003
Joe Gold—March 10, 1922, to July 11, 2004
Paul Demayo—September 12, 1967, to June 2, 2005
Irvin "Zabo" Koszewski—August 20, 1924, to March 29, 2009
Dennis Hopper—May 17, 1936, to May 29, 2010
Dennis Tinerino—December 23, 1945, to May 7, 2010
Phil Burns—May 2, 1931, to February 8, 2012
Michael Clarke Duncan—December 10, 1957, to September 3, 2012
Joe Weider—November 29, 1919, to March 23, 2013
Bobby Scura—Passed away in 2015
Lynn Conkwright—May 30, 1954, to June 14, 2017
Shawn Perine—1966 to December 11, 2017
Kent Kuehn—1936 to June 30, 2019
David Paul—March 8, 1957, to March 6, 2020
Shad Gaspard—January 13, 1981, to May 17, 2020
Rick Drasin—July 12, 1944, to August 30, 2020
Eddie Van Halen—January 26, 1955, to October 6, 2020
Paul Grzymkowski—Passed away on April 1, 2021
Jay Strong—Passed away in 2022
Jeff Campbell—Passed away in 2022
Ruth Silverman—Passed away in December 2022
Eddie Giuliani—Passed away on May 3, 2022
Matt Mendenhall—June 26, 1960, to August 28, 2021
Shawn Rhoden—April 2, 1975, to November 6, 2021
Chris Dickerson—August 25, 1939, to December 23, 2021
Joe Ruggiero—Passed away on March 29, 2022
Ray Liotta—December 18, 1954, to May 26, 2022
James Caan—March 26, 1940, to July 6, 2022
Bill Pearl—October 31, 1930, to September 14, 2022

Doug Brignole—Passed away on October 13, 2022
Rainer Schaller—January 4, 1969, to October 21, 2022
Jeff Henry—Passed away on November 17, 2022
Eric Fleishman—Passed away on November 24, 2022
Tonya Knight—March 24, 1966, to February 7, 2023
Mike Quinn—November 18, 1961, to May 30, 2023
Doug Andrewski—April 13, 1955, to August 11, 2023
Carl Weathers—January 14, 1948, to February 2, 2024

I'm so grateful that so many Gold's Gym family members who I've been seeing for the last thirty to forty years are still with us and working out. Here they are:

Paul Abasal	Franco Carlotto	David Hughes
Martin Alamango	Frankie Cassavetes	Clint Hummel
Alexander Andrecs	Ed Chang	Alex Jamal
Alex Ardenti	Kirk Chittick	Lena Johannesen
Jim Arrington	Ahmad Clayton	David Johnson
Armand Azurdia	Bill Comstock	Sean Kahler
Craig Balkkam	Gilbert Coppage	Dan Kennedy
Samir Bannout	Cookie Cruz	Elyse Kent
Pedro Barron	Steve Davis	Marianne Kopie Liggett
Brian Bean	Joe Delia	Chuck Krall
Nikko Bean	Les De'Morst	Daisy Lang
Edwin Benton	Flavio De Oliveira	Kristoffer Lassen
Dr. Bill Bergman	John Diaz	Brad Lecraw
Matthias Boldt	Nathan Dixon	Mark Lewis
Reginald Brantley	Shay Dunpay	Susie Lin
Kammy Burnett	Lorena Gonda	Gloria Lopez
Randy Campbell	Carly Gregson	Michael Lukich
Geno Carignan	Big Will Harris	Scott Macrillo
Heidi Carignan	Gary Hartunian	Johnny MaDonia
Leslie Carleton	Matthias Hues	Paul Major

Steve Manak
Arina Manta
Tom Marcoccia
Rico McClinton
Gary Michelson
Rich Minzer
Stanley Mitchell
Bruiser Neal
Michon Neal
Chelan Nour, MD
Mike O'Hearn
Harold Parker
Brianna Patterson
Dayton Patterson
Lorenzo Perkins
Tito Raymond
Craig Ribeiro
Juan Richardson
John Richling
Robby Robinson
Adam Rodriguez
Jeff Roncone
John Rosen
Mike Ryan
Silvio Samuel
Matt Schaffer
Ronald Scott
Michael Shea
Marcus Shirock
Sebastian Siegel
Ryan Smith
Val Streit
Tino Struckmann
Heide Sutter
Craig Tapscott
George Thibault
April Thompson
Cathy Tieri
Mike Torchia
Dean Tornabene
Annabelle Troster
Leslie Weisenberger
Greg Wrangler
Bijan Zadeh
Dominique Zimmerman

Living is a process of adaptation. How you respond to what life throws at you is essential to living a happy and healthy life. For instance, let's take a look at how I train now. Because of various injuries I've had over the years, I've had to change my workouts. I can't go heavy doing six to eight reps because my joints don't like it, and I don't feel that much of a pump in the body part I'm training.

So, I had to make some changes. What I found that I really like is training with high reps. I train one body part per day. This includes four movements hitting the body part from different angles. I do three sets for each movement. I do fifty to 150 reps per set. When you train with high reps, the burn and the pump in the muscle is amazing. You have to be hyperfocused when counting out a hundred reps. You can't think of anything else. It's a great release.

Once I'm done with the weights, I train my abs, followed by forty minutes on the treadmill. That's my happy place.

Every morning, I remind myself of all the things I'm grateful for:

1) I'm alive.
2) I have my health.
3) I have a roof over my head.
4) There's food in my refrigerator.
5) I still have friendships with people I grew up with.

When I think of Ansonia, I realize how fortunate I am to still have my cousin Mark and his mother, Auntie Teresa, in my life. I also think about how lucky I was to have lifelong friendships with three of the guys I grew up with—Joe Cardella, Gary Taylor, and Roger Ings. They all did their best in training the next generation of kids. Joe also regularly speaks at Alcoholics Anonymous meetings, inspiring others to continue their journey of sobriety.

I regret to write that Gary and Roger have passed away. I had received a call in April from Joe, who was crying and told me that Gary had passed. Then about a month later, Roger tragically passed in a car accident. Rest in peace, Gary and Roger.

A lot has changed at Gold's Gym Venice. The gym culture has changed. That camaraderie we had in the eighties and nineties has changed. People are not as connected to one another as they were back then. Gym etiquette seems to be a thing of the past. Back in the day, whenever I asked someone if I work-in on a piece of equipment they're using, they'd always say, "Sure." And before you knew, we'd have a friendly competition going, be it heavier weight or more reps. It was fun.

Roger and Gary

But in today's world, whenever I ask a younger person if I can work-in, they say, "No." When I ask how many sets they have, they say, "Well, I just started."

So I find some other machine to use, but when I return, I'll see that person sitting on the equipment, fiddling around with their phone for ten to fifteen minutes between sets. What I'd like you all to know is that you don't own whatever piece of equipment you're using. We all have a right to use it because we all have memberships.

Having said all of that, I still think of Gold's Gym Venice as my home away from home. Despite all the changes, it's an overwhelmingly positive place, and I'm invigorated each day I walk through its doors. I don't think there's any such thing as "the perfect gym," but Gold's comes pretty darn close. I always have a great workout and enjoy catching up with my friends. Isn't that why we go to the gym?

It's important for this young generation to know that followers on social media will never replace authentic friendships. I could have never succeeded like I did in life had I not actually connected with the people around me. Stop looking at your damn phone and start looking people in the eye more often. You might be surprised at how many people you could meet who have your same interests and who may even have some career opportunities for you. You can't buy that kind of connection with fake followers.

I'm so grateful that I've been lucky enough to work out at Gold's Gym Venice for forty-three years. I learned so much about working out, eating healthy, doing cardio—you name it, I've learned it.

GOLD'S
GYM
FAITH
Rick Valente
Blessed
elite
THE MECCA OF BODYBUILDING

THE MECCA
NPC WEST COAST
BE POSITIVE
LAGUNA

Recently, Bill Grant messaged me that he was coming to town with his son Jason and Rich Tuma, and they wanted to have a high-rep arms workout with me at Gold's Gym. It was so much fun to work out with Bill and Rich! Bill's son even recorded our workout. Bill and Rich are both in amazing shape. Thank you both for a great workout!

Bill Grant, Rich Tuma, and me

A few days after that, I met a young woman named Athena Vas at the gym. We had started talking about different workouts, and one day, she told me she wanted to work out with me, so we trained arms together. I was impressed that Athena would do fifty rep sets for arms.

Then I had her stretch and flex in between sets. She loved it and wanted me to get her in her best shape so she could enter a Miss Olympia bikini show.

We now often work out together, having a lot of fun and challenging each other to get more reps. I'll never forget one day we did an ab machine, and I started at 150 reps. Then I did 250 reps, and then she did 300 reps, which will blow your mind.

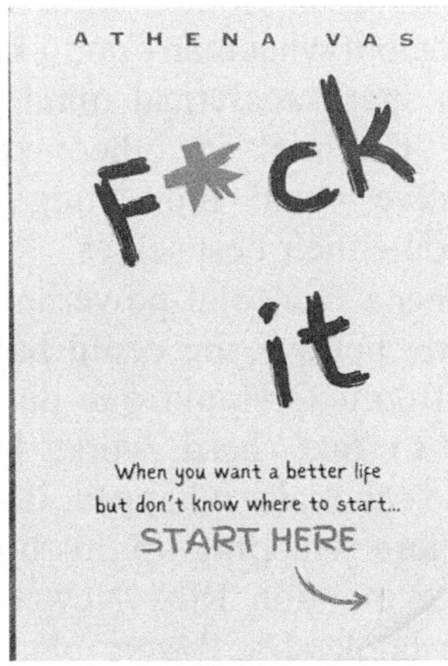

Athena Vas

Athena recently handed me a book she wrote. It's called *F*ck It: When You Want a Better Life but Don't Know Where to Start, Start Here.* Let me tell you, it's an incredible read. If you're looking for something to challenge your mindset and inspire real change, this is the book for you.

I've read hundreds of self-development books in my life, but Athena's book stands out because it doesn't just motivate you—it gives you the tools to actually change your life. Athena's book is packed with exercises and journaling prompts that help you shift your mindset and take actionable steps forward. It's all about saying "fuck it" to the things that no longer serve you and realizing that your biggest challenges can become your greatest blessings. She shows you that when one door closes, another one opens.

You can find her book on Amazon and Barnes & Noble. Go check it out!

Beyond her writing, Athena is one of the coolest and most inspiring people I know. She's fun, bubbly, and always joking around, with a contagious energy that makes everyone around her feel alive. Some might underestimate her based on her exterior, but what many don't know is that she's a mathematician with a sharp analytical mind. She has this incredible gift for seeing potential in others—things they don't even see in themselves—and motivating them to become their best selves.

Me and Athena at the gym

Athena is a total powerhouse. I honestly believe she could become Miss Bikini Olympia one day. It's going to take hard work, but if anyone can make it happen, it's her.

Before wrapping up this book, I have to mention Rick Newcombe, whose book, *The Magic of Lifting Weights*, was a huge inspiration for me to create my own book. I was introduced to Rick by my friend Jimmy Gisondo, whom I had met through Tom Marcoccia.

Rick's book has over 250 photos, which blew my mind! It made me realize that when a book has that many amazing photos, it makes the story feel so much more factual. I think both Rick and I have many amazing stories that people would not believe had we hadn't had pictures to prove them!

I encourage all my friends to also write their own book about their lives. Create an accurate account of your life's journey and thoughts. When we're gone, all that is left of us is memories and the impacts on those we left behind.

I was devastated to learn that my good friend Chuck Woolery had passed away on November 23, 2024. I trained Chuck for years, and we had developed a great friendship. We'd often have lunch together after his workouts, and he put me on a few of his TV shows. And on so many holidays, Chuck would invite me to his home for dinner.

I will miss Chuck so much. RIP, Chuck. You will always be loved, respected, and missed.

And then—boom!—I was blindsided once more when wildfires exploded in LA this January. Thousands of people lost their homes, and countless thousands of acres were burned. At least a dozen of my friends lost everything. It was another lesson in learning how to move forward and find a solution, rather than wallow in the tragedy of losing everything.

Thank you for reading this book. Remember, you're responsible for the energy you bring into a room. The more positive vibes you send out, the more you will receive. Keep moving, and keep playing in your passion. Good things will come from it.

ACKNOWLEDGMENTS

Thank you, Mom and Dad, for bringing me into the world. You showed so much love and respect to each other every day. I love you both forever.

Thank you, Derek Barton, for everything you did for marketing Gold's Gym, and for booking me on all kinds of gigs I never could have gotten on my own.

Thank you, Pete Grymkowski, for making me the face of Gold's Gym during the eighties and nineties.

Thank you, Tim Kimber, for comping my gym membership for life.

Thank you, Joe Pytka, for booking me on so many commercials and for being a true friend.

Thank you, John Traetta, for booking me on *BodyShaping*. It changed my life.

Thank you, Gary Winnick, for showing me a world I probably would never have seen. And thank you, Karen, Adam, Alex, and Matt for continuing to treat me like family.

Thank you, Jimmy Caan. There's so much I want to say that I don't even know where to begin. You were a paisano.

Thank you, TR Goodman, for always having my back.

Thank you, Frankie Cassavetes, for being an all-around stand-up guy.

Thank you, Bobby LeVine, for getting me out of Ansonia and into Florida. It changed my entire life.

Thank you, Magic Schwartz and Reggie Bennett, for the first friendships I developed when I first arrived at Gold's Gym. You helped me get started in so many ways.

Thank you, Mike Christian, for motivating me in bodybuilding and all the memories and good times we had.

Thank you, Dennis Alexio, for your friendship and all the time you shared with me during our training sessions. I will always appreciate your great talent.

Thank you, Bobby Scura, for being a true *goombah*. You

helped me in so many ways that I'll be forever in your debt.

Thank you, Tonya Knight, for being such a beautiful soul. You got me back on my feet after my pec tear. I'll always cherish the time we had together.

Thank you, Rich Minzer, for getting Gold's Gym new equipment and for laying it out in a logical and functional manner.

Thank you, Gregory Hines, for being an incredible friend. Your generosity knew no bounds. I will never forget all the times you invited me to a set to watch you work, or the many shows you took me to. Thank you for allowing me to train you for ten years. You will always be missed.

Thank you, Eddie Giuliani, for being so much fun to be around, as well as recounting the history of bodybuilding.

Thank you, Mike Quinn, for all the training we did together and for allowing me to put together some music and help you with your posing routines.

Thank you, Lyle Alzado, for everything you did for me, like when I tore my pec and you took me to the Raiders' surgeon. I was honored to be part of your inner circle of close friends.

Thank you, Rainer Schaller, for buying Gold's Gym. Your enthusiasm for the gym and its history was infectious. I always had a great time hanging out with you whenever you were in town.

Thank you, Jimmy Vane, for the friendship we shared from the sixth grade and all the way through high school. We always had each other's back.

Thank you, Suzanne and Allan Migdall, for allowing me to work at your amazing club, Summers, and for talking me into entering my first bodybuilding competition.

Thank you, Rick Wayne, for getting me my first magazine cover and for writing such nice things about me.

Thank you, Zabo Koszewski, for your friendship and for sharing your bodybuilding knowledge with me. We always had fun together.

Thank you, Kay Baxter, for our time spent training together, laying in the sun together, and having lunch together. It was always a great time.

Thank you, Don Ross, for writing articles about me and for letting me train with you. You were an animal in the gym.

Thank you, Lisa Lyons, for being the first female bodybuilder and for putting on a bodybuilding art show that featured me, Charles Glass, and Katie Arnoldi.

Thank you, Chuck Zito, for writing your autobiography. It inspired me to write my own. I always enjoy watching your films.

Thank you, Ray "Boom Boom" Mancini, for always helping to raise money for Shad Meshad's National Veterans Foundation, as well as writing your own book about your life.

Thank you, Artie Zeller, for always telling me jokes whenever you'd see me at Gold's Gym and for taking pictures of me training. You were an amazing photographer and always fun to be around.

Thank you, Paul Grymkowski, for growing the number of Gold's Gyms from one to more than five hundred, and for booking me for appearances and seminars at so many of those Gold's Gym openings.

Thank you, Van Halen, for selecting me for the *5150* album cover. It's definitely one of the high points of my career. I always listen to your music.

Thank you, Rick Newcombe, for giving me the opportunity to publish my book. I read your autobiography and thought it was great, and I love that you had more than two hundred and fifty photos in it.

Thank you, Alex Nagy, for all your help with putting the finishing touches on this book. You are a talented editor and a wonderful person.

Thank you, Amy Wang, for handling all the photos in this book. You helped bring my vision to life. And thank you for your service in the U.S. military.

Thank you, Jimmy Gisondo, for being another one of my Italian buddies for over thirty-five years, and thanks for introducing me to Rick Newcombe.

Thank you, Joe Weider, for inviting me to your office, the great conversation we had, and for booking me for so many photoshoots for your magazines. You did so much to help so many bodybuilders.

Thank you, Shawn Ray, for inspiring me in bodybuilding, and for being such a great poser and friend.

Thank you, Lee Haney, for motivating all of us to win the Mr. Olympia and for being such a class act.

Thank you, Mike Ryan, for your friendship and always inviting me to watch boxing and UFC matches, and whatever parties you're throwing at your house.

Thank you, John Ryan, for always grabbing lunch with me and having great conversations.

Thank you, Chuck and Katie Arnoldi, for helping me when I first moved to California. You both did so many things for me that I will always be grateful.

Thank you, Matteo Baker, for always having my back when you managed Gold's Gym. Then, when you opened your owns gyms, you always let me train for free.

Thank you, Joe Bucci, for helping me when you managed the Marina Pacific Hotel. Whenever I'd need a hotel, you'd hook me up. We've been friends for more than thirty-five years and you're always there for me.

Thank you, Joe Gold, for the conversations we had at World Gym. You said you knew who I was and you let me train there. I always respected you and will always be grateful you created Gold's Gym.

Thank you, Sandy Taylor, for a thirty-five-year friendship and introducing me to your mother, who always had nice things to say.

Thank you, Van Cotright, for thirty-four years of friendship. You are one of the only people I still talk to all the time.

Thank you, April Thompson, for your friendship, many great workouts together, and many meals, too.

Thank you, Dr. Rand McClain, for being my longevity doctor and most importantly for being a good friend for the past thirty-five years.

Thank you, Bill D'Addio, for getting me jobs and always reminding me that I have a place to stay should I ever return to Florida.

Thank you, Sergio Delgado, for your friendship and for always helping me with any tech issues.

Thank you, Neal Spruce, for your friendship over all these years.

Thank you, Alex Ardenti, for being such a great friend.

Thank you, Lorenzo Perkins, for all our amazing workouts together.

Thank you, Lou Ferrigno, for being a lifelong inspiration of mine.

Thank you, Samir Bannout, for a forty-two-year friendship. It's great seeing you at Gold's Gym. I always appreciate our great, fun conversations about life.

Thank you, Robby Robinson. You are an amazing bodybuilder who has inspired me my whole life. You still look fantastic. It's always fun having lunch with you.

Thank you, Ron Beckerfeld, for our wonderful friendship. I have so many great memories of all the incredible parties you would invite me to through the years.

Thank you, Joe Cardella, for your lifelong friendship. I love talking with you.

Thank you, John Richling, for always going on casting calls with me and booking a half-dozen commercials with me. It was great working with you, and it's always a pleasure seeing you at Gold's Gym.

Thank you, Rico McClinton, for a friendship that's spanned four decades. It's still great seeing you at Gold's Gym.

Thank you, Lenda Murray, for doing the seminar with me at

Gold's Gym Venice. In my opinion, you were one of the best female bodybuilders of all time.

Thank you, Jim Manion, for all the great conversations we had over lunch. It's always been fun for you and me to share different books about exercising your mind and being grateful every day you wake up.

Thank you to all the *BodyShaping* cast members. Kiana, Deprise, Mary Jean, Kendell, Jennifer, Dr. Pete, and Paige, working with all of you was one of the best experiences of my life. I'm very grateful that we're still friends to this day.

Thank you, Chas, for being an amazing brother who taught me so much about life. Rest in peace. I love you.

Thank you, Frank Yip, for your friendship and for doing my taxes for the last thirty-five years.

Thank you, Brian Moss, for doing so many photoshoots with me. You are so creative!

ABOUT THE AUTHOR

Rick Valente is a celebrated figure in the fitness and bodybuilding world, best known for his role as a charismatic host of ESPN's *BodyShaping*, the groundbreaking TV show that brought fitness into millions of homes during the 1980s and 1990s. Rick earned the prestigious title of Mr. Los Angeles early in his career, solidifying his place among the sport's elite.

Originally from Ansonia, Connecticut, Rick pursued his dreams with relentless determination, moving to Los Angeles to immerse himself in the heart of the fitness industry. Training at the iconic Gold's Gym in Venice, he honed his craft, becoming a sought-after fitness model and appearing in top publications such as *Muscle & Fitness* and *Flex*. His image graced countless national ad campaigns and even the album cover of Van Halen's *5150*.

Beyond his achievements on stage and screen, Rick has dedicated his life to inspiring others to embrace health and fitness. As a personal trainer, motivational speaker, and mentor, he shares his wealth of knowledge and passion for living a balanced, grateful lifestyle.

Rick lives in Los Angeles and continues to train daily at Gold's Gym Venice.

MY LIFE'S RIDE
is also available as an e-book
for Kindle, Amazon Fire, iPad, Nook and
Android e-readers. Visit
creatorspublishing.com to learn more.

CREATORS PUBLISHING

We find compelling storytellers and
help them craft their narrative,
distributing their novels and collections
worldwide.

Printed in Dunstable, United Kingdom

67838686R00262